W9-BML-157

Edinburgh Law and Society Series

Music and Copyright

edited by

SIMON FRITH

EDINBURGH UNIVERSITY PRESS

Edinburgh University Press Ltd
22 George Square, Edinburgh

Typeset in Linotron Plantin
by Koinonia Limited, Bury, and
printed and bound in Great Britain
by Redwood Books, Trowbridge

A CIP record for this book is
available from the British Library

ISBN 0 7486 0481 2

Contents

List of Abbreviations vi

Introduction ix
SIMON FRITH

1 Music and Morality 1
SIMON FRITH

2 Copyright and the International Music Industry 22
DAVE LAING

3 Technology, Economy and Copyright Reform in Canada 40
PAUL THÉBERGE

4 Music and Copyright in the USA 67
STEVE JONES

5 Bette Midler and the Piracy of Identity 86
JANE M. GAINES

6 Making it Visible: The 1990 Public Inquiry into Australian Music Copyrights 99
MARCUS BREEN

7 Copyright and Music in Japan: A Forced Grafting and its Consequences 125
TÔRU MITSUI

8 The Problem of Oral Copyright: The Case of Ghana 146
JOHN COLLINS

APPENDICES

1 Copyright: The Dark Side of the Music Business 159
FRANCO FABBRI

2 Coyright in Germany 164
SIMON FRITH

Notes on contributors 167

Indexes 169

Abbreviations

ACTU	Australian Council of Trade Unions
AMCOS	Australian Mechanical Copyright Owners Society
AMPAL	Australian Music Publishers Association Limited
APRA	Australian Performing Rights Association
ARIA	Australian Record Industry Association
ASCAP	American Society of Composers, Authors and Publishers
BIEM	Bureau International de L'Edition Music-mecanique (France)
BMI	Broadcast Music Inc.
BPI	British Phonographic Industry Limited
CAPAC	Composers, Authors and Publishers Association of Canada (formerly CPRS)
CISAC	Confédération Internationale des Sociétés d'Auteurs et Compositeurs (France)
CPRS	Canadian Performing Rights Society
CRIA	Canadian Record Industry Association
DAT	Digital Audio Tape
EC	European Community
GATT	General Agreement on Tariffs and Trade
IASPM	International Association for the Study of Popular Music
IFPI	International Federation of Phonogram and Videogram Producers (formerly International Federation of the Phonographic Industry)
IIPA	International Intellectual Property Alliance
ILO	International Labour Organisation
JASRAC	Japanese Society for Rights of Authors, Composers and Publishers
MCPS	Mechanical Copyright Protection Society (UK)

NAFTA	North American Free Trade Area
PPCA	Phonographic Performance Company of Australia Limited
PPL	Phonographic Performance Limited (UK)
PROCAN	Performing Rights Organisation of Canada (formerly BMI-Canada)
PRS	Performing Rights Society (UK)
PSA	Prices Surveillance Authority (Australia)
RIAA	Recording Industry Association of America
SACEM	Société des Auteurs, Compositeurs et Editeurs de Musique (France)
SIAE	Società Italiana degli Autori ed Editori
SOCAN	Society of Composers, Authors and Music Publishers of Canada (a merger of CAPAC and PROCAN)
TPC	Trade Practices Commission (Australia)
TRIPS	Trade Related Aspects of Intellectual Property Rights, Including Trade in Counterfeit Goods
WIPO	World Intellectual Property Organisation

Introduction

SIMON FRITH

> Jane Gainsborough, a specialist in copyright law at Columbia, stated that when she started to specialise in copyright law five or six years ago, her colleagues thought her 'bohemian' (translation; you will never make any money); now, though, they tell her that she is in a 'coming' branch of the law (translation: you will make lots of money). (Docherty, 1987)

There are two broad reasons for the growing professional (and academic) interest in copyright law in the last decade: first, new technologies for the storage and retrieval of knowledge, sounds and images have posed complex problems for legal definitions of their authorship and use; second, the (related) globalisation of culture has given multi-national leisure corporations pressing reasons to 'harmonise' copyright regulations across national boundaries. Either way, the legal definition of 'intellectual property' and its financial value has become an issue. In the specific case of the music industry this has meant a kind of analytic redefinition: what was treated in the 1960s and 1970s as manufacture, an industry primarily selling commodities to consumers, came to be treated in the 1980s as a service, 'exploiting' musical properties as baskets of rights. Academic researchers were rather slow to grasp the implications for the industry itself (see, for example, Frith, 1987), and even slower to grasp the implications for taken-for-granted assumptions about industrial statistics and policy making.[1]

The original purpose of this book was simply to reflect on the problems of music and copyright from a number of international perspectives. Unfortunately (for this book), what makes the topic interesting to academics (and lawyers) is precisely what also makes it interesting to music industry lobbyists and politicians, and the field kept changing as we sought to map it. The book therefore took much longer to put together than I had expected, and there are still areas of contingency: if most countries (for example, the UK, USA, Australia, Canada and Japan) have new legislation in place (or in the pipeline), it is still too early to know how such laws will be interpreted and applied in case practice. The most dramatic legal changes since these essays were commissioned occurred in East Germany,[2] but all the countries discussed here face unresolved problems of their own, whether about blank tape levies, moral rights or the legality of sampling, and international agreements, even after the various 1990s free trade agreements, remain as difficult (and as fraught) as ever.

I'm sure, nevertheless, that this collection will be useful, not just for its descriptions of specific music copyright rules and issues, but also for its emphasis on the importance of copyright law for the analysis of both contemporary musical institutions and, more surprisingly perhaps, contemporary musical aesthetics. I should stress that this is not a book written by lawyers, but by music researchers and journalists; it is not, that is, any sort of substitute for the various substantive guides to copyright law (see, for example, Bagehot, 1989; Dworkin and Taylor, 1989; and McFarlane, 1989). But for that very reason, I believe that the essays here do focus and clarify cultural issues that are often obscured in purely legal debates. If one purpose of this book is, then, to persuade music sociologists (and fans) that the 'narrow' subject of copyright is actually the key to cultural analysis, another is to remind lawyers that the 'common sense' of copyright, how the public understands it in principle (if not in detail), can sometimes be at startling odds to its legal meaning – one reason, as we'll see, for certain sorts of dispute. As Jessica Litman puts it:

> Copyright law turns out to be tremendously counterintuitive; that is why it is fun to teach it, and why it can be such a good substitute for small talk and other species of cocktail party conversation. Some of the reasons why lay people (by which I mean lawyers and non-lawyers and authors and non-authors; indeed, everyone but the copyright specialist) find copyright law hard to grasp could be its mind-numbing collection of inconsistent, indeed, incoherent complexities. But there seems to be nothing inherent in the subject of law about copyright that should violate people's intuitions. Although writers have suggested that members of the public find the idea of property rights in intangibles difficult to accept, there seems to be little evidence that members of the public find the *idea* of a copyright counterintuitive. Rather, the lay public seems to have a startlingly concrete idea of what copyright is and how it works, which idea has little to do with actual copyright law. (Litman, 1991, pp. 3–4 – my emphasis)

Music copyright is a particularly fascinating topic of party conversation because of its various anomalies, many of which are discussed here, but some of which are not – for example, the issue of collaboration.[3] This question becomes even more complicated when collaboration involves translation: what are the rights of the original lyricist in the translated version? (My favourite cocktail anecdote here concerns Italy, where the translator can claim a right in the original song. To translate Bob Dylan songs in the 1960s, for example, was to get a share of the rights income from the Italian sales and performances of Dylan's own words!) Or take the problem, just beginning to hit the record industry, of works coming out of copyright. One of the implications of digital technology not discussed here is that record company control of master tapes no longer gives them *de facto* control of out-of-copyright recordings; over the next thirty years we can therefore expect multiple issues of classic Presley, Dylan and Beatle tracks, just as we take for granted multiple editions of books by Kipling, Hardy and Woolf, as they go out of literary copyright.

It is the possibility of different national solutions to the same copyright problems that makes the international regulation of intellectual property so difficult. From the music industry point of view, 'harmonisation' is crucial, whether the problem is piracy – and the international enforcement of copyright protection – or trade – and the most profitable flow of sounds across national boundaries. Harmonisation is not pursued for aesthetic or ethical reasons, for all the musical metaphor. Rather, international companies seek to spread 'best practice' (translation: most profitable practice) everywhere. Hence, for example, MTV (Europe)'s ongoing battle to change the European system of blanket licences[4] to the American system of individually negotiated, 'exclusive rights'.[5] If the difference between the two systems reflects, as we'll see, philosophical and political differences between Europe and the USA, MTV favours the American system for purely financial reasons: using it they would get the same number of video hours for less money.

The harmonisation of European copyright law equally involves questions of economic interest as well as legalistic neatness (see Table I). From the music industry point of view, the aim is not only to bring the various figures in line, but also to work out which national legislative framework is most profitable and to establish that as the EC norm. The problem then arises as to which part of the music industry we're talking about. In 1991, for example, the British Copyright Tribunal had to adjudicate a dispute between the Mechanical Copyright Protection Society (MCPS) and the British Phonographic Industry Limited (BPI) – that is, between record companies and music publishers (in many cases different divisions of the same leisure corporations) – which precisely hinged on MCPS's attempt to bring the level of UK mechanical rights payments up to those elsewhere in Europe (see Copyright Tribunal, 1991)

From the common sense point of view, justification for copyright law rests on two different sorts of assumption, both of which have been called into question by recent developments. It seems obvious that the author of

TABLE I.1: European Copyright Laws.

	Auth/ Comp	Pho/ Pro	Rent Proh	BTL	Rome	Berne
Belgium	50	none	TBI	TBI	No	Yes
Denmark	50	50		Yes	Yes	Yes
Eire	50	50			Yes	Yes
France	70	25		Yes	Yes	Yes
Germany	70	25	Yes	Yes	Yes	Yes
Greece	50	none			No	Yes
Italy	50	30		TBI	Yes	Yes
Luxembourg	50	none			Yes	Yes
Netherlands	50	none	TBI	TBI	No	Yes
Portugal	50	50			No	Yes
Spain	60	40			No	Yes
UK	50	50	Yes		Yes	Yes

Key: Auth/Comp: years of protection after death of author/composer
Pho/Pro: years of protection for phonogram producer
Rent Proh: prohibition on record rental
BTL: blank tape levy
Rome: signature to Rome Convention
Berne: signature to Berne Convention
TBI: to be introduced

Source: *Music Business International*, II/1, January 1992, p. 28.

a work has first rights in it. The question is: who should benefit when a work doesn't have an obvious author; and who should benefit when the author doesn't produce an obvious work. The first question is discussed here by John Collins, writing from Ghana, where the working Western definition of individual copyright – music is in the public domain when no composer is likely to sue, because they're dead, far away or anonymous – is becoming increasingly problematic as global record companies (and musicians) exploit 'world music' (and local 'folk' sounds) for their own commercial ends. The second question follows from the increasing twentieth-century ability to fix (and unfix) the 'transient' aspects of music (sound, style, performance).[6] In this respect, technology has changed the organisation of not only music, but also image and dance. Until video recording, for example, the only way to establish copyright in choreography was through conventional notations (and under the 1956 UK Copyright Act, the notator had to declare legally that he or she was not the dance's author).The 1988 Act made video registration possible, but defining a musical or theatrical work in performance remains problematic. How much can be changed from show to show before a new work is produced? Isn't the performer just as much as the composer, author or choreographer, the 'creator' of the 'work'?[7] These questions are addressed here by Jane Gaines in her examination of American legal arguments about *the voice* as property.

But the recurring issue here, the recurring debate in the music industry itself, is digital sampling (discussed by Simon Frith, Paul Théberge and Steve Jones, from British, Canadian and American perspectives). All three writers suggest that the arguments around sampling mark a striking shift in what one might call the common sense *ideology* of copyright. The pop consensus used to be that copyright was a good thing, a necessary protection of authors from publishers and publishers from pirates; rock'n'roll tales of corruption and exploitation emerged from the bottom end of the industry, featured the manipulation or evasion of copyright law by devious music hustlers and lawyers. Naive artists handed over composer credits; the most unexpected people – managers, publishers, promoters, DJs – turned up as songwriters.[8] Nowadays, as Dave Laing's essay here explains, the nastiest arguments occur at the top of the industry, as international corporations seek to protect their rights through trade negotiations, using USA or EC commercial power to bring obdurate small countries into line.[9]

Hence, I think, the increasing scepticism about, if not downright hostility to, copyright protection among music consumers and even musicians. Certainly, from an international perspective, copyright can be seen as a key plank in Western cultural and commercial imperialism – thus, Toru Mitsui's essay here traces the history of Japanese copyright law as an imposition of Western concepts on the Japanese understanding of authorship, while Marcus Breen, writing from Australia, shows how a national economic policy for the music industry depends on the political use of copyright as corporate regulator. In short, if copyright law has always had as much to do with market ideology as with concepts of creativity, then in the last decade the sources of tension *between* artist and industry have changed. A law which could once be justified as protecting artists and publishers against exploitation or piracy, is increasingly seen as a weapon used by the multinationals against small nations, on the one hand, and against creative musical consumers and producers, on the other. The most pressing legal problems now concern definitions of public domain and fair use.

NOTES

1 For a brief comment on this from an Italian perspective, see Franco Fabbri's 1989 note, reprinted here as Appendix 1.

2 These changes have continuing ramifications for musicians – see Appendix 2.

3 The song writing norm of lyricist/composer is handled differently in different legislations: one copyright or two? See Krasilovsky, 1987.

4 The company pays an annual fee for the right to so many hours of music video broadcasting to the video rights collecting agency, Video Performance Limited, VPL, which, in turn, distributes the

income to the rights holders in the videos eventually programmed.

5 Individual payments for the exclusive right to play each video are paid directly to the rights holders.

6 Legal definitions of the musical property are rooted in nineteenth-century technology: music as notes, the score.

7 For discussion of copyright and the performing arts see Parry, 1988; Auslander, 1992.

8 For a classic case, made complicated by US law on the re-registering of titles, see the Frankie Lyman story, Trillin 1991.

9 For a detailed account of this process, see Uphoff 1991.

REFERENCES

Auslander, Philip (1992), 'Intellectual property meets the cyborg. Performance and the cultural politics of technology', *Performing Arts Journal* 40, 30–42.

Bagehot, Richard (1989), *Music Business Agreements*, London: Waterlow Publishers.

Copyright Tribunal (1991), Decision on Reference CT 7/90 to the Copyright Tribunal, 1 November.

Docherty, David (1987), 'Nasties that cut directors to the quick', *Guardian*, 10 August.

Dworkin, Gerald and Taylor, Richard D. (1989), *Blackstone's Guide to the Copyright, Design and Patents Act 1988*, London: Blackstone Press.

Frith, Simon (1987), 'Copyright and the music business', *Popular Music* 7/1, pp. 57–75.

Krasilovsky, M. William (1987) 'Implications of collaboration in determining rights to royalties for musical composition', *Media Law & Practice* January 123–9 (First published in *New York Law Journal*, 7 and 14 January 1986).

Litman, Jessica (1991), 'Copyright as Myth', paper presented to conference on 'Intellectual Property and the Construction of Authorship', Case Western Reserve University, 19–21 April.

McFarlane, Gavin (1989) *A Practical Introduction to Copyright*, London: Waterlow Publishers, 2nd edn.

Parry, Jann (1988), 'Sir Fred's will be done', *Observer*, 18 September.

Trillin, Calvin (1991), 'You don't ask, you don't get', *New Yorker*, 25 February, pp. 72–81.

Uphoff, Elizabeth (1991), *Intellectual Property and US Relations with Indonesia, Malaysia, Singapore and Thailand* Ithaca, NY: Cornell University Southeast Asian Program.

1

Music and Morality[1]

SIMON FRITH

My starting point is that the meaning of art depends on a specific conjunction of aesthetic, ideological, economic and legal institutions. Until recently, for example, it was taken for granted that 'music' (a particular organisation of sound) was constituted as something fixed, something authored, and something that exists as property. These assumptions reflect the two sides of the bourgeois ideology of art, its simultaneous stress on individual creativity and individual ownership, on the Romantic-capitalist ideology which has survived both the rise of the mass media and the development of electronic means of cultural reproduction. During the last two hundred years, though, the contradictions involved in this account of art have become harder and harder to manage – hence the huge elaboration of legal and institutional mechanisms to contain them, to sustain the belief that a work of art expresses an individual sensibility (even when collectively produced, as in the cinema, television and recorded music), and to keep in balance the theory of intellectual property (something abstract, 'owned' by its creator) and the practice of the intellectual commodity (creativity realised in a material object, something to be 'owned' by its consumer).

The challenges to art thrown up by technology and commerce have been seen off historically by a variety of economic, legal and ideological institutions – by copyright laws, by publishing and production companies, by the academy, by literary and other forms of criticism. Their success is not guaranteed. It depends on specific political and economic struggles which, in turn, need to draw on specific ideological and moral arguments. Here I want to focus on the moral debate about the latest technological developments in music production and use. Two issues in particular have dominated recent music industry attempts to change copyright laws: home taping and digital sampling.[2]

HOME TAPING

In the last fifteen years or so record companies around the world have mounted campaigns for some sort of levy to be placed on blank audio and video cassette tapes and/or recording equipment. In some countries (Austria, France, Germany and Scandinavia) they have been successful, in others (USA and UK) they have not; in the latter the fight goes on. All the campaigns have had the same economic premise: the increased sales of blank tapes (which are used to copy pre-recorded tracks and albums) are correlated with the declining sales of those tracks and albums.

I don't want to go into the statistical validity of this argument here (it is more problematic than it might seem) but, rather, to look at the rhetoric with which the record industry mounted its blank tape campaigns, at the moral articulation of economic interests. Two figures of speech recur: home taping is theft; home taping is murder. On the one hand, then, home-tapers are accused of taking pleasure from an artist's work without paying for it; on the other hand, home-tapers are accused of eating into musicians' and record companies' potential profits and thus killing creativity itself. Home-tapers, that is, remove the financial incentive for artists to create in the first place, and, in particular, threaten the 'creative community' (ASCAP's term), the marginal and minority music makers who depend on buoyant overall profits for their continued record company subsidy. 'Home taping is killing music!' as BPI put it. 'Home taping is eroding our cultural base!' as the Canadian industry argued, with characteristically national self-consciousness.

Campaigners against a blank tape levy (the various Tape Manufacture groups) use a different kind of imagery. Their arguments revolve around the rights of the consumer to do what she or he likes with their property, and they proclaim the democratising effects of home taping as a cheap and accessible way of diffusing knowledge and culture (its role, for example, in Eastern Europe). In Britain the pro-tape lobby raised awkward questions for the record industry, summoning up images of company snoopers and company cartels: how would home taping be monitored? How would levy income be distributed? Would the musicians being taped really be the musicians to be rewarded? Wouldn't the levy simply reinforce the corporate power structure of the industry? Would those 'marginal' artists really notice any difference?[3]

The campaign for a blank tape levy became a political campaign because governments had to be persuaded to change laws. The political arguments revolved around competing definitions of property. As James Lardner shows in his entertaining study of the VCR wars between Hollywood and the Japanese electronics industry, software and hardware manufacturers have rather different notions of consumer rights. Lardner notes that the first video cassette recorder to be marketed in the USA was

Cartridge Television Inc's Cartrivision (which went on sale in June 1972). It came complete with a catalogue of 111 black cassettes (for sale only) of programmes such as *Erica Wilson's Basic Crewel* and Chekhov's *The Swan Song* ('the first dramatic work made expressly for cartridge television') and 200 red cassettes (for rental only) of Hollywood films like *Casablanca* and *Dr Strangelove*. The movie box had a locking device which made it impossible to rewind. Only retailers had a rewinding machine, and this was equipped with a counter so that every resetting was noted – Hollywood studios weren't about to change the principle that they 'lend' movie prints, take a cut of *every* showing.

In the event, the Cartrivision was a bit of a flop. Customers were much more interested in the red than the black cassettes and soon found their disadvantages. In Lardner's words,

> if a screaming infant summoned a viewer away from his Cartrivision set in a hurry and made him miss a few minutes of a movie, there was no way to recapture those minutes without a return trip to the store – and no way for the store to rewind the cassette without reporting a fresh transaction to the Cartridge Rental Network. (Lardner, 1987, pp. 82–4)

Further disaster struck in November 1972, when the company's tapes 'spontaneously began to decompose'. By mid–1973 Cartridge Television Inc was filing for bankruptcy and the video boom, which began with the launching of Sony's Betamax in 1975, was entirely dependent on Japanese hardware. The Japanese VCR manufacturers and their US allies were not willing to give up precisely those features of video technology that consumers wanted just to suit the film studios, and so the dispute was fought out in the courts. Hollywood wanted to establish that the home copying of films was illegal; it wanted both to control the film rental business and to exact some sort of royalty from the sale of VCR machines and tapes (the campaign prefigured record companies' 1980s positions on audio taping).

Two kinds of property right were, then, in conflict: copyright holders' right to exploit their 'creativity' and VCR owners' right to do what they liked with their machines. The subsequent legal battles suggest that this conflict is, in fact, at the heart of intellectual property law. A lower court's robust populist decision for Sony was overturned by a higher court's supercilious finding for MCA/Universal. 'It is noteworthy', Judge Kilkenny wrote, 'that the statute does not list "convenience" or "entertainment" or "increased access" as purposes within the general scope of fair use' (Lardner, p. 134). But his ruling was, in turn, set aside by a split Supreme Court, which recommended the issue be considered by Congress. It was there that consumer and small business interests (at this stage video rental stores were still small-scale, as local entrepreneurs rushed to satisfy an obvious market need) defeated the film industry. And, as Lardner makes clear, the argument in Congress was conducted in straight ideological terms. The film studios may have claimed to represent film 'artists' and 'creators', but because store owners and customers so obviously stood for the American entrepreneurial ideal, they were, in the end, able to out-lobby Hollywood interests – the VCR campaign may have been financed and run by the Electronics Industry Association of Japan, but the Motion Pictures Association could hardly play the xenophobic card against mid-Western mom-and-pop stores.

The failure of the film and music industries in Britain and the United States to persuade governments to introduce a blank tape levy (the British government changed its mind on this several times) reflects their failure to win the moral argument, to persuade either politicians or voters that, in this instance, 'creators' had more significant rights than consumers. I have never met anyone who felt they were doing *wrong* by home taping someone else's record, and I have never met anyone who thought they were harming the artist (rather than record company) by doing so.

SAMPLING

Of all technologies, digital storage probably poses the trickiest questions for conceptions of copyright. I will focus here on the issue of sound sampling, but digital technology has similarly complicated the ownership and use of imagery – Scitex, for example, transforms the storage (and potential manipulation) of photographs; film 'colourisation' has led to bitter arguments about authors' rights in films; the Lexicon audio time compressor enables films to be speeded up without affecting sound quality, confusing the relationship between the 'original' and the 'TV version'. In all these cases what's at issue is the definition of 'the work'; in all cases the traditional copyright assumption of a shared legal interest between a work's 'creator' and its 'owner' is called into question. The situation is particularly complicated in the field of music.

Take the case of the British sampling group, the Justified Ancients of Mu Mu, JAMS (who later became KLF, the Kopyright Liberation Front). JAMS' Bill Drummond defines sampling as follows: 'Sampling is to digitally record a sound, any sound; by using a computer these sounds can be trimmed, EQed and programmed before being committed to tape, which is the basis of making all "modern" records.'[4]

Such 'straight' technology opens up a host of problems. To quote another sampling musician, John Oswald, 'A sampler, in essence [both] a recording [and] transforming instrument is simultaneously a documentary device and a creative device, in effect reducing a distinction manifested by copyright' (Oswald, 1987).[5]

What are the implications of this? I'll begin by following the fortunes of JAMS. Their first single, 'All You Need Is Love', issued in 1987, was initially available only as a promo record, sent to critics and DJs. It was designed as a taster of JAMS' upcoming LP for WEA (a subsidiary of the major corporation, Time-Warner), to whom the group had just signed. WEA was appalled by the potential cost of getting the permissions to use the sampled bits of the Beatles, MC5, Samantha Fox, etc. A high powered legal meeting was held to determine the precise legal constraints on sampling: the conclusion was that no-one really knew. As John Brooks, then legal and corporate affairs director at CBS (UK), commented;

> The [then 1956] Copyright Act says that if you copy a *significant part* of any piece of music then that is a breech of copyright. This rule has an almost arbitrary interpretation in the courts because of its flexibility and the nature of music composition itself, as there are only so many notes to go round. But as far as *sound* is concerned, technically even copying a sliver is an infringement although the courts will apply the *de minimis* rule and will consider other factors like recognition, skill, flair, loss of earnings, and so on.

I'll come back to these other factors shortly, but in the JAMS case the immediate issue was the meaning of 'substantial', and WEA lawyers' meetings focused on the maximum *length* of quotes JAMS could use. An (arbitrary) 'sliver' of sound was agreed; when the LP came out it still had recognisable samples, but in much smaller quantities. In this legal version of *1987* the group merged the 'original' samples with their own (completely legitimate) *copies* of the various tracks (and the result was decidedly less powerful). The group's troubles, though, were not over. On the track 'The Queen and I', the confusion between the sample and the copy of Abba's 'Dancing Queen' was such that when Abba demanded appropriate payment, and threatened an injunction, WEA took fright: *1987* was withdrawn from the shops, and WEA agreed to destroy all remaining copies and the master tapes. The final, really legal version of the LP contained silences and an explanatory note:

> This record is a version of our now deleted and illegal LP *1987, What the Fuck is Going On?* with all the copyright infringing 'samples' edited out. As this leaves less than 25 minutes of music we are able to sell it as a 12-inch 45.
>
> If you follow the instructions below you will, after some practice, be able to simulate the sound of our original record. To do this you will need three wind-up record decks, a pile of selected discs, one t.v. set and a video machine loaded with a cassette of edited highlights of last week's *Top of the Pops*. Deck one is to play the record on, the other two are to scratch in the selected records …

There follow detailed instructions on how to fill each sound-gap, and the notes end with a WARNING:

> We must inform you that to attempt any of the above in the presence of two or more paying or non-paying people could be construed as

> a public performance. If the premises that you are in do not have a music license you will be infringing the copyright laws of the United Kingdom and legal action may be taken against you. Under no circumstances must your performance be recorded in any form ... (JAMS, 1987)

The legal fuss around JAMS coincided with another sampling case that generated considerable publicity. At the end of 1987, Pete Waterman, of production team Stock, Aitken and Waterman, brought an action against M/A/R/R/S, whose chart-topping single, 'Pump up the Volume', allegedly contained a direct sound lift from the SAW produced, 'Roadblock'. M/A/R/R/S replied with a counter-suit, alleging that Sybil's 'Red Ink Mix', another SAW production, took sound from 'Pump up the Volume'. Waterman was joined in his suit by other artists (Trouble Funk, James Brown) and by various industry bodies: the MCPS (the agency formed by music publishers to collect the fee income from the licensing of songs for recording); the BPI (the record industry's trade body); the PRS (the agency formed by music publishers and composers to collect the fee income from licensing songs' public performance). M/A/R/R/S was represented by Britain's top showbiz lawyers, and the case looked set to provide a crucial legal clarification of the sampling situation.

In the event it was settled out of court: M/A/R/R/S agreed a royalty deal for SAW. I'll come back to the settlement and its implications later. First, I want to discuss the two issues involved in the case as it was originally set up: using a musical sound without paying for it was allegedly *a breach of copyright;* passing off someone else's sound as original (and benefiting from it financially) was allegedly a form of *plagiarism.*

The first question to ask is: how was what M/A/R/R/S did any different from the usual pop practices of copying, quoting and indeed, plagiarising? Hasn't pop always been, in Charlie Gillett's words, 'a magpie form'? Haven't pop writers and producers always used musical elements eclectically, taken sounds and ideas from wherever they could find them? Putting it simply: why is *sampling* a bass line different from *imitating* it?

Pete Waterman himself has suggested two sorts of difference. First, a qualitative difference: copying means creating something different by imitation; sampling means using the same sound to the same effect. Yes, rock has always been bound up with copying (and cover versions), but no one can exactly re-produce the original; the Rolling Stones sounded different to Muddy Waters; Vanilla Ice sounds different to Ice-T. Stock, Aitken and Waterman themselves started out 'copying' Minneapolis producers Terry Lewis and Jimmy Jam's rhythmic riffs, but SAW inevitably created their own sound, reflecting their own abilities, equipment and personalities. Rock history has always been about musicians finding their own voices in the process of trying *unsuccessfully* to sound like someone else. Samplers, by contrast, are simply using other people's voices; it's just a question of pushing the right buttons.

It follows, second, that the appeal of a sample record (the reason for its sales and profitability) may well lie in the appeal of the original, sampled sound, rather than in what someone has done to or with it (and in this musical world the sound matters more than the tune – which was the basis of the appeal of cover versions in the 1950s). Waterman thus goes along with the legal distinction between sounds that are 'recognisable' and those that are not; their very recognisability is what enables sounds to give a track its distinction, its market edge. In other words there can be no objection to sampled hi-hat pulses or bass lines *that are not noticed.* Recognisability is a more significant concept in this context than 'substantial'. A micro-second of James Brown's voice may be 'recognisable – give a track its distinction; a three-minute rhythm guitar pattern may not.

This is to beg questions about 'recognisable' (as defined by common sense listeners – and judges) and 'characteristic' sounds (which may be the source of a record's appeal even if listeners can't describe them), but British record producers seem to agree with Waterman's view of sampling ethics:

> 'You're not nicking a drummer's performance, you're nicking his sound,' says Waterman, 'and anyway by rights that sound belongs to the engineer.' ... 'You can't talk about who actually hit that hi-hat eight years ago and pay him a "royalty",' says [Stephen] Hague.
>
> Where does this new generation of producers draw the line then? Can sampling ever be wrong in their eyes?
>
> 'Yes,' says [Martyn] Ware. 'The Rubicon to be crossed is stealing the *hook* from a song and using it in only a slightly different context. That's wrong.' Hague agrees, adding that 'the principles behind sampling something like a James Brown scream are shaky. You are taking the personality. I wouldn't do that.' (Sutcliffe, 1987; and see Porcello, 1991)

In the case of the M/A/R/R/S record, then, Pete Waterman claimed that the sound allegedly stolen – the snatch of a woman's cry – while not defining the 'personality' of 'Pump up the Volume', did determine its pop appeal, did help sell the record, did put it into direct competition with his original (which was now taken to be the copy!).[6] He therefore claimed 50 per cent of the record's earnings (but probably settled for less).

The real issue here, of course, was money. Sampling only becomes an issue when a record is successful, when there is money to be made, and music industry observers concluded that the Waterman–M/A/R/R/S case was settled out of court because the industry didn't want a formal ruling that might make sampling either cheaper or more costly by firmly *defining* concepts like substance and recognition. After all, major record companies all now issue records that use sampling technology, and the value of samples has become just another issue to be negotiated, company to company, lawyer to lawyer, behind the scenes, with the claims to a cut coming in only as a record begins to sell.

In this respect, sampling is easily enough absorbed into the music business tradition of copyright wheeling and dealing. One consequence (to which I'll return) is that the possible defence of sampling in terms of fair use has not yet been mounted. Rather, a kind of working convention has emerged that clearances for samples should be sought in advance (their costs a matter of negotiation – and subsequent sales), which means that a sampler has little defence if clearance has not been granted. Hence the notorious case of Gilbert O'Sullivan vs Biz Markie, in which a US judge came down clearly *against* samplers (Christgau, 1992, p. 79). Another consequence is that samplers have adopted the long established pop rule of thumb about 'folk music' – a song is in public domain if its author is unlikely to sue you. And so sample records make extensive use of sounds lifted from obscure old tracks and from so-called (far away) 'world' music; lifted, it seems, without needing clearance. The ethics of sampling, in short, cannot really be discussed without reference to the contradictory morality of copyright law itself.

WHOSE MUSIC?

Begin with a simple question: what is actually *copyrightable* in music? What is being protected? And a simple answer: music copyright is rooted in nineteenth-century literary property law. What is protected is what can be *notated*, stored in written form – notes and words, a lyric, a melody, an arrangement. The development of recording technology, at the turn of the century, complicated the situation. Recording was another way of fixing or storing sounds, and copyright law had to be adapted to protect record makers from piracy and copying, while reserving the print definition of music as that which could be represented in a score. (Even under the 1956 Copyright Act, to register authorship of a song meant providing a transcription.) This situation is further complicated by digital storage. Music can now be 'written down' in computer language; one can now retrieve a sound exactly *and* manipulate it at will; it is now possible to remove sounds from *within* a record and use them for oneself.

Actually, what's at issue here is not possibility but ease. Taking another example, people have always been able to copy books; but until mechanical printing (and then photocopying) it was hardly economically worthwhile. Similarly with sampling. In the words of Mixmaster Morris, 'Sampling doesn't theoretically offer you anything you can't do with a razor blade and a spool of tape. It's just that you're less likely to cut your fingers, it takes a lot less time and the process is reversible' (quoted in Gray, 1987).

The ease of sampling should not be exaggerated, though. It is not as straightforward as I've been suggesting: which means, on the one hand, that it is not likely to be as widely used as is sometimes implied (it's still *easier* to play a violin into a tape deck than to cue in a sampled violin effectively); and, on the other hand, that samplers certainly do display flair and skill. How does the law protect or encourage them?

In his comprehensive study of the implications for samplers of the 1988 Copyright, Designs and Patents Act, Lionel Bentley concludes that any successful applications for injunctions against them are likely to rest on two rather different sorts of argument (Bentley 1989).

First, there are arguments deriving from the (new) concept of the author's moral right, written into the 1988 Act to bring the UK in line with the Berne Convention and most European states (but not the USA). This clause gives creators 'the right to be identified as the author' (a 'paternity' right which remains the author's regardless of what happens to the work's copyright), and consequently 'the right to object to derogatory treatment of the work' (the right to protect its 'integrity') and thus to object to any 'treatment, mutilation or distortion of the work' which might 'prejudice either the honour or the reputation of the author' (Bentley, p. 114). Such rights would undoubtedly favour the original artist over the sampler.

But there are, secondly, arguments about competition. According to previous copyright case law, artists would have to show that the sampler had damaged their earnings (as Waterman claimed in his case against M/A/R/R/S). This, suggests Bentley, might be a tougher proposition: if the original record was unknown then its sales could well be *increased* by being sampled (a common enough effect in recent pop history); if the record is already well known enough to have 'recognisable' bits, then it has probably sold well enough already! In competitive terms, then, the British courts are quite likely to find for the sampler.

As Bentley points out, the place of moral rights in the treatment of copyright issues in competitive terms has yet to be tested in British courts, and he concludes that the 1988 law is unsatisfactory because it doesn't give the sampler clear guidelines:

> The sampler may take only a small amount, stretch it, change it and add to it, and produce what is for all purposes a creation worthy of encouragement. He can then have the profits he makes from it taken away from him in an action for infringement and costs defending the action. (Bentley, p. 412)

The uncertainties concern what is meant by a 'derogatory' use of the work, on the one hand, and by a substantial use of it, on the other. With regard to the former, some clues to British legal thinking may be found in the judgement of the Copyright Tribunal in the 1991 dispute between the MCPS and the BPI concerning the licensing arrangements (the 'Scheme') for recording songs. The Tribunal notes that Chapter IV of the 1988 Copyright Act creates 'moral rights' in respect of, *inter alia*, musical works:

> It is an aspect of these rights that works should not be subject to 'derogatory treatment' as defined, namely, in the case of a musical work, an arrangement (other than mere change of key or register) which amounts to a distortion or mutilation of the work or is otherwise prejudicial to the honour or reputation of the composer. We take it that the right does not forbid any arrangement: after all, arrangements are a commonplace feature of recordings and any arrangement may be said to distort the original – that is the point of re-orchesrating or making a variation of a musical work. It is only arrangements which are prejudicial to the honour or reputation of the composer which are prevented by the moral right. Probably as a practical matter this could generally apply only to the lyrics of a song. (Copyright Tribunal, 1991, pp. 20–1)

The Tribunal goes on to find the clause in the proposed MCPS licensing scheme which allows record companies to make those 'modifications' to a song necessary for the process of a recording, but not those which 'alter the character' of the work, unreasonable: 'The Scheme also forbids any alterations whatever to lyrics, "dramatico-musical works" or classical works, whether the alterations are derogatory or not. Again we find this unreasonable.' The MCPS 'say that the composer should be able to choose what arrangements are made of his work.'

> We reject the MCPS argument. As a practical matter it was acknowledged that arrangements 'have to happen every day.' So as a practical matter, just as the Scheme must cover the distribution right, so it must cover arrangements, and the only question is what limit should be put on arrangements. The meaningless or near meaningless 'alter the character' ... seems to have no point. What matters is that the arrangement should not be derogatory.
>
> It was particularly suggested that a classical composer might object to any arrangement at all. We wonder if this is really so provided that the arrangement is not derogatory and royalties are paid. 'Pictures at an Exhibition' has been re-arranged and varied many times by other (many great) composers. No harm has been done to the original work. Certainly we have not been made aware of any significant evidence from any composers, classical or otherwise, on this point. (Copyright Tribunal, 1991, pp. 21–2)

The Tribunal therefore supported the BPI proposal that 'the record company should be able to make any modification which it considers necessary to satisfy the requirements of the relevant recording subject only to the moral rights protected by the act' (p. 21), noting that the BPI also provides that 'the record company is not to get any share of what might be called the "arrangement copyright" unless otherwise agreed.' (i.e. that the record company cannot claim to be creating a 'derivative' work in the necessary changes it makes to a work in order to record it) (p. 22). In short, if the Tribunal reflects judicial common sense, then composers might well find it hard to prove that a 'distortion' of their work is 'derogatory', and cases are more likely to focus on words than music.

As far as issues of musical substance are concerned, Bentley suggests that samplers, just as much as the people they sample, need legal protection.

> We are told that intellectual property rights are intended to be incentives to create and innovate. Taking a small amount as the sampler does, does not reduce the rewards of the author: the author will either have reaped all the rewards of this creation, or may be promoted by inclusion in the sampling record.The record will in no way be a substitute for or change the market for the original work. Thus the sampling does not affect the degree of incentive to the creator of an original song or record. The sample record is itself a creation, and the copyright law is at present at least in part creating a disincentive to produce such works. On a straight utilitarian policy ground, sampling should be permitted or even encouraged. Two possible ways of effecting the change can be suggested: first, emphasising the fact that loss of reward to the plaintiff is a crucial factor in assessing substantiality; secondly by introducing a general defence of fair use as in the United States (rather than the restricted defences of fair dealing for specified purposes); the latter was suggested in debates and rejected, perhaps too peremptorily. (Bentley, pp. 412–13)

The rejection mentioned here partly reflects the fact that copyright cases in Britain have always put more emphasis on the private, contractual aspect of copyrights than on the public interest. As the Copyright Tribunal put it, in assessing the various claims by the BPI and MCPS to represent the public good,

> We are not entirely sure about a question of 'pure' public interest (e.g. in a substantial and healthy record industry as such, or lower record prices to the public as such). We say we are not sure because what is being licensed is a private right and the public interest as such is not self-evidently a relevant consideration to that. (Copyright Tribunal, p. 42)

If samplers are, as Bentley argues, as creative as authors, and need their own financial incentives and legal protections, then the public has as much interest in the flow of sounds as record companies, and it is to the public interest that I now want to turn.

CONTROL

Who has the right to control the use of a song or a record or a sound? Until the 1988 Act, music in Britain was subject to a compulsory license clause; that is, once a *song* had been published in recorded form anyone else had a legal right to record it too – all a record producer had to do was pay the fixed royalty rate to the song's author and publisher; to grant a license to record was to grant a blanket license to record. This was in contrast to the rules on the use of a *record*. Here license holders can deny the use of a record (on a soundtrack, for example), even if it has been so used before. They can negotiate each such use on its own terms; they can charge arbitrary and unpredictable fees – hence the incentive to advertisers and film makers, to copy a record rather than use the original recording itself. From a listener's point of view the difference is often unnoticeable. How many TV viewers realised, for example, that it *wasn't* Marvin Gaye singing 'I Heard It Through the Grapevine' on that famous Levi's ad.; that it *wasn't* Elvis Presley and Neil Sedaka on Jeff Goldblum's radio in *The Tall Guy?* As Jane Gaines points out in her chapter in this collection, a similar strategy in the USA (which still has a compulsory license for recorded songs) was eventually challenged not by copyright law but in terms of the invasion of privacy and a judgement more akin to a trademark regulation. As the US Appeals Court ruled in the Bette Midler sound-alike case: 'when a distinctive voice of a professional singer is widely known and is deliberately imitated in order to sell a product, the seller has appropriated what is not theirs' (Stevenson, 1989, p. 19).

The arguments about imitations, in other words, focus not on the fact of copying, but on the meanings of 'distinctive', 'professional' and 'deliberately', and whereas the Midler judgement stressed the direct economic exploitation of her voice, other US actions have involved attempts to prevent the unlicensed use of an original name or sound or image for *any* reason (see Gaines, in this collection, and Lange, 1981).

In Britain, despite the demise of the compulsory license, on the one hand, and the emergence of an author's moral rights, on the other, such arguments are likely to refer to conventional usage already worked out in negotiations among record companies, that is, to 'custom and practice'. Here too, then, control of copyrighted works (and working definitions of fair and competitive use) are likely to be defined in ways that suit record company practice more obviously than they promote creativity. Note, for example, how quick record companies have been to apply digital technology to their own back catalogues, reissuing, remixing, even sampling the work of their artists without much reference to their works' integrity at all. There are occasional rumblings of discontent (musicians unhappy about their old work appearing in material forms not covered in their original contracts; stars unhappy about the sound of their digital versions) but as far as I know there has not yet been a successful challenge to the record companies' right to do to their own copyrighted works what they like. If copyright law is explained in terms of the protection and promotion of creativity, then the concept needs further investigation.

CREATIVITY

In looking at the implication of creative rights (the right to benefit financially from one's own creation) for sampling, we have to draw a distinction between creativity and originality; one can, after all, be 'creative' with a set of musical elements even if one didn't 'originate' them (and British copyright law has always recognised that copyright can be claimed in the arrangement of existing material if such arrangement displays sufficient 'skill and flair'; this has been the standard way for folk performers and publishers to establish a financial stake in songs in the public domain). This is essentially an economic rather than aesthetic argument – a 'creative' arrangement is defined as one which *can* be rewarded (we're back to the question of recognition) – and two definitions of 'creativity' are involved here. On the one hand, there is the flair with which the original song is transformed – and samplers can certainly claim that they are 'arranging sounds' just as musical arrangers arrange tunes (and samplers claim copyright in their 'finished' works accordingly); on the other hand, there is what one might call 'creative exploitation' – the question is whether or not the 'arrangement' directly competes with the original, whether or not it will have a detrimental effect on its sales. To be 'creative', in this respect, is to spot a market possibility the original author hadn't. Thus Abba once failed to prevent the issue of 'unauthorised' Abba tee shirts because the group hadn't previously had this money-spinning idea themselves. The tee shirts certainly used Abba's image but could not be said to be detracting from Abba's income. A sampler who transforms, say, Carl Orff's *Carmina Burana* into a dance floor hit (a notorious Dutch case) could thus claim to be bringing Orff's music to a market not previously thought of.

If sampling can be seen as either a form of creative arrangement or as a form of creative exploitation, it can also be thought of as a form of creative criticism, which is to raise different questions (and, possibly, to bring the sampler up against the concept of moral rights). In the 1950s, the US comedy duo, Buchanan and Goodman, made records by splicing together extracts from hits. (The Barron Knights made similar records ten years later in Britain though, symptomatically, they copied the hits rather than using the records directly.) When Buchanan and Goodman's first single, 'The Flying Saucer', started selling in 1956, the duo was instantly sued by seventeen labels! Buchanan and Goodman claimed that 'Saucer' was a burlesque, and thus effectively a new work. They won their case not just because they had clearly 'transformed' the original but also because their joke record could not possibly detract from the sales of its well-established sources.

The point here, of course (and the same could be said of many sampler records) was that recognisability was precisely the point of the new work – the joke depended on the familiarity of the quotes – and burlesque was therefore defined legally as a species of fair use. There is a precedent for certain sorts of sampling here although, on the other hand, Buchanan and Goodman's burlesques (like the Barron Knights') were essentially friendly; and added to hits' promotion. Many of the most active samplers, by contrast, have been attracted to the process by its cheapness, by the opportunity it offers for independent, individual production (ironically, these days the samplers match the image of the lonely romantic artist rather better than the average pop or rock star). Their comments on the records used (and on the record industry) may not be friendly at all.[7] Negotiations for clearance, in other words, may involve not just negotiations over costs but also over the uses of sounds, and record companies, just as much as artists, may play the 'derogatory' card. This is the context in which samplers might be better off employing a different argument, denying that record companies have any rights in the sounds at all.

PUBLIC DOMAIN

A familiar argument in copyright courts (the most famous recent case concerned recordings of the Lambada) is that a tune is in the public domain, that there is no-one who can claim to be its originator. Sampling suggests another reading of the public domain: certain sounds exist in the public soundscape, we are compelled to listen to them whether we like them or not, and we should therefore also have the right to use them to our own ends (just as we assume we can use our audio and video cassette players, our walkmen, our home digital mixers). Such 'public' records are 'found sounds' just as much as a dog bark or a police siren. As David Lange argues about the case of *DC Comics, Inc.* v. *Board of Trustees* (in which a group of students was sued for calling their newspaper the *Daily Planet*),

> When the proprietor of a mark presumes to intrude into the relationship which the subject of the mark may have contracted with the public in some setting essentially beyond the proprietor's own undertakings – as Superman and all his friends and enemies have a place in the estimation of the American public that simply has nothing to do with the parochial interests of DC Comics, Inc. – the proprietor goes well beyond any purpose legitimate in the law of trademarks and begins, indeed, to engage in an appropriation of its own. It is tempting, but inadequate, to see this as simply a corollary of the rule that trademarks are lost as they take on generic signifi-

> cance. The lesson in the *Daily Planet* case ought to derive instead from a more fundamental recognition of separate rights in the public domain. (Lange, 1981, p. 168)

The corollary for music would be that some records ('Whole Lotta Love', say) become so ubiquitous that they too take on a 'generic' significance. But there is another issue here, which again suggests that the new technology, far from challenging copyright holders' rights, threatens to extend them unreasonably.

Some samplers have argued that their music represents not only a 'democratic' challenge to corporate control but also a new aesthetic. The technology makes possible a form of musical production (best used by rap artists) which captures a new sort of listener experience of urban noises, of the constant bombardment of musical fragments. But such sonic experience has always been an aspect of urban modernism. What's changed by technology is the corporate ability to capture the passing sounds and images on film and tape. As Lange says, once upon a time the Marx Brothers put together an act by drawing on, imitating and quoting a host of long forgotten music hall and burlesque acts; now a theatre company can be sued for using the 'image' of the Marx Brothers now owned, on film, by a studio. The value of that image, in other words, depends on its being fixed in film and thus prevented, it seems, from playing freely in the public domain. 'As access to the public domain is choked, or even closed off altogether, the public loses too: loses the rich heritage of its culture, the rich presence of new works derived from that culture, and the rich promise of works to come' (Lange, p. 165).

Robert Christgau has made exactly the same point about sampling, suggesting that copyright law is being used as a form of censorship: 'the issue is who gets to use this stuff, and for what – whether the public has any claim on the output of public artists whose creation would mean nothing without it' (Christgau, 1986, p. 42). For Christgau, as for Lange, the issue is the power of corporations to appoint themselves as guardians of their artists' 'interests', defined as *all* potential earnings. As Lange puts it,

> The resulting protection guards against the adverse consequences of unfair competition, as it always did, but it does more than that, by far: in effect, it runs against any diminution in the value of any hypothetical interest, and thus it converts each interest into a mutable species of mutant property distastefully reminiscent of *The Alien*. (Lange, p. 168)

AGAINST SAMPLING

This picture of the corporate Goliath and the sampling David is not the only available moral narrative. For example, Bruce J. McGiverin concludes his 1987 survey of sampling and American law as follows:

> Digital sound sampling represents a threat to the livelihoods of an increasing number of acoustic musicians. The current copyright law is equipped to handle the challenges posed by the most extreme abuses of the new technology. The concept of substantial similarity and dubbing may legitimately be interpreted to prevent harm to copyright owners through the direct reproduction of or derivation from something less than the entirety of a recorded work. Moreover, a plaintiff whose work had been sampled for commercial purposes should withstand a defence of fair use. However, when musicians do not own the underlying copyright to their recordings or a use of a sample is insufficiently similar to satisfy a copyright claim, musicians may still obtain relief under state law if state courts extend the right of publicity to sound and voice. State courts should extend this action to offer relief against sound sampling whenever such actions would not be preempted in federal copyright law. (McGiverin, 1987, p. 1745)

This is in striking contrast to the arguments put forward by Bentley, Christgau and Lange for a number of reasons. McGiverin suggests that copyright law should be used to protect the livelihood of 'acoustic musicians'; he assumes that sampling is by nature a kind of 'harm'; he concludes that if such harm cannot actually be recognised in copyright cases, then other forms of law should be invoked. He starts from the premise, that is, that sampling 'poses a threat both to the value of musicians' recorded work and to their professional identities' (p. 1723). The picture here is of the individual musician, struggling to make a living from their unique and fragile talent, and the prowling, faceless sampler, quick to seize the opportunity to make money out of someone else's ideas. It's a picture that seems misleading in both its aspects. On the one hand, the sampler (unlike the pirate) is just as self-conscious an artist – a source of original ideas – as the sampled musician; on the other hand, the 'authors' of a record's sound include *all* those people (performers, arrangers and engineers) needed to turn a song into a disc. In practice, these various authors 'sell' their rights to the recording company which then has exclusive copyright in the record, acknowledging the creative contribution of the performers, producers, etc. through royalty deals (and the basic distinctions between performers and 'session musicians', between producers and engineers, refer less to their actual contributions to a record's sound than to how they are paid for them). The implications of this collaborative process were made clear when the 1971 Sound Recording Act was being drafted in the American congress:

> The copyrightable elements in a sound recording will usually, though not always, involve 'authorship' both on the part of performers whose performance is captured and on the part of the record

> producer responsible for setting up the recording session, capturing and electronically processing the sounds, and compiling and editing them to make the final sound recording. There may be cases where the record producer's contribution is so minimal that the performance is the only copyrightable element in the work ... [T]he bill does not fix the authorship, or the resulting ownership, of sound recordings, but leaves these matters to the employment relationship and bargaining among the interests involved. (Quoted in Thom, 1988, p. 307)

Record 'authorship', in other words, is a matter of contract not creativity; images of individual expression and personality are misleading – what's at issue is their value as commodities. The words of the British Copyright Tribunal seem apposite:

> We also heard particularly sterile evidence and debate as to the relative *creative* roles of composers on the one hand and record companies and performers on the other. What song the siren sang may not be beyond all conjecture, but what certainly is beyond us is any assessment as to whether there has been any change in their relative importance over the years. (Copyright Tribunal, 1991, p. 49)

The Tribunal is right to point to a confusion. Thom, for example, who is well aware of the realities of the recording studio, nevertheless asserts that even taking a sax line from a big band record is theft: 'Each musician on the album has a copyright in his work, which usually has been purchased by the record company. Therefore, the sampling of the tenor sax is an infringement of the saxophonist's copyrightable work' (p. 329). But the copyrightable work at issue is no longer the saxophonist's but the record company's, to whom he has already handed over the right to manipulate, to *exploit* his sound, for their own ends. The sampler, to use Thom's imagery, is not robbing the saxophonist but his record company; the goods (the sax notes) have already been stolen (and there is far more evidence in the history of popular music of musicians being ripped off, deprived of the rightful returns of their work, by their record companies than that any individual musician has ever actually been done out of income by a sampler).

For Thom, though, sampling is simply 'a pirate's dream come true and a nightmare for all the artists, musicians, engineers and record manufacturers' (except, presumably, those artists, musicians, engineers and record manufacturers engaged in sampling). If the US Sound Recording Act of 1971 fails to assert the recording artist's implicit right 'to control recorded performance', then 'an incongruous result of a copyrighted work which is both protected by copyright but also part of the public domain will occur' (Thom, pp. 301, 336).

Thom suggests that previous piracy cases make the situation clear, in two respects:

> First, the unauthorized duplication of copyrighted sound recordings constitutes misappropriation (theft) of another's commercially valuable intellectual property. Second, the only legal process of reproducing the sounds fixated on a copyright recording is by imitation or simulation utilizing one's own studio and musicians. The sounds on a record *are* the genius and talent of the musical laborer. (Thom, 1988, p. 320)

We've already seen the odd consequence of this argument in British law. What's in dispute, it seems, is not what we hear (I doubt if many judges could distinguish between a sample and a soundalike) but how it was produced. Thom distinguishes between compositional copyright (notes as tools) and sound copyright (notes as copyrightable in themselves) but I can't help feeling that there is also a whiff of moral puritanism here. Samplers are taken (mistakenly) to be somehow *idle*, people who just can't be bothered to do the work of re-arranging, re-playing, re-recording the music for themselves.

What I find interesting about Thom's anti-sampling argument, then, is that even though he is discussing the rights involved in the ownership of recorded sound – 'sounds are not ideas but the expression of ideas' – he still uses the imagery of the live performance, he still draws on the moral authority of the performer's personality and spontaneous expression.

> To illustrate this point consider the two words 'hey you.' Suppose a pirate [*sic*] sampled these two sounds from separate Elvis songs. He then puts them into a new song and they are repeated only twice among the sounds independently created by other musicians and vocalists. Would this be an infringement? Perhaps this is trivial. However, what if the sampler used the words 'hey you' two-hundred and seventeen times, building a song around the phrase, which is modified and speeded up so that it sounds different each time. In essence Elvis becomes the vocalist … (Thom, p. 330)

Does he?

CONCLUSION

The American copyright historian, Lyman Ray Patterson, has argued that the recurring problem of copyright law – the reason that it is an unsatisfactory law – lies in its origins: 'copyright was developed as a private concept by a private group; subsequently, it was embodied in a statute.' Judges have, then, been 'bound by the language of the statutes … Their task was to resolve disputes under the statute, not to formulate guiding principles.' And he points to the subsequent 'forgotten ideas of copyright': 'the danger of monopoly from the publisher rather than the author, the differing interests of the publisher and the author, and the right of the individual user' (Patterson, 1968 p. 29).

To put this another way, the moral rhetoric of copyright (the references to creativity, rights, protection, etc.) conceals the basic point that copyright was designed to protect publishers not against authors or users but against other publishers, against piracy: 'this suggests that copyright should be limited again to its traditional functions of protecting the entrepreneur, not the work itself.' There is little reason, Patterson suggests, 'to limit the author's protection to that of the publisher' (Patterson is in favour of separate moral rights for authors, if only as a way of limiting the publisher's monopoly) or to extend the publisher's protection against economic competitors to a protection against 'use' in general: the individual should have the right 'to make whatever use of a copyrighted work he desires, except for competing profits' (p. 228).

Patterson was writing twenty-five years ago about publishing, but his points remain at the heart of the arguments about music, even after the various new copyright bills of the 1980s and 1990s. Again, the moral rhetoric conceals the *different* interests of record companies and their artists, the potential *contradictions* between the use of a musical work as a source of profit and its use as the basis for further creativity. In the end, the legal challenge of digital technology is, as John Oswald argues, that it blurs the boundary between production and consumption, and thus between the different sorts of artistic rights that define music as a commodity: the rights of the commodity creators – authors and publishers, and the rights of the commodity owners – consumers. Indeed, the sampling aesthetic originates, as David Sanjek points out, in the work of cutting and mixing disc jockeys – consumers as producers; producers as consumers (and in Jamaica, where, many of the scratching and dubbing practices began, 'derivative' producers and DJs can hardly be distinguished from 'original' musicians). The art of sampling, in short, is as dependent on samplers' musical knowledge, as consumers, as on their technical abilities, as producers. Sanjek quotes John Leland:

> The digital sampling device has changed not only the sound of pop music, but also the mythology. It has done what punk rock threatened to do: made everyone into a potential musician, bridged the gap between performer and audience. Being good on a sampler is often a matter of knowing what to sample, what pieces to lift off what records; you learn that by listening to music, which makes it an extension more of fandom than musicianship. (Sanjek, 1991, pp. 2–3)

And here is the final threat to orderly ways of making money out of music: in its digital form a 'work' is no longer firmly fixed; it is no longer clearly authored. It is no longer certain, that is, what it means to define music – to store it – as a 'property'.

NOTES

1 Thanks to Robert Christgau and Jon Savage for clarifying my arguments in this paper.

2 As will become evident in this book, record industry trade associations, whether national (BPI) or international (IFPI), are almost exclusively concerned with copyright issues. Even their PR work, their good deeds, are designed to curry favour from politicians. The British School of the Performing Arts, for instance, was bankrolled by the BPI as part of an (unsuccessful) attempt to persuade the Thatcher government to introduce a blank tape levy.

3 This point has been partially recognised in some countries. In Denmark, Sweden and France, for example, a portion of levy income goes not to the record companies but to a state fund which is used to support local music and musicians. On the whole, the industry has opposed such moves, not wanting to confuse a levy (which is, in their terms, a statutory income, the 'fee' paid by the consumer for a blanket license to home tape copyright material) with a tax (money raised by a government for its own policy purposes).

4 Unattributed quotes come from interviews conducted by Jon Savage and myself for the *Observer* in 1987.

5 For further discussion of John Oswald's 'Plunderphonics' see Paul Théberge's essay in this book.

6 It is no accident that most sampling arguments concern dance records, in which the 'gimmick' effect of a specific sound is particularly important: on the dance floor, a rhythmic phrase or repetition matters far more than a tune or linear arrangement.

7 The American band, Culturcide, for example, has as its slogan: 'Home taping is killing the music industry ... so keep doing it!' Their album, which did not even use samples, but simply the group mixed in over the top of other people's records, remained strictly illegal.

REFERENCES

Bentley, Lionel (1989), 'Sampling and Copyright: is the Law on the Right Track?' *Journal of Business Law*, March and September.

Christgau, Robert (1986), 'Down by Law', *Village Voice*, 25 March.

—— (1992), 'Tale of Two Weirdos', *Village Voice*, 21 January.

Copyright Tribunal (1991), Decision on Reference CT 7/90 to the Copyright Tribunal, 1 November.

Gray, Louise (1987), 'Fairlight Robbery', *New Musical Express*, 11 July.

JAMS (1987), *1987*, 12-inch Single JAMS 25T.

Lange, David (1981), 'Recognizing the Public Domain', *Law and Contemporary Problems*, 44 (4)

Lardner, James (1987), *Fast Forward, Hollywood, the Japanese, and the VCR Wars*, New York: W. W. Norton.

McGiverin, Bruce J. (1987), 'Digital Sound Sampling, Copyright and Publicity: Protecting Against the Electronic Appropriation of Sounds', *Columbia Law Review*, 87.

Oswald, John (1987), 'Plunderphonics', *Re Records Quarterly*, 2 (1), Spring.

Patterson, Lyman Ray (1968), *Copyright in Historical Perspective*, Nashville: Vanderbilt University Press.
—— (1991), 'Understanding Fair Use', paper presented to conference on 'Copyright and Authorship', Case Western Reserve University, April.
Porcello, Thomas (1991), 'The Ethics of Digital Audio-Sampling: Engineers' Discourse', *Popular Music* 10 (1).
Sanjek, David (1991), '"Don't Have to DJ No More". Sampling and the "Autonomous" Creator', paper presented to conference on 'Copyright and Authorship', Case Western Reserve University, April.
Stevenson, Richard W. (1989), 'Midler Case Stirs Debate on "Alikes"', *New York Times*, 1 November.
Sutcliffe, Phil (1987), 'Sound wars', *Q*, December.
Thom, J. C. (1988), 'Digital Sampling Old-fashioned Piracy Dressed Up in Sleek New Technology', *Loyola Entertainment Law Journal*, 8 (2).

2

Copyright and the International Music Industry

DAVE LAING

The Christian Church was Europe's first transnational institution and its liturgy gave music an international dimension as early as the Middle Ages. In the fifteenth Century, for example, the Duke of Milan sent a court musician to England to procure the services of choristers trained by the religious composer, John Dunstable (Sanjek, 1988, p. 6). From the Renaissance period, secular music also became increasingly international as composers, choir-masters and orchestra leaders crossed national boundaries and a pan-European corpus of classical works developed. These musicians and composers operated in an economy of patronage which gradually gave way to a market economy in music in the eighteenth and nineteenth centuries. Copyright systems played an increasingly important role as a new breed of publishers established the sheet music industry to provide repertoire for the growing domestic market of parlour pianos. In each country across Europe, the music business joined other copyright interests in lobbying for legal protection. Since music, more than other arts, easily crossed national linguistic and cultural boundaries, the issue of copyright protection in foreign countries became particularly significant.

During the nineteenth century there were two ways to get payment for foreign uses of work: to appoint licensees to exploit the rights under any relevant national legislation in the foreign country, and to persuade governments to sign bilateral copyright treaties with other countries. The difficulties of enforcing exclusive rights in foreign works against publishers who had printed and distributed copies without permission of the author was demonstrated in the case of the British publication of Bellini's opera, *La Sonambula*. In the mid-1840s, the music publisher Boosey & Son had been granted British publication rights by the Italian publisher Ricordi. The UK had passed an International Copyright Act in 1838. Its provisons were extended to musical works four years later. To protect their rights in *La Sonambula*, Boosey followed the provisons of the 1842

Copyright Act regarding the registration of the work and its 'simultaneous publication'. The popularity of the work led three other London publishers to print copies of songs taken from it. Boosey took each to court. In one case he successfully defended his exclusive rights but he lost the others. One, *Boosey* v. *Jeffries*, went on appeal to the House of Lords where, in 1853, British judges decided that foreign authors were not entitled to British copyrights (Barnes, 1974, pp. 162–72).

Similar cases could be found in other European countries. However, the relationship between the United States and European copyright interests provided a different slant on the management of international copyright. As part of a relatively new nation state. United States publishing interests were antagonistic to attempts to enforce payment to foreign authors when the US itself had little copyright material for export. It was not until the 1890s, when the songs of Stephen Foster and others had gained substantial popularity and sheet music sales in Britain, that the US government agreed to protect the rights of foreign composers and publishers. Prior to this, the prevailing view in the US was that such royalty payments would be a 'tax on knowledge' and would cause a balance of payments deficit in the cultural field. Ironically, such arguments have been deployed in more recent times by governments of Asian and African countries against the demands of US copyright interests for extended protection for US works.

By the last decades of the nineteenth century, the growth of the music industry in Europe and North America was such that the pressure for international copyright regulation became irresistible. The activities of the international music industry in this sphere since that time can be divided into three phases:

From the 1880s to the 1930s, the process of copyright reform was dominated by the interests of composers and songwriters, together with those of literary and dramatic writers. The principal vehicle for the international recognition of their rights as authors was the Berne Convention for the Protection of Literary and Artistic Works.

The growth in the importance of mechanical and electrical media such as the cinema, the phonograph and the wireless triggered the second phase, that of the extension of 'neighbouring rights', in the international arena. These rights were those which underpinned the contribution to cultural production of such interest groups as performing musicians and singers, recording companies and film studios, and radio and televisons broadcasters.

US film and music interests have played a commanding role in the third phase of the international copyright process, which gathered momentum in the 1980s. This phase has been characterised by an emphasis on the commercial and trading role of the cultural industries and on the contribution of copyright protection (or the lack of it) in the creation of a 'level playing field' for the global trade in films, music and audio-visual programming. While the protagonists of phases one and two concentrated much of their efforts on establishing and strengthening international copyright conventions, phase three is focused more closely on bilateral treaties between governments or international trading agreements such as the General Agreement on Tariffs and Trade (GATT).

THE RIGHTS OF THE AUTHOR

National organisations devoted to the assertion of the rights of songwriters and composers grew up slowly during the second half of the nineteenth century. The first to be founded was Société des Auteurs, Compositeurs et Editeurs de Musique (SACEM) in France in 1850. The catalyst for SACEM's formation was the need for composers to be granted performing rights in their work. Several composers were drinking in a Paris café when they recognised their tunes in the repertoire of the café orchestra. Enraged at receiving no payment for this use, they refused to pay their bill and took and won a court case against the café proprietor. (Attali, 1985, pp. 77–8).

The number of national authors' societies similar to SACEM grew slowly. By the end of the nineteenth century, only Italy and Austria had followed the French example. Four more societies, including the PRS and ASCAP, were formed before the outbreak of the First World War. This initial reluctance to form national organisations was due to differences in attitude towards the importance of receiving payment for the performance of music. While SACEM regarded this as of equal significance to the sale of copies of songs, in the UK music publishers for many years refrained from charging singers or music hall owners. This was because they regarded the publicity given to their songs through public performance as of prime significance in generating sales of sheet music. This argument was later to be echoed in debates over the radio airplay of pop records and the television screenings of video clips.

The divergence between the approach of SACEM and of the British publishers came to a head in 1890. In that year SACEM appointed a UK representative whose job was to charge fees for the public performance of works by French composers. The lack of co-operation from the British music industry was such that SACEM contemplated reporting the UK to the committee responsible for administering the Berne Convention to which both France and Britain were signatories (Ehrlich, 1989, pp. 6–7). That Convention, signed in 1886, had been the outcome of bilateral meetings between cultural workers. These were frequent in the late nineteenth century and it was from one of these – between French and German writers – that the notion was born of an international treaty binding goverments to a common level of support and protection for all authors.

Despite its title, the Convention was in essence a treaty whose purpose was to protect *authors'* rights in literary and artistic works. Since 1886, the Berne Convention has been amended six times. The main purpose of the amendments has been to enable authors' rights to keep pace with new uses of their works brought about by technological change. The Berlin revison of 1908 incorporated references to photography, the cinema film and sound recording. The Rome Act of the Convention in 1928 extended authors' control of their work to sound broadcasting, while television was brought within the scope of the Convention at Brussels in 1948. The concept of an author's 'moral rights' was first included in 1928. Later revisions in Stockholm (1967) and Paris (1971) concentrated on such issues as the 'compulsory licensing' of films and possible exemptions from parts of the Convention for Third World countries.

Nine countries signed the original Berne document, seven of them European. By 1993, there were almost 100 signatories. In principle, the effect of acceding to the Convention is that each signatory agrees to incorporate its provisions into its national law. But there are significant limits to this process and to the protection a Berne signatory can provide for works of citizens of other Berne states. The Convention lays down minimum standards of protection which may be increased in national law. In addition, a number of its provisions are optional. A case in point is the granting of 'moral rights', such as the right of an author to be properly identified and to insist that any editing of a work preserves its integrity. When the United States finally joined the Berne Convention in 1989, pressure from film industry interests ensured that the country opted out of the moral rights part of the treaty.

Although the purpose of the Berne Convention is that each country should provide protection for foreign authors within its own copyright law, these rights can be adopted into national law in two distinct ways. 'National treatment' for foreign authors means simply that these copyright owners will receive the same level of protection as domestic authors. But a Berne Convention member can also decide to grant 'reciprocal treatment'. This means that foreign authors will get only the level of protection which is granted in their own country. The most prominent current example of reciprocal treatment for authors concerns the private copying or home taping levies which exist in a number of European countries. The only foreign composers entitled to share in the distribution of these levies are those from countries which also have a blank tape levy in place.

Another crucial 'opt-out' for national governments was written into the Berne Convention clause concerned with broadcasting. The general rights of authors granted by the Convention gave them the power to 'authorise or prohibit' the use of their work. By the late 1920s, the radio industry had itself become a powerful force in Europe and music was one of its most important sources of programme material. When the issue of broadcasting rights for composers was considered by the Berne Convention nations, there was a strong lobby for the alternative of a 'compulsory licence' to be substituted for the right to prohibit. Under this system the copyright owner is compelled by law to allow works to be used, subject to appropriate payment from the music user. Rather than substitute the compulsory licence procedure for the right to authorise or prohibit, the Berne Convention countries decided to allow each national government to opt for one or the other in relation to broadcasting.

By allowing countries to operate a compulsory licence procedure, the Convention ensured a constant supply of music for radio, even when there was a dispute over royalty payments. Songwriters and publishers were obliged to permit broadcasters' use of their work, subject only to the payment by radio stations of 'equitable remuneration'. The ultimate decision on what constitutes equitable remuneration is taken in most countries by a government-appointed tribunal or special court. The definition of authorship itself came into question in 1928, when the nature of cinematographic works was under discussion. Prior to this, the Convention had accepted that an author of a book, play or song was a single individual or a partnership of named individuals. The author had a separate existence from the publisher whose role was to put the work into circulation. While the collaborative nature of film-making made it more difficult to locate a single individual as author, the committee dealing with the revision of the Convention was faced with the fact that both the production of movies and their distribution were under the control of companies, not individuals. The committee was deadlocked on whether the Convention should accept the idea of corporate authorship. It was again decided that the definition of the author of a film should be a matter for decision by each member of the Convention.

These disputes over definitions of authorship and over broadcasting rights have been interpreted by some commentators as a direct reflection of conflicting legal philosophies between the Latin countries of continental Europe and the Anglo-American group of nations. For instance, Vincent Porter writes that 'the Roman Catholic countries of France, Italy, Spain and to a lesser extent Germany, saw the author's right as a human right with almost mystical overtones ... in some countries, this mystic right stretched beyond the grave into eternity' (Porter, 1991, p. 2).

This emphasis on the right of the author as the fundamental and primary right in creative work is reflected in the Berne Convention itself. The text deals solely with authorship and does not acknowledge the interests of other contributors to the creative process. In the jargon of

Latin jurisprudence, they possess 'neighbouring rights' (*droits voisins*), a secondary level of legal right. The rationale of this philosophy was restated in a contemporary context in a 1992 speech by Jean Loup Tournier, president of SACEM: 'The only arms which authors possess to defend their legitimate interests are the rights they draw from the law, since they have no actual means (right to strike, physical prohibition) of opposing the use, the reproduction and thus the pirating of their works. Owners of neighbouring rights, be they performers or producers, do have the physical means of defending themselves' (Tournier, 1992).

The contrasting approach, deriving from English common law, has been described by Porter, somewhat disingenuously, as the 'public interest approach' (Porter, 1991, p. 3). While this view recognises that the Anglo-American notion of copyright tends to give greater weight to the needs of the users of copyright than does the Latin approach, it underplays the extent to which US and UK copyright law has been framed to accommodate the interests of the owners and distributors of cultural products through the granting of primary copyright status to 'producers' of film, television and music products. The advancement of the global interests of this sector of the cultural industries has constituted the second phase of international copyright reform in the twentieth century.

THE NEIGHBOURING RIGHTS ERA

When the Berne Convention was drawn up, the music industry was on the eve of a technological and commercial revolution. In 1886, the only means of exploitation of music were by live performance and by the sale of printed music. Within twenty years, the use of sound recordings had become a powerful new means of communication with audiences. Two decades later, radio supplanted records as the principal user of musical works. Not only did Berne have to contend with these new uses, but these new music users themselves claimed copyright interests in music and other media. In the United Kingdom, the 1911 Copyright Act had acknowledged the ownership of sound recordings by 'record producers'. Although today this term is generally used to refer to a category of specialists who supervise studio recordings, its legal reference is to those who own or control the rights in the recordings. In most cases, these are the record labels and record companies which contract performers, finance recording sessions and issue copies of recordings to the public. The term 'record producer' is used in this sense throughout this article.

In 1933, one such record producer, The Gramophone Company (EMI Records) won an historic case in the United Kingdom against a Bristol restaurant owner, Stephen Cawardine & Co. The change in 1925 from acoustic to electrical means of sound recording had enhanced the quality and volume of reproduction. As a result, a growing number of hotels, bars and other premises had begun to use gramophone records to entertain their customers or clients. Like the French composers eighty years previously, the Gramophone Co. objected to this exploitation without payment of its property. The Cawardine case made the UK the eighth country to recognise a performing right for record companies and recording artists. A new organisation. Phonographic Performance Ltd (PPL) was set up to administer these rights through the issue of licences to users of recorded music.

The Cawardine decision coincided with the formation of an international organisation to represent the recording industry. This was the International Federation of the Phonographic Industry (IFPI) whose first congress in Rome in 1933 was attended by representatives of national trade organisations from Germany, France, Italy and the UK. Over the subsequent years, IFPI has become one of the most skilled lobbyists for copyright reform at the international level. It has established consultative status with the International Labour Organisation (ILO, 1938), with UNESCO (1948) and with the World Intellectual Property Organisation (WIPO). More recently, IFPI has established itself as a consultative body with the European Commission.

One of its initial aims was to achieve a similar treaty to the Berne Convention for owners of neighbouring rights. This was to take almost thirty years, principally because of conflicts of interest among neighbouring rights owners themselves. As Porter has written, the 1961 Rome Convention for the Protection of Performers, Producers of Phonograms and Broadcasting Organisations was, in reality, 'a deft interweaving of three separate minor conventions which afford different levels of protection ...' (Porter, 1991, p. 13). Predictably, the point of view of IFPI itself was somewhat different. According to Stephen Stewart, IFPI's then director general, 'The Rome Convention provided a breakthrough and put record producers and performers on the international map as rights owners, as opposed to rights users' (Stewart, 1983, p. 16).

The Rome Convention confirmed the rights of both performers of music and of record producers to control the reproduction of their work and its public performance. It set a minimum period of copyright protection at twenty years. On broadcasting, the Rome Convention followed Berne and provided for a compulsory licence with equitable remuneration. These latter provisions indicate the extent to which the Convention had indeed been a compromise between different interests. Today, most national laws protect sound recordings for fifty years and the US has a seventy-year period. Both the compulsory licence and the twenty year minimum was something of a sop to broadcasters who wished to see records fall into the 'public domain' and therefore become free of copyright royalties as quickly as possible. Signatories to the Rome Convention could also opt out of granting broadcasting rights altogether. This option has been exercised by Monaco and Luxembourg, two small European countries with powerful music radio stations broadcasting to neighbouring countries.

The Convention left to national laws the basis on which broadcasting royalties should be shared between record producers and performers. This issue has since been made the subject of an agreement between IFPI and the two international unions of performers – the International Federation of Musicians (FIM) and the International Federation of Actors (FIA). Under this agreement, the two parties agree to divide equally any broadcasting royalties collected on their joint behalf. In most European countries, as well as Japan, a single collecting society for performers and producers is in operation.

In the first thirty years of its existence, the Rome Convention was joined by thirty-five states, less than half the membership of Berne after a hundred years. The relationship between 'contracting' and 'non-contracting' states is complex, notably in relation to broadcasting royalties. As with Berne, Rome provides a fundamental national treatment for performers, producers and broadcasters of other contracting states. Rights owners from non-contracting states may also share in royalties if the recording in question received 'simultaneous publication' in the contracting state. 'Simultaneous' is defined here as 'within thirty days' of the recording being released in its country of origin. However any contracting country may drop the criterion of 'publication' of a recording and replace it with one of 'first fixation'. This term refers to the geographical location of the studio, concert hall, back bedroom etc. where the recording was created. To adopt this criterion means to exclude all recordings from non-contracting countries from the share-out of royalties. These details have taken on added significance because the nation which originates the majority of the world's most popular and most played recordings is not a member of the Rome Convention. The broadcasting lobby has to date ensured that the United States does not give broadcasting rights to performers and producers.

To adopt the criterion of 'first fixaton', as such countries as Finland, Sweden, France and Italy have done, means that performers and producers of US recordings cannot benefit from airplay of their works. (Royalties must still be paid to US songwriters.) Additionally, broadcasters in Scandinavia pay copyright fees only for the proportion of airtime devoted to 'protected' (non-US) recordings. This is clearly a disincentive to broadcast records by local artists. This view was shared by the authors of a report commissioned by the UK government in 1989. The survey was undertaken to decide whether to abolish the criteria of publication, a move which could have saved millions of pounds for broadcasters. It rejected the change, partly on cultural grounds. To make US recordings cheaper than British recordings to play over the airwaves would have lessened the opportuntities for local performers (Dept of Trade and Industry, 1989).

According to IFPI itself, performance royalties for performers and producers added up to no more than $ 200 million worldwide compared to the $ 17 billion wholesale value of record and tape sales in 1992. Since the 1970s, performance rights have been a lower priority for the international music industry than piracy and home taping. Like the Berne Convention, the Rome Convention has been outpaced by technological developments in the recording, duplication and distribution of music. These have enabled and accelerated such unforeseen uses of recorded music as home taping or 'private copying', the widespread rental of audio and audi-visual products, digital broadcasting via cable and satellite and piracy. Home taping and rental have been addressed in some national copyright laws of the 1980s and 1990s, while DAB (digital audio broadcasting), which can offer thirty or more channels of non-stop music, did not become a reality until the early 1990s and has not yet been addressed by legislators. The view of IFPI is that the ease with which it can enable home copying means that DAB should not be treated as a new form of broadcasting but as a method of distributing music comparable to the retailing of records and tapes.

These three topics were all put on the agenda of a committee set up in 1991 to consider the feasibility of a 'protocol' to the Berne Convention. This Berne Protocol would seek to codify a comprehensive set of rights for performers and producers, comparable to that which the Berne Convention provides for authors. Even if this protocol comes about, however, it is unlikely to be ratified by national governments until the late 1990s.

The issue which rose most quickly to the top of the music industry agenda after the Rome Convention, however, was piracy. While the Convention provided broad protection against copyright infringement, it was drafted at a period when the piracy of sound recordings was still a relatively minor problem for the music industry. Although unauthorised copies of vinyl records had been produced in earlier decades, it was the arrival of the compact tape cassette in 1963 which provided the technology for music piracy to become big business. The new technology was smaller in scale than the heavy industrial plant required for vinyl manufacturing. Tape duplication equipment was far cheaper to purchase than the heavy duty presses for vinyl discs. Apart from its cumbersome reel-to-reel predecessor, the compact cassette was also the first mass-produced pre-recorded music format that could also be used to make recordings.

By the end of the 1960s, it was clear that the piracy and counterfeiting of pre-recorded cassettes was becoming endemic and IFPI decided to follow up the Rome Convention with a proposal for a new international treaty specifically designed to deal with piracy. The result was the 1971 Convention for the Protection of Producers of Phonograms against Unauthorised Duplication of their Phonograms, known more briefly as the Phonograms Convention. This treaty added new import and distribution rights to those already granted in the Rome Convention. Record producers could now stop illegal imports and take action against wholesalers and retailers as well as those who manufactured illegal copies.

The Phonograms Convention had gained the adherence of thirty-six countries by 1983 and forty-three by 1993. After its passing, the international record industry devised a three-stage global strategy to control piracy. According to IFPI's director general, Stephen Stewart: 'Stage I was protecting the major markets; Stage II protecting minor markets in the record-producing countries and thus throwing a *cordon sanitaire* around 90 per cent of the world's production. Stage III was clearing the countries which were very largely piratical and are mainly, but not entirely, situated in the developing world.' In 1983, Stewart was able to add that while Stages I and II had largely been achieved. 'Stage III has merely begun' (Stewart, 1983, p. 17).

For the purposes of achieving Stewart's Stage III, the system of international conventions has proved to be less effective than a different kind of lobbying which harnesses the economic and political weight of certain nation states and trading blocs to the demand for anti-piracy action by governments in the developing world. For this type of lobbying the commercial importance of music as an export industry counts for more than the legal rights of copyright owners.

THE AGE OF ECONOMIC RIGHTS

The rise of piracy and home taping coincided with a 'globalisation' of popular music and the record industry. The success of The Beatles and other performers in the 1960s significantly increased the share of world record sales taken by Anglo-American performers and songwriters. Nowadays many national trade organisations measure the percentage of record sales attributable to foreign repertoire. In 1991, this ranged from 22 per cent in Japan to 77 per cent in the Netherlands (*Financial Times*, 1993, p. 7). Across continental Europe, foreign records account for an average of 40–50 per cent and most of this foreign repertoire originates in the United States and the United Kingdom. While there are no official music industry calculations of world market share on the basis of national origins, it is likely that recordings originating in the UK and US represent around one half of current record sales.

Coinciding with this cultural change, US-owned recording companies took on an international role in the 1960s and 1970s. In the past, such firms as CBS, WEA, MCA and A&M had been content to contract local companies to market and distribute their recordings outside North America. Now they have branches in Europe which take direct responsibility for selling their own repertoire and in many cases also make a bid for a share of the local music market by signing local artists. Over the past twenty years, too, the growth of music markets in Europe and Asia has caused a steady decline in the percentage of the world market held by US domestic sales. In 1971, this figure was approximately 45 per cent. By 1981 it had shrunk to 37 per cent and in 1991 to 32 per cent (Hung and Morencos, 1990, pp. 84–5).

Taken together, these factors have caused a greatly increased awareness of the importance of foreign markets for US copyright music and recordings. They have coincided with a similar growth in sensitivity to international markets on the part of the United States film and television industries. A survey of US copyright industries by Stephen Siwek and Harold Furchgott-Roth of Economists Incorporated estimated that 'core copyright industries' were responsible for export earnings of $34 billion in 1990. Of this amount, $5.4 billion was generated by the music business. The survey showed that the copyright industries were the third largest exporters in the US behind agriculture and aircraft and ahead of computers and electronics (Economists Incorporated, 1992).

The focus on world markets has led to special scrutiny of those countries believed by US industries to maintain trade barriers to American exports of films, music and TV shows. In some cases the barriers take the form of quotas, restricting the amount of broadcasting time taken by foreign material. The television regulations of the European Community have come under attack for this reason, as has the exclusion of US copyright owners from home taping royalty payments in France and Germany. Some nations also have punitive currency export regulations or corporate ownership rules which make it very difficult for US companies to operate. But the principal 'trade barrier' faced by the US is the existence of weak copyright laws and even weaker enforcement.

Led by the Motion Picture Association of America (MPAA), the US copyright industries have banded together to form the International Intellectual Property Alliance (IIPA). The Recording Industry Association of America (RIAA) and the National Music Publishers Association are among the member organisations of the IIPA. Since the election to the presidency of ex-actor Ronald Reagan, the IIPA has had an increasing influence on America's foreign trade policies. The principal instrument for pressurising foreign governments has been the so-called Special 301 provision of the 1988 Omnibus Trade and Competitiveness Act. This permits the United States Trade Representative (USTR) to nominate

'Priority Foreign Countries' whose trading practices are alleged to be harmful to US industries, including those like music which are dependent on the protection of intellectual property. Once designated, nations can be subject to trade sanctions if they fail to improve their commercial and trading rules.

As a preliminary stage of its activities, the USTR in 1989 set up a Watch List and a Priority Watch List of countries felt to be unfair trading partners of the United States. Two years later, three countries – Thailand, China and India – were the first to become Priority Foreign Countries for their failure to adequately protect us copyright material. An intensive six-month period of negotiation and investigation followed. Afterwards, the governments of China and India announced plans to improve copyright protection. China joined the Berne Convention in 1992 while the Indian government agreed to ease restrictions on the operations of foreign companies. In subsequent years, the list of 301 Priority Foreign Countries has been lengthened to include Taiwan and South Korea.

Inspired by the success of us pressure on Asian governments, the European Commission was persuaded by the music industry to adopt a similar approach in relation to Indonesia in 1986. The extent of piracy of foreign recordings had been highlighted when bootleg cassettes of the 1985 *Live Aid* concerts in London and Philadelphia were discovered in Indonesia. Subsequently, the EC accepted a complaint from IFPI against Indonesia under a relatively obscure 1984 Regulation related to the Common Commercial Policy of the EC. This gave the EC the right to use such sanctions as import restrictions and increased customs duties. The EC subsequently initiated an inquiry into piracy in Indonesia and the Indonesian government eventually agreed to improve the level of protection. A new copyright law was introduced in 1988. From a 100 per cent rate, the piracy of foreign recordings had fallen to 30 per cent in 1991. In 1992, the EC began a similar inquiry into the piracy of European sound recordings in Thailand.

An ambitious attempt to incorporate these trade-related aspects of copyright protection was made as part of the Uruguay Round of the GATT treaty. First negotiated in 1948, GATT is an international treaty designed to promote and police free trade on a worldwide basis. The GATT treaty is renegotiated about every ten years and the 1986 round of discussions, named after the country in which they started, incorporated trade in intellectual property for the first time.

The talks on the so-called TRIPS (Trade Related Aspects of Intellectual Property Rights, Including Trade In Counterfeit Goods) were marked by fierce disagreements between exporting countries led by the US and EC and those developing countries with a negative balance of trade in 'intellectual property', led by Brazil and India. In these debates, the concept of intellectual property included not only artistic works such as music and films but products derived from patents in the fields of computers and electronics. In economic terms, the latter were of great significance. A 1993 report, for example, detailed some $4.6 billion in alleged losses to American companies from 'copyright piracy'. Of this, almost half ($2.2 billion) came from unauthorised copying of computer software. Pirated music accounted for one-quarter of the total (*Financial Times*, 1993, pp. 1–2).

By the end of 1991, a draft TRIPS treaty had been devised. Many of its seventy-three clauses echoed the Berne and Rome Conventions in providing fundamental rights for authors, performers and producers. It included detailed provisions on the role of customs services and courts in dealing with piracy. The treaty made allowances for the difficulties of developing countries by permitting them to phase in the trips provisions over five or ten years. Broadly, it pleased Western copyright owners by opening up Third World markets in a more comprehensive way than before. The TRIPS proposals remained frozen during 1992 while disputes over other parts of the GATT treaty were dealt with. They will only be adopted by the over 100 countries which are members of GATT when these disputes over agricultural exports have been resolved.

This trend towards the incorporation of music copyright issues into the framework of international trading policies was also reflected in regional programmes for free trade which were developed in the late 1980s and early 1990s. The two most important of these are likely to come into force before agreement is reached on GATT. They are the North American Free Trade Area (NAFTA) and the Single European Market programme of the EC. The NAFTA treaty will end trade barriers between Mexico, the United States and Canada. Under it, the three countries will give national treatment to each other's copyright owners. However, NAFTA specifically permits the continuation of the Canadian government's programme of state support for the arts, which includes an airtime quota for Canadian music.

The EC programme for a single market was intended to be completed by January 1993, a target date which was not fully met. Among those parts of the single market project which were not in place by the 1993 deadline was a scheme to harmonise the copyright laws of its twelve member countries. This consisted of a number of directives which, once agreed, would be incorporated in each country's national law. Those of direct interest to the music industry include directives on rental, private copying, the duration of copyright protection and the transborder aspects of cable and satellite broadcasting. By early 1993 only the directive on the rental of videos and compact discs had been adopted by the EC Council of Ministers. Like the other EC directives, this was broadly favourable to the interests of copyright owners, granting them the right to prohibit rental, an issue of particular concern to the German music business. In Germany, CD rental had become a profitable sideline for video rental stores in the late 1980s.

EC proposals on private copying levies and the duration of copyright protection set future Europe-wide levels at the highest existing national rates of royalties on blank tapes and the longest protection periods for authors and neighbouring rights owners. The approach of the European Commission officials who drafted these directives showed the continuing influence of the *droit d'auteur* philosophy, something which was not lost on representatives of the US media industries. American commercial interests in general were already concerned about a possible protectionist, 'Fortress Europe' dimension to the single market. Now, leading officials of US-based conglomerates have launched attacks on the copyright harmonisation proposals on the grounds that their commitment to reciprocal treatment for foreign rights owners would deny revenues to US companies and individuals. In a hard-hitting speech, Robert D. Hadl, vice president and general counsel of MCA Inc, spoke in 1992 of the EC 'creating a crisis in international copyright' (Hadl, 1992).

Hadl argued that the majority of video rentals in Europe were of US films. But the EC rental directive was so worded that the producers and authors of these films could not share in any revenues paid to collecting societies by video rental outlets. This was because US law does not allow control over video rental. Hadl had a further complaint against the EC approach. By making the author's and performer's right to 'equitable remuneration' from rental and private copying royalties inalienable, he said, 'freedom of contract would be subverted'.

Hadl was referring here to the EC's intention to monitor the flow of royalties to ensure that authors and performers are properly rewarded. In the view of MCA and other corporations, this amounted to governmental interference in the right, for instance, for a performer to agree by contract to 'cross-collateralise' income from rental or private copying with that from other sources. In the music industry, this could mean recording artists agreeing that home taping royalties would be set against recording studio advances due to record companies instead of being paid directly to the artists themselves. Ironically, a safeguard against cross-collateralisation was built into the United States' own legislation on private copying royalties, the Digital Audio Home Recording Act of 1992. This states that private copying monies will be paid directly to artists, although it does not forbid future recording contracts from including clauses under which artists might agree to some form of cross-collateralisation.

The US Act was the first substantial piece of copyright legislation to be agreed in America for over a decade and its success was due to a relatively new approach to international copyright reform. This is a type of copyright diplomacy which has taken place not between governments but between the multinational companies which dominate both the music and the electronics industries. The 1992 Act was thus made possible by an unprecedented agreement made a year earlier between the various representative bodies of the US music industry and the Electronics Industry Association (EIA), whose members are the importers and manufacturers of CD players, cassette recorders and other domestic recording and playback equipment. The two sides had spent many years of deadly combat in their lobbying of bemused Senate committees which invariably became deadlocked over the issue of home taping. In 1991, however, the music business and the EIA put together a set of proposals for a limited levy on digital blank tape and equipment. Through their unanimity, the proposals were able to become law.

This process of convergence between the two industries was a global one which began fitfully in the mid-1980s. The point at issue was the intention of hardware companies to place a Digital Audio Tape (DAT) recorder on the market. The music industry saw this as extremely damaging to the then fledgling CD market. DAT, they argued, could be the basis of an explosion in digital home taping which would affect sales of CDs. The dispute was made more acute by the fact that the most powerful companies in the hardware industry were Japanese-owned whereas the music business at that time was controlled by US and European firms. This was a time when Western antagonism to allegedly unfair (and highly successful) Japanese trading practices was at its height. The DAT controversy was coloured by this antagonism so that Japanese companies were accused of an indifference or hostility to the rights of artistic creators.

In these circumstances, it was not surprising that it took many months before IFPI (on behalf of the record industry) could persuade the Electronics Industry Association of Japan (EIAJ) to meet to discuss the DAT issue. An initial conference meeting finally occurred in Vancouver in December 1986. IFPI officials had expected to have private talks in an atmosphere of secrecy. They arrived to discover that the EIAJ delegation, which included the heads of all the main electronics firms, had already held a press conference to announce that they would persevere with DAT. The failure of the Vancouver talks led to a harder line by the international music industry which deployed two tactics to thwart the launch of DAT to consumer markets. The first was the development of a so-called 'spoiler' mechanism which could prevent or limit the use of digital audio tape for copying recorded music. The specific mechanism chosen by the record industry was the Copycode system developed by CBS. When Copycode was demonstrated to the European and US media, it received a hostile reception because of its impact on the sound quality of recordings and, after its rejection by technical advisers to the US government, it was abandoned.

The record industry's second tactic was more successful. It involved a simple refusal to supply repertoire for release on pre-recorded DAT tapes. Following the marketing patterns of the existing analogue compact cassette format and of Compact Disc, the electronics industry needed to have available a full range of pre-recorded music in order to persuade consumers to invest in a DAT system. When all of the major record companies denied access to their catalogues, attempts to sell DAT on the consumer markets of Europe and the US were abandoned. Instead DAT became almost entirely a professional format, used universally in recording studios.

The lessons of the DAT saga were not lost on the major Japanese manufacturers. They were now forced to acknowledge the need for the co-operation of owners of copyright material in the successful marketing of future generations of audio playback and recording hardware. This realisation was dramatically illustrated in 1987 when Sony Corporation of Japan purchased CBS Records for $2 billion. Overnight, one of the more intransigent hardware companies had become the world's largest owner of copyright recorded music. Two years later Japan's largest consumer electronics company, Matsushita, followed Sony and acquired the MCA Entertainment group for $6 billion. As well as a major film studio, MCA owned one of the big three music companies in the US.

Sony and Matsushita lined up alongside the Dutch-owned hardware company, Philips (owners of PolyGram), as multinational companies whose interests included both hardware and music software. The stage was set for a new series of more positive negotiations which resulted in the Athens Agreement of 1989 between IFPI and the international consumer electronics business. This 'memorandum of understanding' involved an historic compromise between the two industries on the private copying issue. In a carefully worded clause, European electronics companies led by Philips accepted the principle of royalties on blank tape and recording hardware while their Japanese counterparts acknowledged 'the extreme importance' placed by the copyright owners on the royalty principle (Davies, 1991, p. 7). All sides agreed that a new digital Serial Copy Management System (SCMS), developed by Philips, should be added to the technical specifications of digital recording machines. The SCMS chip permits one copy to be made of a recording but does not allow further copies to be cloned from the initial copy.

The terms of the Athens Agreement were designed to act as guidelines for national legislation throughout the world and they formed the basis of the EC directive on private copying as well as the US Audio Home

Recording Act. Progress on copyright reform was slower in Japan, although government regulations have made it mandatory for DAT recorders offered to the public to include the SCMS chip. Elsewhere, the music industry was intent on ensuring that the new Digital Compact Cassette (DCC) and Mini Disc machines would be equipped with SCMS. DAT, DCC and Mini Disc are only the first of numerous innovations in the distribution of digitally recorded music, and the parties to the Athens Agreement have set up a continuing working party on the copyright implications of such formats as CD-R (recordable) and CD-WORM (write once-read many). These are all variants of the optical disc of which CD was the prototype. And while the optical disc is likely to become the global standard for multi-media playback and interactive systems, the music business is faced with further technological challenges in the 1990s. These include the possibility of electronic delivery of recorded music via fibre optic cable into the consumer's home, and the reality of multi-channel CD quality DAB radio.

Having forged one unlikely alliance – with electronics manufacturers – the music industry is faced with the need to protect its copyrights on further fronts. Although collaboration with electronic retailers and broadcasters may seem a distant hope, so did co-operation with hardware firms a decade ago. The late 1990s may see further deals between multinational entertainment firms acting as blueprints for copyright legislation across the globe.

REFERENCES

Attali, Jacques (1985), *Noise. The Political Economy of Music*, Manchester: Manchester University Press.

Barnes, John J. (1974), *Authors, Publishers and Politicians: The Quest for an Anglo-American Copyright Agreement (1815–1854)*, London: RKP.

Davies, Gillian (1991), 'Digital Audio Tape and New Technology', in Kingston, M. (ed.) *IFPI Review: the Challenge of the 1990s*, London: IFPI

Department of Trade and Industry (1989), *Copyright Protection of Foreign Sound Recordings, Report by National Economic Research Associates*, London: HMSO.

Economists Incorporated (1992), *Copyright Industries in the US Economy. A Report Prepared for the International Intellectual Property Association*, Washington DC: IIPA.

Erlich, Cyril (1989), *Harmonious Alliance. A History of the Performing Right Society* Oxford: Oxford University Press.

Financial Times (1993), 'Music and Copyright Newsletter', 12 March.

Hadl, Robert D. (1992), 'The Crisis in International Copyright', unpublished speech to the 38th Congress of the International Federation of Societies of Authors and Composers (CISAC), Maastricht, October.

Hung, Michele and Morencos, E. G. (1990), *World Record Sales 1969–1990, A Statistical History of the World Recording Industry*, London: IFPI.

Porter, Vincent (1991), *Beyond the Berne Convention*, London: John Libbey.

Sanjek, Russell (1988), *American Popular Music and Its Business. The First 400 Years*, vol. 1, Oxford: Oxford University Press.

Stewart, Stephen (1983), 'The Years 1961 to 1979', in Borwick, J. (ed.), *IFPI. The First Fifty Years*, London: IFPI.

Tournier, Jean Loup (1992), unpublished speech to the 38th Congress of the International Confederation of Societies of Authors and Composers (CISAC), Maastricht, October.

3

Technology, Economy and Copyright Reform in Canada

PAUL THÉBERGE

> Don't you see what perpetual copyright implies? It is perpetual racial memory! That bill will give the human race an elephant's memory. *Have you ever seen a cheerful elephant?*
>
> (Robinson, 1984, p. 12)

Spider Robinson's science fiction short story, 'Melancholy Elephants', portrays a time in the not-so-distant future when it has become increasingly difficult to write music without inadvertently infringing on someone else's copyright. The situation has become desperate: copyright submissions are subjected to computer analysis and the rejection rate is so high that some noted composers are driven to suicide while others content themselves with being able to publish something new once in about every five years.

Like most science fiction however, Robinson's story is not so much about some possible future as it is about the present and the recent past: the inspiration for this science fiction tale would appear to have been the much publicised case during the late 1970s and early '80s in which George Harrison was convicted of *unconsciously* plagiarising the Chiffon's 1960s hit, 'He's So Fine'. Harrison was certainly not the first musician who, in the normal practice of his craft, had purposely or (as he had claimed) unknowingly borrowed from other sources. But his unexpected encounter with the legal and economic system known as copyright (which cost him 75 per cent of the profits to 'his' song, 'My Sweet Lord') would certainly appear, to the casual observer, to be the stuff of fiction as much as reality.

In fact, in the realm of music copyright , I suspect that truth is often stranger than fiction and certainly more complex. Copyright law attempts to define 'ideas' and their 'expression';[1] it assigns both 'authorship' (no matter how many people were involved in a particular production); it attempts to establish which 'uses' of a work are permissible (in an environment in which new uses are being created with increasing rapidity); and tries to determine when damages or remedies may, or may not, be required (mere 'copying' does not inevitably lead to charges of 'infringement'). Moreover, recent innovations in technology (a realm in which even science fiction would seem to have difficulty keeping pace) have called into question the basic definitions of musical expression, authorship and use, and many countries have been forced to re-evaluate their copyright legislation.

As this process takes place it has become clear that the legal and moral principles upon which new copyright laws will be based are far from self-evident, but rather, they must be negotiated within the political arena where a variety of social and economic interests struggle for power and influence. Even within the music industry itself there is little consensus as regards copyright issues and one's point of view is often influenced by one's position vis-à-vis conventional artistic divisions (for example song writers v. performers), one's location in the occupational hierarchy (session musicians and engineers v. producers), or one's creative strategies (rap sampling practices v. mainstream pop production).

The socially contested nature of copyright certainly does not end when legislation has passed into law. Copyright laws tend to be rather vague and, once enacted, become subject to a wide range of interpretation by the courts where oversimplification and a misunderstanding of even the most basic elements of musical structure are common.[2] And finally, in order for the legal framework of copyright law to become the basis for a realised economic right it must be operationalised by various institutions – including government agencies (copyright tribunals), collective bodies (performing and mechanical rights societies) and others – where the day-to-day business of negotiating the monetary value of musical works and their use actually takes place.

In the following pages I approach the problem of copyright law from three different perspectives: firstly, I discuss a number of important issues in the historical and institutional development of copyright law and performing rights societies in Canada. The present moment (the early 1990s) is particularly important because copyright law in Canada is currently in the process of revision and amendment and because the two previously separate performing rights societies have just undertaken a corporate merger – the new society is known as the Society of Composers, Authors and Music Publishers of Canada, or simply SOCAN. These two events have brought to the fore a number of tensions and contradictions that have been ignored for many years.

Secondly, I look briefly at some of the copyright problems raised by the use of new technologies in musical production. The issue here is that new technologies are not simply a threat to existing copyright, but they create the conditions for the possible extension of copyright protection to areas of musical activity not previously considered as economically exploitable under copyright law. It is the tension between social actors engaged in these various areas of musical activity and the very real problems – both theoretical and practical – of attempting to extend copyright while remaining within the framework of its traditional definitions, that has caused the current state of chaos in the revision of copyright law.

Finally, I discuss the case of a Canadian musician, John Oswald, whose reworking of copyrighted material through digital sampling and other techniques left him vulnerable to legal action from the recording industry. As in so many other instances of alleged infringement that have arisen in recent years as the result of studio sampling, the case was never brought before the courts. But its peculiar nature and outcome make Oswald's case a particularly salient example of some of the contradictions embodied in copyright law – where the definition (and economic exploitation) of musical objects takes precedence over compositional practice. These contradictions are the result of an ongoing misconceptualisation in copyright legislation as regards the social context of music-making and of creative activity in general.

> Now tell me: what's so damned awful about extending copyright to meet the realities of modern life? Customarily I try to listen to both sides before accepting a campaign donation but this seemed so open and shut, so straight forward …
>
> (Robinson, 1984, p. 9)

For all its rhetoric concerning the importance of individual creative activity, copyright legislation remains, above all, an economic régime – a régime organised as much for the benefit of large-scale corporate cultural enterprises as for struggling poets and composers. And like the modern economic order, copyright is an international system (albeit one administered at the national level) where certain players profit more than others. This is especially apparent in countries like Canada, where artistic output is limited (in part, because of controlled access to the channels of both national and international distribution) and the capacity for consumption is relatively high (while the Canadian population is small it is nevertheless one of the highest per capita consumers of recorded music in the world). Thus, a recurring theme in virtually all discussions concerning the extension of copyright to new areas of artistic endeavour in Canada is its impact on the balance of payments – the net outflow of capital to foreign interests. And at the centre of this economic tension are the collection societies that implement copyright law: in their attempts to increase the level of user tariffs they augment not only the monies paid to domestic copyright owners but those paid to foreign owners as well.

In the following pages I will outline some of the history and the idiosyncrasies of both copyright legislation and performing rights societies in Canada. Throughout this discussion I place a certain emphasis on the influence of international interests in the development of domestic legal rights and their implementation. Particular attention is paid to recent amendments concerning new technology and artistic practices in subsequent sections of this essay.

Drafted in 1921 and enacted into law in 1924, the Copyright Act established performing rights in musical works in Canada. While government studies and discussions concerning revisions to the Act have been ongoing at least since the mid-1950s, the Act remained substantially unchanged until 1988 when Parliament passed Bill C-60, the first of a series of promised amendment packages. These amendments are based largely on the recommendations of a House of Commons Sub-Committee report, 'A Charter of Rights for Creators' (Canada, 1985), which was the culmination of some fourteen individual studies and a government White Paper published between 1980 and 1984. Taken as a whole, the recommendations place an emphasis on the extension of rights for creators and, increasingly, for corporate enterprises as well. This emphasis, I would argue, has the potential for significantly shifting the balance between creator, corporate and user rights in Canadian copyright law.

As in other areas of Canadian law, the original Act of 1924 was heavily influenced by previous legislation in Britain. This has not been without its pitfalls: for example, the definition of a 'musical work' contained in the Act – which restricts music to any combination of melody and harmony, or either of them, printed, reduced to writing, or otherwise graphically produced or reproduced – is unnecessarily limiting both with respect to its exclusion of rhythm, timbre and other essential elements of music and to the requirement of fixation in the form of a musical score (Mosher, 1989). The definition itself was drawn from a previous British law that had already been abandoned by Britain in 1911 (*ibid.*, p. 69). From the outset then, the Canadian Copyright Act was not only derivative but also out of date.

Music is the only type of artistic work to be specifically defined by the Copyright Act; other types are described through examples and illustrations, which allows for greater flexibility in the application of the law. With regard to music, this leaves copyright overly committed to a 'strategy of forms' (*ibid.*). Even with the 1988 amendments to the Act, parts of the original definitions remain intact and the graphical fixation requirement was used as a kind of legal red herring as recently as 1990 by cable television networks in a bid to stall tariff payments to music copyright owners (*Probe*, April 1991).

The Copyright Act of 1924 also recognised a copyright in sound recordings, piano rolls and other mechanical devices 'as if such contrivances were musical, literary or dramatic works'.[3] But this recognition has posed a number of problems: firstly, the law makes a conceptual distinction between mechanical reproductions themselves and the underlying musical (or other) work contained therein (this distinction has more recently become the basis for the arguments of broadcasters that their signals – their 'broadcast day' – attract copyright protection independent of the content itself) As musicians have come to rely on technology as an integral part of their musical practice however, such distinctions have become increasingly problematic.

Secondly, copyright in mechanical reproductions was vested in the owner of the original plate. In Canada, this is usually held to be the record company but, depending on contractual agreements, may also be the artists themselves or an independent producer (recent recommendations for revision of the law have argued that the author of a sound recording should be 'the person principally responsible for the arrangements undertaken for its making' – the producer). In either case, there is a fundamental problem in the manner in which the claim of authorship is made: in the case of a musical work, an artist is conceived of as an individual and their claim is based on having made the work (they may assign their economic rights to another party but the actual claim of authorship is relatively straightforward); in the case of a sound recording (a work resulting from a collective process), it is the contractual agreement between the producer or record company, on the one hand, and the musicians, arrangers and engineers, on the other, that sets one party off as employer/copyright owner and the other as employee/wage labourer. In cases of sampling, the compatibility of interests between these two parties, or a lack thereof, has a direct bearing on the degree of protection offered to musicians (Desjardins, 1990, pp. 140–1).

Thirdly, all copyrights are not created equal and, although the original law would appear to have given sound recordings equal status with other works of art, the possibility of exercising performance rights in sound recordings (often referred to as 'neighbouring rights') was never actually taken seriously in Canada until 1968. By that time, the issue of neighbouring rights was firmly on the international agenda: a number of countries, including Britain, had long been collecting performance and broadcast fees for recordings and had already formulated a set of international agreements – the Rome Convention of 1961. But in Canada, where 90 per cent of the records manufactured during this period were of foreign origin, it was feared that substantial royalties would soon be pouring out of the country. On the recommendations of a report by the Economic Council, the government amended the Copyright Act in 1971 to restrict the copyright in sound recordings to a simple reproduction right (as was the case, for example, in the US), thus preventing the exploitation of sound recordings as generators of income from performances and broadcasts and, in the process, creating a legal imbalance in the quality of protection afforded two forms of music media – print and recording. Music publishing continues to be valorised over sound recording in the copyright law of many countries despite the fact that its role in musical culture has been drastically reduced since the rise of the record industry (see Fabbri, 1991, p. 110). Furthermore, the legal treatment of sound recordings in the amendment created a basic inconsistency in Canadian copyright law regarding other forms of mechanically reproduced work, such as film, which continued to enjoy a full régime of protections.

Subsequent government studies criticised the report for placing economic issues rather than creative rights at the centre of copyright policy. But it seems to me that such moves need to be understood in the context of other nationalist policy initiatives of the same period: such as the Canadian Content regulations which set quotas for Canadian material broadcast on radio and television. In this sense, the Economic Council Report could be interpreted as placing copyright within the purview of broader issues of cultural policy rather than the narrow, legal focus of individual property rights.[4]

The role of copyright as a single component within an overall cultural and economic strategy was raised again in 1985 by the dissenting member of the Sub-Committee on the revision of copyright. The reinstatement of neighbouring rights for sound recordings and the creation of new rights for performers, which are still contentious issues, would result in a major outflow of capital; the dissenting member questioned the logic of recommendations which would result in such an outflow of funds precisely at a time when government support of the cultural sector was dwindling.

The balance of payments issue is not likely to disappear from copyright debates: in Canada, over 50 per cent of all music performance royalties go out of the country;[5] prior to the introduction of the Canadian Content regulations the deficit figures were considerably worse (the impact of such regulations on the distribution of copyright income suggests that copyright law be studied within the broader matrix of government institutions and policies). The situation is likely to worsen, however, as new categories of copyright are approved: for example, as a result of the Canada-US Free Trade Agreement, the Copyright Act has been amended so that cable television and radio companies will now pay royalties on the retransmission of broadcast signals (because of the manner in which it was worded, speciality services such as the non-broadcast music video channels are not even covered by the amendment – a situation which has been taken up in the courts by SOCAN). Beginning in 1990, these royalties will amount to just over $50 million a year: of this amount, 57 per cent will go directly to a collective society representing mainly American producers;

the remaining 43 per cent will be divided among a number of other collectives which represent Canadian and American television networks and a variety of other interests (including music copyright owners). Thus, the cable retransmission royalties exiting the country could easily exceed 80 per cent of the total amount. In an effort to control further capital outflows that will result from the possible implementation of neighbouring and other new rights, the revisions Sub-Committee has proposed a reciprocity scheme whereby payments will be made only to countries having similar rights legislation; a stopgap measure at best, the proposal will partially stem the outflow of royalties only so long as certain key nations, such as the US, do not grant similar rights.

The setting of tariffs is a complex process mediated by a government body known as the Copyright Board. Established in 1938 through an amendment to the Copyright Act and originally known as the Copyright Appeal Board, the body is charged with balancing the interests of users and creators.[6] The concept of a government tribunal of this type is perhaps one of the only truly Canadian innovations in copyright legislation and has since been adopted elsewhere in countries such as Australia, Britain and the United States.

Most commercial users of copyrighted material agree, in principle, that creators should be compensated for the use of their work;[7] but the details of how such compensation should be organised (through per use fees, blanket license and the like) and how much should be paid is a constant process of negotiation and, often, litigation.[8] Each year the Copyright Board receives and publishes the tariff proposals from the rights societies and, after hearing the objections, if any, from prospective users it approves or modifies the tariffs. For music, there are currently nineteen different tariff categories covering uses in radio and television broadcasting, concert halls, clubs, discos, skating rinks, commercial aircraft, background music systems, sports arenas, fitness clubs and other venues. Some forty-two objections were filed in reference to the 1990 tariff proposals ranging from outright denial of the obligation to pay royalties (as in the case of the cable television networks, mentioned above, which has resulted in litigation in the Federal Court) to much less contentious issues.

The organisation and distribution of copyright tariffs has become especially problematic with regards to the issue of home taping. Indeed, the attempt to deal with home taping through copyright law is perhaps misguided in the first place: the whole system of copyright law and collective societies is based on the possibility of identifying specific uses of copyrighted material (even if this can only be done on a statistical basis, as with radio airplay) and the compensation of specific copyright owners; but with home taping it is impossible to know who is taping what, for what purpose (certain limited, private uses of copyright material are permitted under the law) and to whom, if anyone, compensation should go. Levies on the sale of audio equipment or blank tape have relatively little to do with copyright law as it is currently practised; they are, at best, a pragmatic solution, 'a form of rough justice', 'a somewhat regressive and "post hoc" form of protection' (Elrifi, 1988, pp. 420, 422).

Nevertheless, industry pressure has led many countries to adopt levies in one form or another. The Canadian Sub-Committee report has taken the stand that a royalty, to be divided amongst copyright owners, is preferable to a tax. But once again, the dissenting Sub-Committee member drew attention to the more flexible (though state-controlled) alternative: a tax would offer greater scope in terms of the redistribution of the funds throughout the cultural sector and contribute to increased opportunities for (domestic) creative work. However, given recent agreements made between the American consumer electronics and music industries that propose a system of levies for digital audio tape (DAT) that would see compensation paid on the basis of record sales and airplay, the Canadian record industry is hoping that Canada will also opt for the royalty system in the next phase of copyright revisions (*Probe*, August 1991).

The Sub-Committee's recommendations for a royalty on audio hardware and software are a reflection of the neo-liberal attitude towards the sanctity of individual and corporate property rights that permeates the report as a whole; and nowhere is this more evident than in the recommendations concerning the extension of moral rights (several of which became law in the 1988 amendment package). Specifically, the new law states that any unauthorised modification of an artistic work is automatically assumed to be prejudicial to the creator's honour and reputation and thus an infringement of the moral right of integrity (under the previous Act, it was necessary for the artist to prove that the modification in question was prejudicial); unlike economic rights, moral rights cannot be assigned though they may be waived by the artist. Furthermore, the Sub-Committee has recommended that corporations be recognised as possessing the same economic and moral rights as individuals. While the amendment is primarily intended to be implemented with regard to 'original' works, such as paintings or sculptures, the possibility that it could be applied to sound recordings (where the notion of the original is less relevant) has important implications for musicians who engage in sampling, remixing, or similar forms of compositional activity. I will return to this point later.

Taken as a whole, the recommendations of the Sub-Committee represent an important shift in outlook in that the original intent of copyright – to offer incentive to creative effort while not limiting public access to cultural goods – has virtually been abandoned. In the view of the Sub-Committee, the cultural industries are so fully developed today that the need for incentives is obsolete. The role of copyright should instead be to recognise and sustain success through further economic reward:

> There is an important characteristic of copyright as an income-generating mechanism: it rewards popular success rather than just effort. In this sense copyright provides a very democratic reward system because its outcome is the result of a cumulative process of choices ...
>
> ... the copyright system helps reinforce and sustain those who develop and nurture the cultural goods that the nation approves of and enjoys. (Canada, 1985, p. 5)

Thus the primary function of copyright today is to reinforce and legitimate the status quo of the market-place.

But while this popular rhetoric and faith in the democratic principles of the market-place may be used to support the extension of copyright into new realms, there appears to be little attempt to balance these new rights with greater access for users. Indeed, at every point there appears to be an effort to close down avenues of access. For example, as in most Commonwealth countries, Canadian copyright law contains a 'fair dealing' clause which allows unauthorised use of protected materials but limits those uses to private study, research, criticism, review or newspaper summary (the clause is not intended as a blanket authorisation but as a defence against charges of infringement). The Sub-Committee flatly rejected the possibility of extending these sanctioned uses and also specifically rejected any suggestion that Canada adopt the more broadly-based use concept of 'fair use'.[9]

And where avenues of use have not been foreclosed, they have been made more complex and expensive. For example, in an attempt to balance the interests of the early publishing and recording industries and to prevent monopoly control over musical works, the Act of 1924 contained a compulsory licensing clause for mechanical reproductions: once a work has been recorded, anyone was allowed to record their own version of the work provided they paid a royalty of two cents per playing side (the actual amount of the royalty, which was rooted in the technology of the day, has, in industry practice, been increased in recent years). There are similar clauses in the legislation of a number of other countries and their existence has been, no doubt, a contributing factor in the development of the 'cover' version which has become something of an institution in contemporary popular music. Under the new law, the compulsory license had been abolished in favour of free negotiations between interested parties. The law has been welcomed as an enhancement to the degree of control that individual authors may exercise over their work and as a potential source of additional revenues; in practice, negotiations take place on a collective basis and new rates have already been established by the mechanical rights societies.

But in the areas where mechanical rights societies currently have no jurisdiction, the impact of the abolition of the concept of compulsory licenses could be very different. Compulsory licenses have been one among a number of schemes proposed as alternatives to current practices within the record industry regarding sampling: at present, there is no objective way in which to determine the value of a sample taken from a well-known recording and the industry appears to be pursuing a policy of charging whatever the market will bear when approached by artists seeking permission to sample from their repertoire (Rosenbluth, 1989). The law could potentially be used as a kind of legitimation of such practices and, in future, fix the dividing line between those who can, and those who cannot, afford to sample certain popular songs.

> 'Your organization is large and well-financed and fairly efficient ... and there's something about it I don't understand.'
> 'What is that?'
> 'Your objective.' (Robinson, 1984, p. 7)

The creation of new rights inevitably gives rise to the need for mechanisms of management for those rights and, following the long history of success of the performing rights societies in music (which were the only collectives specifically mentioned in the original Act), Bill C-60 has given its blessing to the concept of the collective administration of rights in a variety of other areas of the arts as well. But if Canadian law is, by virtue of its colonial heritage, indebted to the British legal system, then it should come as no surprise that the origins of the economic administration of performing rights in Canada are closely tied to Canada's relationship to the more powerful economies of both the UK and the US. To understand the nature of copyright as an international system, it is instructive to examine, if only briefly, the history and function of the Canadian performing rights societies.

Following closely on the heels of the passage of the Copyright Act, the Canadian Performing Rights Society (CPRS) was established in 1925 as a wholly-owned subsidiary of Britain's Performing Rights Society (PRS). Of course, the initial interest of PRS in Canada had less to do with the protection of works by Canadian composers and lyricists *per se* than with the collection of royalties for their British counterparts. The precedent for such a manoeuvre had already been set during the late nineteenth century by Britain's first performing rights organisation, the Dramatic Authors Society: it was the opinion of the Society that theatrical performance rights (stemming from the British Act of 1833) applied not only to performances on British soil but to productions throughout the Dominions and on this basis it appointed colonial agents to collect all due fees (McFarlane 1980, pp. 70–1). While its practices vary considerably from country to country, the extensive overseas operations of PRS, which continue in many developing countries to this day, have led Wallis and Malm to consider it as something of a latter-day 'empire' in itself (1984, pp. 203–7).

The influence in Canada of PRS was quickly followed by that of ASCAP when it became part owner of CPRS in 1930. As joint owners of CPRS, the two agencies were in a monopoly position to set tariffs as they saw fit; subsequent disagreements between CPRS and copyright users led to the creation of a Royal Commission in 1935 whose recommendations included the establishment of the Copyright Appeal Board discussed above. No appeal mechanism existed in the US however and tariff disputes there eventually led radio broadcasters to set up their own rights society, Broadcast Music Inc. (BMI) in 1940; BMI was unique in that it was the first such society not directly linked to the music publishing industry and the only rights organisation owned by users rather than copyright owners (its distribution system, based on per play payments, also differed from most other societies, where revenues are pooled). BMI Canada Ltd was established that same year in order to collect fees in Canada for the parent company's repertoire and did so almost exclusively during the first years of its existence. Canadian composers who wanted to benefit from the activities of the society did so by becoming affiliates of the US organisation; it wasn't until 1947 that BMI Canada began to take a more direct, active role on behalf of its Canadian affiliates.

Thus, the history of Canadian copyright collectives is not studded with colourful myths (as in the US) of composers who banded together to demand recognition from a populace that supposedly allowed even its most well-known composers to die penniless, or with histories of musical and industrial conflict. Instead, their story is basically one of branch-plant operations and government arbitration. Over the years however, both performing rights societies did become deeply involved in the promotion of Canadian music, both at home and abroad, through the sponsorship of concerts, workshops, competitions, recording grants, and other programmes. BMI Canada even opened its own publishing division (which was established in 1947 and operated until 1969 when it was sold) to promote Canadian popular and serious music; significantly though, the division also acted as the Canadian agent for a number of foreign publishers. Foreign ownership of Canada's performing rights societies continued for many years: CPRS, whose name was changed to the Composers, Authors and Publishers Association of Canada (CAPAC) in 1945, was held by its joint owners until 1963; and BMI divested itself of its subsidiary in 1976, at which time the society became known as the Performing Rights Organisation of Canada (PROCAN).

Although the competitive relationship between ASCAP and BMI in the US was carried over into Canada in a somewhat muted fashion, the existence of two performing rights societies in a relatively small market did have its effects on the quality of services offered by the societies. Firstly, the duplication of administrative activities led to higher operating costs: in 1988, when CAPAC and PROCAN announced their intention to merge operations, it was estimated that the eventual savings in administrative costs that could then be made available for distribution would amount to about $5 million annually. Secondly, and more importantly, competition combined with foreign ownership had always placed certain limits on the kinds of promotional activities (mentioned above) that the two societies could engage in on behalf of their Canadian affiliates. Under international agreements, performing rights societies may deduct up to 10 per cent of the money they collect for use in the development of local and national music; though the percentage deducted varies from country to country, most societies have taken advantage of these agreements for the purpose of funding domestic projects – the notable exceptions have been the North American societies and in Britain (Matejcek, 1988). In Canada, several million dollars annually (far more than either society had ever spent on their promotional activities) could be diverted for domestic use; it remains to be seen whether the new Canadian society will adopt such a nationalist policy.

Of course, if additional monies could be made available the problem would then become how they should be distributed. Most of the countries that retain a percentage of their tariffs do so in order to support 'serious music' in some fashion. This is not surprising given the preferential treatment that art music appears to have enjoyed for many years within performing rights societies generally, and is a reflection of how 'genre hierarchies' work within the day-to-day implementation of copyright (Fabbri, 1991, p. 113). Although revenues from concerts of serious music probably amount to less that 2 per cent of the income of the Canadian societies (Matejcek, 1988), various means have been used to increase the actual amounts distributed to composers of serious music: for example, a percentage of general licensing revenues (such as those from clubs and cabarets) may be rolled into the concert pool, or money earned as interest on the investment of general tariffs may also be used to augment the pool for serious music. The amounts paid are often in dispute however and, since the merger of the two Canadian societies, organisations representing concert composers have begun to fear that their portion of royalty payments may be diminishing (competition between the two societies for legitimacy and prestige may have been one of the reasons for maintaining the system of unequal payments).

But apart from the distribution structure, serious music composers have always been allotted a certain amount of power within the collectives. When the first slate of candidates for the election of the Board of Directors of the newly merged Canadian performance rights society, SOCAN, was put forward in 1990 it was decided that the Board should be both geographically and stylistically representative: each region of the country would be represented and, in addition, composers and publishers of 'serious music' would be guaranteed a number of seats. Interestingly, serious music was the only style of music to be singled out in this way: neither jazz, nor country, nor any specific form of popular music enjoys special status on the Board.

Other hierarchies exist both within the organisation (in the above elections, members' votes were weighted by income – one vote for every $500 in earnings up to a maximum of twenty votes) and in its external relations. Of the latter, the conventional division between composer/song writers and performers has recently become a site of potential conflict over copyright income: now that the debate concerning the establishment of neighbouring rights is on the agenda for Phase Two of the copyright law revisions, SOCAN has found itself in the position of having to support, in principle, the idea of new rights while at the same time opposing any attempt to divide up present tariffs among SOCAN and any future performers' collective. So while rights societies pay lip-service to equal representation and the abstract principles of copyright, in practice, the administration of copyright monies is always one of negotiation between competing interest groups.[10]

As is perhaps evident in this brief summary, even with the first phase of copyright revisions in place, Canada maintains only the most basic levels of copyright protection: the government appears to have been reluctant to sign the more recent texts of the Berne and Universal Copyright Conventions (it is signatory to the earliest versions only) most likely because to do so would require a greater international obligation (and an increased outflow of capital) on the part of Canada (Keyes, 1988). In the area of neighbouring rights in particular, Canada (along with the US and a number of other countries) lags far behind. In part, this is due to an ongoing concern with the outflow of funds but also reflects the antiquated and ideologically loaded categories of copyright law and the nature of the interest groups that make up the performing rights societies.

However, the lack of protection in the area of neighbouring rights poses particular kinds of problems with regard to technological change: in music production, the number of interest groups making claim to protection under copyright law seems to expand with every technological development but there remains little legal basis in Canada, or the US, for such claims. At the same time, the 'strategy of forms' to which copyright law is committed becomes increasingly problematic as technologies transform the nature of musical objects and practices. And it is this specific set of problems that I would now like to address.

> More new art forms have been born in the last two centuries than in the previous million years ... and they are generating mountains of new copyrights. (Robinson, 1984, p. 16)

While copyright law may be rooted in concepts of property rights and plagiarism that date as far back as the ancient worlds of 'Greece and Rome, it should be understood that modern notions of copyright are meaningful only in relation to market economies and to the technologies of mechanical reproduction: the first copyright laws were introduced in order to govern the relations between authors and publishers and, similarly, performance rights in music only became an issue once the foundation of a mass-oriented industry in popular song sheets was established. As noted above, the advent of sound recording necessitated a second, distinct area of copyright – one for musical 'work' and another for the recording itself – which was based on different notions of authorship and ownership resulting from the collective nature of the recording process; the legal and economic implications of such a distinction have never been fully resolved in the copyright laws of Canada, the US and a number of other countries.

The introduction of digital technologies in music production during the past decade has resulted in the development of new kinds of creative activity that have, on the one hand, exacerbated already existing problems in the conceptualisation of music as a form of artistic expression and, on the other, demanded that even further distinctions be made in copyright legislation. Three broad categories of activity are of interest here: firstly, in conjunction with digital synthesizers and samplers, the development of a market for individual sounds (whether programmed or pre-recorded); secondly, through the use of digital devices known as 'sequencers', the separation of the human gestural aspects of musical performance from its manifestation in sound; and thirdly, the reworking of entire recorded works, or parts of works, in 'mastermixes' and related forms.

Here again, technical possibilities are closely linked to economic opportunities: for example, prior to the introduction of digital synthesizers and samplers, no real market existed for individual sounds but now that there is such a market, issues of economic and artistic rights have come to the fore. Perhaps it is precisely because such a large gap presently exists between new technology, musical practices and market conditions, on the one hand, and Canadian and American laws, on the other, that a considerable body of comment and opinion has already appeared in recent years, both in the popular and industry press.[11] As regards these problems, Canada, with its lack of neighbouring rights legislation, has more in common with US than British law.

Throughout these debates there have been a number of recurring issues that touch on basic problems in the conceptualisation of music as form, expression and sound. For example, under the present law a musician's sound can in no way be considered as equivalent to a musical 'work'; and as mentioned above, musicians seldom own the copyright in their recorded performances because of the contractual agreements made with producers and record companies. Thus, issues of the appropriateness of granting copyright protection to musicians' sounds and the question of actual ownership have been raised by a number of authors.

But even if Canada were to bring neighbouring rights in musicians' performances into legislation, it is doubtful whether they could be used to protect musicians from certain uses of sampling. Samplers allow one to make digital recordings of acoustic sounds or pre-recorded sounds, manipulate them in various ways, and then play them from a keyboard, a computer or other device; typically, only a few milliseconds of sound might be recorded and, once incorporated into the rhythm, melody or harmony of a musical work, the precise origins of the sound may be difficult to identify. Proof of ownership and violation of the neighbouring right would thus, in many cases, become almost impossible. In conventional cases of infringement of musical works, it has often been the role of the so-called 'expert witness' to establish whether copying has taken place (Der Manuelian, 1988). In cases of sampling however, where the recording process is so complex and the possibilities for manipulation so great, musician Frank Zappa (who spends a great deal of time creating and customising his own samples and doesn't want to see them lifted from his records) has suggested that computer analysis may be the only means of establishing similarity between a sound and its copy. But even when ownership can be established, the duration of most samples raises the question of whether the actual amount of material copied is substantial enough to support a claim of infringement.

Similar problems exist with synthesizer programmes as well: because it is possible, in theory, for almost anyone to stumble upon the same set of parameters for a synthesizer sound, conclusive proof of copying may only be possible when bugs or other mistakes present in the originals also turn up in the copies (Tomlin, 1986). In such contexts, ownership becomes defined in negative terms rather than positive attributes. And given that computer software packages designed for editing synthesizer sounds often contain utilities that allow for the random generation of new sounds, the concept of 'originality' in this domain can sometimes appear meaningless.

But in the case of sampling, the critical questions are not merely technical ones concerning whether or not the identity or originality of a sound can be established; indeed, in many cases, well-known performers have been sampled precisely because their sounds are unique and recognisable. In infringement cases involving musical works it has always been necessary to prove 'substantial similarity' – usually taken to mean a certain quantitative or qualitative amount of musical material – between an original and a copy. But in using a recognisable sample, no matter how brief (for example, the use of less than a second of James Brown's scream in the middle of a rap record), quantitative criteria become more or less irrelevant. McGraw (1989, pp. 161–5) refers to the concept of 'fragmented literal similarity' (perhaps one of the most succinct descriptions, legal or otherwise, of this use of sampling technology) in describing such instances where similarity is both evident and intended. When recognition is intended, the most relevant question becomes the degree to which unauthorised appropriation constitutes improper use; and to date, there have been no cases that firmly establish either the boundaries of what might be considered as 'fair use', or the monetary value of a sampled fragment of sound.

In most discussions, the tendency has been to give vocalists a special status denied instrumental performers: because the human voice has such immediately recognisable tonal qualities, it is often regarded as the carrier of individuality, personality and identity; vocalists are thus considered by many as having a special moral right in their sounds that instrumentalists do not enjoy to nearly the same extent (Porcello, 1991, pp. 77–8). But to consider the voice in such existential terms rather than legal ones risks mistaking mere physical attribute for artistic creativity. And in this regard it is significant that the main argument for the protection of musicians from unauthorised digital sampling has not been in terms of copyright (which protects only specific artistic creations) but in relation to common law rights of publicity. These laws guarantee individuals the right to exploit their personality, image or name for commercial purposes (as in the case of product endorsements by entertainers and sports figures) and a number of American states and several Canadian provinces permit such exclusive marketing rights (McGiverin, 1987; Desjardins, 1990). This line of argument clearly places the issue of sound rights outside of the realm of creativity *per se* and into the sphere of notoriety and entrepreneurship.

The problem for instrumentalists is that they are recognised as much by their phrasing as by their sound (McGiverin, 1987, p. 1740) – a quality that is seldom captured by the brevity of most sampling techniques. The distinction is not a trivial one because it really concerns how the law should define value in the recording of musical performances. Some argue that the creation of new, interesting sounds (such as Phil Collins's trademark snare drum sound) has become so important in the music business today that individual sounds should be protected under copyright law (e.g., McGiverin, 1987). Others argue that the individual object is less important than the musical context in which it is placed (Keyt, 1988).

But what may appear to be simply a difference of aesthetics could have important implications. (The debate over the uses and abuses of sampling has created an inflated value in sounds as objects of exchange and has obscured other, equally essential aspects of performance as a form of musical practice.) Today, digital sequencers allow musicians to record virtually every nuance of their performances on digital keyboards, drum machines and other devices without actually having to record the sounds produced on the specific instruments themselves; data generated by the performance can then be edited, arranged and reorchestrated at a later time. Thus, the underlying character of a performance can be fixed in a technical form without any reference to sound at all.

A market for popular songs, arranged and performed by session musicians and stored in the form of digital sequences, has already begun to develop. Furthermore, performances stored in sound recordings can also be translated into digital data and it has become quite commonplace for remix engineers to use recorded performances in conjunction with sequencers to simply trigger synthesized or sampled sounds; in this way, the style and phrasing (the sense of timing and the 'feel' of a live drum track for example) can be retained while the sounds are changed in such a way that they bear little if any, resemblance to the original recording. Again, even if Canadian law supported neighbouring rights in performances, these two uses of sequenced data pose significant problems: conventional neighbouring rights are conceived of in terms of recorded sounds, and the protection of performance gestures that have been translated into digital form might require yet another layer of definition regarding this type of fixation; and even once this was in place, the burden of proving ownership, originality, the act of copying, and improper use in cases of infringement in this domain would indeed be formidable.

But in another sense, these new technical capabilities pose a dilemma that remains far beyond the horizon of most present-day copyright concerns: the problem lies at the root of the conception of music as a set of fixed forms – scores, recorded sounds, or even digital sequences – rather than a specific kind of creative activity with its own particular modes of expression. If understood in this way, copyright legislators might become less concerned with concepts of originality and the ownership of cultural goods and develop a more flexible attitude towards different kinds of musical activity – including not only composition but also performance, digital sampling and sound recording – and the various relationships that exist between creation, convention and norm.

> Artists have been deluding themselves for centuries with the notion that they create. In fact they do·nothing of the sort. They discover... As a species I think we will react poorly to having our noses rubbed in the fact that we are discoverers and not creators. (Robinson, 1984, p. 16)

Copyright law defines musical works as original creations and in this way gives legal weight to romantic notions of individuality and creative genius. But as a musician and composer, I am often all too aware of the well-worn character of the scales, rhythms, instrumental sounds and other materials with which I 'compose' music; at such moments, it is clear to me that music is, above all, a profoundly social and historical process – a process in which myriad influences and borrowings, some conscious, others not, coalesce to create 'the work' that I call my own. Furthermore, in the instances when I have purposely made use of pre-existing material (and like many musicians who sometimes make use of sound recordings as an integral part of their musical materials, I have 'borrowed' openly – and thus honestly – on occasion), I have never felt that the resulting work was any less 'original' than when I have 'created' my materials from scratch. The problem for copyright law is in determining whether, and under what conditions, such activities might be considered legitimate.

But, on the whole, the law has tended to disregard the social context of music-making where various forms of borrowing have always been sanctioned: themes and variations, certain types of improvisation, the uses of folk music in classical compositions etc.[12] If put in historical perspective, even the sampling of rap, dance remixes, and other popular forms might appear as only the most recent (and controversial) of a whole series of practices that have been characteristic of music-making for centuries.[13]

It has been suggested that if one of the purposes of copyright law is indeed to stimulate different forms of artistic creation, then the law must adapt itself to the different social rules, criteria and expectations of each medium of expression in determining the balance between creator and user 'rights' (Keyt, p. 422). It follows that to deny 'fair use' of recorded sounds actively discourages various uses of sampling as creative endeavour and thus goes against one of the dominant purposes of copyright (*ibid.*, see also McGraw, 1989, pp. 167–9). But as discussed earlier, recent revisions in Canadian copyright law have discarded the idea of stimulating creation while reinforcing the right of ownership and control over artistic products. The potential inhibiting effects, on creation, of an imbalance in the rights of owners and users is illustrated in a recent Canadian case where the aesthetic of sampling was pushed far beyond its conventional limits.

During the 1980s, composer John Oswald had made an aesthetic out of editing, manipulating and reconstructing recordings of well-known (and not so well-known) pieces of music: some of his work drew on eclectic sources – classical music, jazz and music from different parts of the world – but, increasingly, he turned to recordings of popular music as raw material precisely because of their capacity for listener recognition – their ability to engage the listener at a variety of levels. However, unlike most contemporary uses of sampling in popular music – where songs might contain literally dozens of brief, though still recognisable snatches of sound from other recordings, film and television soundtracks and the like – Oswald's technique often involved the reworking of an entire recorded song (and in legal terms this precluded any possibility of a defence on the basis of the samples being insubstantial). Oswald used the recordings like a jazz musician uses a song chart: the melodies and harmonies of a song are the bare bones framework within which a musical process – the improvisation – evolves; for Oswald, recordings of popular music were simply the pretext for a different kind of music-making – the technical and aesthetic transformation of sounds and cultural artifacts. But Canadian copyright law, with its emphasis on fixed forms had never been very kind either to jazz musicians (their performances have never enjoyed the kinds of protection given to published songs) or to various kinds of experimental music (Mosher, 1989) and Oswald clearly realised that the distribution of his work put him in potential conflict with copyright owners (indeed, his views on sampling and the law seem to have evolved in tandem with the musical works themselves – Oswald, 1986, 1988).

Oswald called his work, 'Plunderphonics' – a term loaded with the kind of associations that would certainly not help him in his eventual negotiations with the recording industry – and released two recordings under that title during the late 1980s: an EP and a CD (the former seems to have gone relatively unnoticed by the industry whereas the latter was to become the object of considerable protest). The source material for each selection on the recordings was openly acknowledged and documented with meticulous care in the liner notes; in this sense, there was not plagiaristic intent, nothing hidden or deceptive in their presentation. In addition, in place of the standard copyright symbol the recordings contained a 'shareright' notice (not unlike those commonly used in the world of computer enthusiasts) instructing users that the recordings could be freely copied but neither bought nor sold. In the context of the home taping controversy, this aspect of the works would also be regarded as a form of provocation by the record industry.

As a defence against possible prosecution, Oswald decided that the works would be distributed to public outlets – libraries, broadcasters, periodicals – free of charge. In conventional cases of infringement it is usually necessary for the plaintiff to prove that the potential market for their work has been damaged by the presence of the infringing copy; by not putting his records up for sale, Oswald hoped to circumvent prosecution simply by claiming that he did not profit financially from the work.[14] Oswald also sent copies of his work to Michael Jackson, Paul McCartney and other pop stars whose songs he had reworked. While not exactly asking permission for the use of their material (the work was already completed), he hoped that they would be convinced enough by the integrity of his work to waive their moral rights or, at the very least, not to invite negative publicity upon themselves by attempting to stop what was, for all intents and purposes, a harmless activity as far as the market for their songs was concerned (Oswald, 1990b, pp. 18–19). The problem with Oswald's twin strategy – financial on the one hand and moral on the other – was that its intent was primarily to deflect legal action rather than to act as a real defence should the project ever come before the courts.

In actual fact, Oswald had very little basis for the defence of his activities under Canadian law. As mentioned earlier, the concept of 'fair dealing' is quite narrow and mainly applies to private uses of copyrighted material; his decision to distribute his work, free or otherwise, may have ruled out recourse to this defence. But although Canada has rejected the broader, US concept of 'fair use', there still remains some acknowledgement of the use of copyrighted works for the purposes of parody. The problem here is that the concept of parody is as old as copyright law itself and only *imitations* of the style or character of a performer or work are considered, not actual appropriation of material from the parodied work itself. To plead that his work used recordings of popular songs for the purposes of parody would require that Oswald convince a court that the technical manipulation of actual recorded material could, in particular instances, be considered as an essential element in this form of expression and thus challenge the very definition of parody as it currently exists.

The vulnerability of Oswald's position was made clear almost as soon as industry protest against the CD project surfaced in the fall of 1989. Interestingly, the opposition did not come directly from any of the interested parties, but rather, from a proxy: the Canadian Recording Industry Association (CRIA), essentially a production and marketing organisation for international record companies. CRIA threatened to take legal action and to have all copies of Oswald's CD recalled. Eventually, in an out-of-court settlement, Oswald agreed to allow CRIA to destroy all remaining copies of the CD, plus the master tapes, and to cease distribution of his work; no recall of copies already distributed would take place.

Oswald made no admission of infringement and the actual legality of 'Plunderphonics' as a form of creative activity remains unresolved.

According to Oswald, CRIA implied that they would indeed pursue legal action on moral grounds and that this convinced him to seek a settlement: it was his understanding that under the new, expanded Canadian legislation in this area not only individuals, but corporations (and their representatives) would be able to claim moral rights (*ibid.*, pp. 19–20). In actual fact, I suspect that such innuendos were something of a bluff on the part of CRIA: even under the new law, moral rights (unlike economic rights) cannot be assigned; only the original owner of the song and/or the recording (which may have included the record company) in question could bring action against Oswald on moral grounds (which is not to say that they would not have chosen to do so). In any case, it is perhaps unreasonable to expect an individual of limited means to take on both the recording industry and the legal system: indeed, threat and innuendo on the part of the recording industry has no doubt been largely responsible for the fact that the brief history of sampling has already been strewn with more curiosities, unresolved questions and out-of-court settlements than with solid legal precedents.

The 'Plunderphonics' case became something of a *cause célèbre* in Canada and to a lesser extent abroad but, to my mind at least, for all the wrong reasons. The controversy was framed as a classic example of art v. commerce and, as such, the really difficult issues of the relationship between art-making and the market-place and copyright as an economic régime were side-stepped in favour of moralist posturing. In part, this was precipitated by Oswald's initial decision to distribute his work non-commercially: his actions were contradictory insofar as he sought public recognition for the work (and was even upset when some reviewers who had been sent copies of the CD chose to ignore it) and, at the same time, insisted on its social and legal autonomy through an artificially-produced economic marginality. Such gestures are perhaps not uncommon in the art world where discussions of copyright are still characterised by romantic notions of creative work, unconstrained by form (Mosher, 1989) or legal/economic structures (Raes, 1988); but for Oswald the strategy may have backfired in that it left his opponents no alternative except to challenge him on moral grounds. Ironically, both sides of the controversy have, in the end, been able to claim moral victory: the record industry, because it believes it has crushed the illicit plundering of its copyrighted materials, and Oswald, because public opinion rallied behind him in the cause of artistic freedom.

Oswald's work was indeed 'art', although he tried to claim that his CD was a 'pop record' by virtue of its content. Of course, it was nothing of the kind: it neither functioned economically (you couldn't buy it) nor socially (you couldn't really dance to it) as pop music. And function could have been a key issue in his defence had he decided to allow his case to stand in court: Oswald had often described his experiments as a form of research, and non-profit research is sanctioned even under Canada's narrow 'fair dealing' clause.

But such a strategy would perhaps be as misleading as the move to distribute the work free of charge in the first place. Ultimately it doesn't matter if a work of this nature is sold or given away or whether it functions as art or pop; and indeed, neither Oswald nor the industry are as uncompromising as their legal strategies and moral rhetoric would make them appear. Shortly after the CD controversy Oswald was contracted by Elektra to create a 'Plunderphonics' version of their 40th Anniversary compilation recording entitled, '*Rubaiyat*'. Again the recording was to be distributed free of charge to radio stations and other selected recipients (mainly, one suspects, because Elektra had no idea of how to divide up the profits if the recording was to be sold to the public) but two important differences set it apart from earlier 'Plunderphonics' works: firstly, the function here was no longer simply artistic but, as far as Elektra was concerned, distinctly commercial (promotional) as well; and secondly, Oswald's 'shareright' symbol had been replaced in this case by Warner Communications' own copyright notice warning against unauthorised reproduction. So obviously, even for Oswald, the issue here was not whether some idealised notion of art-making could survive in the face of a money-grubbing popular music industry and a rigid, outdated legal system: artistic legitimacy and economic and legal status were, to some extent, separate concerns.

And for its part, the industry has been more than willing (as pointed out earlier) to permit sampling provided that would-be samplers are willing to pay for the privilege. But beyond this, especially in the world of dance music, there has been an increasing recognition that remix engineers bring their own distinct 'voices' to the projects they work on. In recent years, prominent remixers have signed long-term recording contracts with major labels; it is the ability to reshape musical material that is considered valuable in these cases, not the ability to write songs from scratch (Flick, 1991).

If the work of remix engineers can achieve such credibility (albeit based on their ability to deliver marketable hits), then surely the work of Oswald and that of other, equally creative sampling musicians (like the 'mastermix' producers described by Christgau, 1986) deserves to be recognised as a legitimate form of creative activity quite apart from the material content of the work. Understood in this way, the really difficult questions become: firstly, in what way do technical transformations of recorded material create a new, separate level of identity in musical works? and secondly, how can copyright law accommodate such processes so as to stimulate, rather than inhibit, new forms of creativity?

Aaron Keyt has suggested that works incorporating sampling should be regarded as something akin to 'the product of a constructive joint authorship' – a product whose construction involves both original material, on the one hand, and a form of original *use*, on the other (1988, pp. 447–8). At a practical level, he argues that this might require that the concept of infringement be replaced by a more flexible notion of 'creative labour' – a notion that recognises all contributions and expressions regardless of the presence of 'borrowing' – and that criteria for the 'apportionment of profits' be developed (*ibid.*, pp. 454–6).

But before this practical level can be reached, the more fundamental conceptual shift away from the notion of the 'work' as fixed in specific forms must be achieved. At present, Canadian and American laws continue to valorise musical scores over recordings, and either over musical or compositional processes: the electronic alteration of a sound or a recorded piece of music does not alter the fact that one has first copied it (Barry, 1987) and this leaves one open to charges of infringement no matter how creative the transformations performed. If copyright law is to accommodate new practices then legislators need to develop a different attitude towards such compositional activities and, in this regard, sound recording itself needs to be understood as a compositional process and not simply a reproductive medium.

> We must do it the way the human race did it for a million years – by forgetting, and rediscovering. (Robinson, 1984, p. 17)

To achieve the kinds of changes in copyright law that seem to be demanded by new forms of creative activity in music, legislators need to think in terms other than simple amendment to existing statutes. What technology has done for musicians is to allow them to 'rediscover' music and sounds in new ways. Nothing less can be expected of the legal system: it needs to redefine the legal concept of a musical work, its value and its social uses in light of present technical and creative realities.

In the area of music production, those realities would appear to be at least two-fold: on the one hand, digital sampling practices have created the conditions for a new form of value in musical sounds. Despite the difficulties of assessing ownership and a fair market value for what often amounts to minimal material, the music industry has already demonstrated its interest in exploiting that value. On the other hand, the same technology allows for new forms of compositional activity that highlight creative forms of 'borrowing' and restructuring of pre-recorded sound. At a fundamental level, these practices are related as much to modes of consumption as they are to modes of production and the key problem regarding copyright law is of striking a balance between ownership and use – between the right of artists to benefit from the products of their labour and the interests of users wishing to explore the creative potential of a new technology. The recent trend in copyright reform in Canada, however, has been to strengthen the rights of creators while virtually ignoring the interests of users; in particular, with the extension of moral rights, there now exists the potential for copyright owners to prevent virtually any re-use of their recorded sounds.

In addition, the increasing use of computers in music production has already created the capacity for a new kind of fixation of musical performance gestures – sequencing – that does not involve the recording of sounds at all. As the next round of Canadian copyright reforms gets under way, the debate concerning the establishment of neighbouring rights for performers has thus far been based on existing definitions of musical performance as sound, around the economic concerns of powerful interest groups (broadcasters and the performance rights societies), and around concerns for the potential outflow of funds. By comparison, the problems associated with redefining the essence of performance as a particular form of musical expression and practice appear relatively abstract and it is unlikely that they will be dealt with adequately during the reform process. Nevertheless, to some extent the old definitions of music based on melody and harmony, the economic interests invested in musical scores and sound recordings, the problem of the balance of payments, and even sound itself, all need to be 'forgotten' if musical performance is to be 'rediscovered' and, indeed, protected as a meaningful form of creative activity.

But it is often difficult, if not impossible, to forget: the resolution of theoretical, legal and practical concerns in music copyright must take place within the already existing matrix of social institutions and always hinges on larger issues of cultural and economic policy – issues that are highly political in nature and, in Canada especially, subject to the influence of a variety of domestic and foreign interests. So while the outcome of the current deliberations on the reform of copyright will no doubt take the form of simple, unwavering statements of musical, legal and moral principle, in actual fact those statements will express the much more complex and variable nature of historical, cultural, political and economic relations in Canada.

NOTES

1 This is a distinction that, in a medium such as music, is questionable at best, especially at the present time when stylistic norms and the material character of the 'work' are constantly in flux; see Der Manuelian, 1988, pp. 135–7; Keyt, 1988, pp. 441–3.

2 Melody is often misconstrued as the sole carrier of musical originality, see Keyt, 1988, pp. 430–38.

3 Again, the wording of this section was almost identical to that of the British Act).
4 Other countries have developed a similar point of view, see Wallis and Malm, 1984, chapter 6.
5 Even part of what stays in Canada goes to the subsidiaries of foreign-owned music publishers, Audley, 1983, p. 165.
6 The original impetus for setting up the Copyright Appeal Board came as the result of complaints from licensed users concerning the rates set by the then unregulated collective society.
7 During the recent revisions process the most vocal opponents of various copyright proposals were the noncommercial users – teachers, librarians and researchers, Keyes, 1988.
8 For an American example, see Kennedy, 1984.
9 This includes such uses as personal relaxation and entertainment – key concepts in the justification of home taping, Elrifi, 1988, p. 417.
10 See also, Frith, 1988, pp. 68–9.
11 For example, Barry, 1987; Bateman, 1988; Christgau, 1986; Considine, 1990; DeCurtis, 1986; Dupler, 1986, Giffen, 1985; Oswald, 1986, 1988; Pareles, 1986; Ressner, 1990; Rosenbluth, 1989; Tomlin, 1986; Torchia, 1987; and, in the pages of respected law journals, see Desjardins, 1990, Keyt, 1988; McGiverin, 1987; McGraw, 1989; Mosher, 1989.
12 Although the boundaries of such activities have changed considerably with historical shifts in the definition of musical ownership and creativity – see Keyt, 1988, pp. 423–8.
13 In every instance, these practices place an emphasis on the (re)structuring of material as opposed to its simple generation (*ibid.*, p. 425).
14 Insofar as Oswald's strategy of non-commercial release was completely at odds with the logic of the marketplace, the argument may have held some weight in, for example, a US court where non-profit use can be one component in a 'fair use' defence; see McGiverin 1987, pp. 1737–8.

REFERENCES

Audley, P. (1983) *Canada's Cultural Industries*, Toronto: James Lorimer & Company.

Barry, H. V. (1987), 'Legal Aspects of Digital Sound Sampling', *Recording Engineer/Producer* 18(4) April, pp. 60–7.

Bateman, J. (1988), 'Sampling: Sin or Musical Godsend?' *Music Scene* 363, September/October pp. 14–15.

Canada, House of Commons (1985), *A Charter of Rights for Creators*, Report of the Sub-Committee on the Revision of Copyright, Gabriel Fontaine, Chairman, Ottawa: Minister of Supply and Services.

Christgau, R. (1986), 'Down by Law', *Village Voice*, 31(12), 25 March, pp. 39–40, 42.

Considine, J. D. (1990), 'Larcenous Art?', *Rolling Stone*, 580, 14 June, pp. 107–8.

Coxson, M. (1984), 'Performing Rights' *Some Straight Talk about the Music Business*, Toronto: CM Books, pp. 117–27.

DeCurtis, A. (1986), 'Who Owns a Sound?', *Rolling Stone*, 488, 4 December, p. 13.

Der Manuelian, M. (1988), 'The Role of the Expert Witness in Music Copyright Infringement Cases', *Fordham Law Review*, 57(1), pp. 127–47.

Desjardins, M. (1990), 'Digital Sound Sampling and Copyright in Canada', *Canadian Patent Reporter*, 33 C.P.R. (3d) pp. 129–57.

Dupler, S. (1986), 'Digital Sampling: Is It Theft?', *Billboard*, 98(31), 2 August, pp. 1, 74.

Elrifi, I. (1988), 'What's DAT – Amstrad Revisited: Canadian Copyright Law and Digital Audio Tape Players', *Canadian Business Law Journal*, 14(4), December pp. 405–22.

Fabbri, F. (1991), 'Copyright – The Dark Side of the Music Business', *Worldbeat*, 1, pp. 109–13.

Flick, L. (1991), 'Remixers Have Found a New Beat: Major-Label Deals Offer Artistic Credibility', *Billboard*, 103(4), 26 January pp. 1, 106.

Frith, S. (1988), 'Copyright and the Music Business', *Popular Music*, 7(1), pp. 57–75.

Giffen, P. (1985), 'A Source of Dissonance', *Maclean's* 98, 29 July, p. 48.

Horowitz, I. (1986), 'Session Wages Drop 7.5%', *Billboard*, 98(31), 2 August, pp. 1, 4.

Kennedy, M. K. (1984), 'Blanket Licensing of Music Performing Rights and Possible Solutions to this Copyright-Artefact Conflict', *Vanderbilt Law Review*, 37(1) pp. 185–216.

Keyes, A. A. (1988), 'Bill C-60: The Battle's Finally Over', *Probe*, 3(4), pp. 2–3.

Keyt, A. (1988), 'An Improved Framework for Music Plagiarism Litigation', *California Law Review*, 76(2), pp. 421–64.

Matejcek, J. (1988), 'Canada's Performing-rights Relations with Other Countries', in Beckwith, J. and Cooper, D. R. (eds), *Hello Out There!: Canada's New Music in the World 1950–85*, Toronto: Institute for Canadian Music, pp. 47–51, 64–5.

McFarlane, G. (1980), *Copyright: the Development and Exercise of the Performing Right*, Eastbourne: John Offord Ltd.

McGiverin, B. J. (1987), 'Digital Sound Sampling, Copyright and Publicity: Protecting Against the Electronic Appropriation of Sounds', *Columbia Law Review*, 87(8), pp. 1723–45.

McGraw, M. (1989), 'Sound Sampling Protection and Infringement in Today's Music Industry', *High Technology Law Journal*, 4(1), Spring, pp. 147–69.

Mills, J. V. (1983), *You and the Music Business*, Toronto: CAPAC.

Mosher, J. (1989), '20th Century Music: The Impoverishment in Copyright Law of a Strategy of Forms', *Intellectual Property Journal*, 5 August, pp. 51–70.

Oswald, John (1986), 'Plunderphonics or, Audio Piracy as a Compositional Prerogative', *Musicworks*, 34, Spring, pp. 5–8.

—— (1988), 'Neither a Borrower Nor a Sampler Prosecute' (guest editorial), *Keyboard*, 14(3), March, 12–14. Reprinted in *Canadian Composer*, 232, July-August, pp. 18–22.

—— (1990a) 'Recipes for Plunderphonic' (interview by Norma Igma, Part 1), *Musicworks*, 47, Summer, 4–10.

—— (1990b) Taking Sampling 50 Times Beyond the Expected', (interview by Norma Igma, Part 2), *Musicworks*, 48, Autumn, pp. 16–21.

Pareles, J. (1986), 'Dissonant Issues of Sound Sampling', *The New York Times*, CXXXVI, 46, 929, 16 October, C23.

Porcello, T. (1991), 'The Ethics of Digital Audio-sampling: Engineers' Discourse', *Popular Music*, 10(1), pp. 69–84.

Probe, April 1991, 2(4), pp. 2–3 (editorial).
—— August 1991, 2(8), 5 (editorial).
Raes, G-W. (1988), 'The Absurdity of Copyright', *Interface*, 17, 145–50.
Ressner, J. (1990), 'Sampling Amok?', *Rolling Stone*, 580, 14 June, pp. 103–5.
Robinson, S. (1984), 'Melancholy Elephants', in *Melancholy Elephants*, Middlesex: Penguin Books pp. 3–19.
Rosenbluth, J. (1989), 'Indie Pubbery Panel Ponders Sampling Trend Pros & Cons', *Variety*, 1 November, p. 70.
Sanderson, P. (1985), *Musicians and the Law in Canada*, Toronto: Carswell Co. Ltd.
Tomlin, B. (1986), 'Bootleg Synthesizer Programs Hurt Everyone' (guest editorial), *Keyboard*, 12(9), pp. 11, 154.
Torchia, D. (1987), 'Sampling Realities: Frank Zappa's experience with his recent Jazz From Hell album', *Recording Engineer/Producer*, 18(4), April, p. 64.
Wapnick, J. (1989), 'McGill University Master Samples: Setting the Record Straight', *The McGill Reporter*, 30 May, p. 3.
Wallis, R. and Malm, K. (1984), *Big Sounds from Small Peoples*, New York: Pendragon.

4

Music and Copyright in the USA

STEVE JONES

Authorship, uniqueness, reproducibility and a host of other issues occupy business and legal transactions in the American music industry. Within that framework, copyright has traditionally been an author's protection against the copying and pirating of music. It has also been a means for record companies and music publishers, who usually own the copyrights to songs, to ensure income during periods of low sales. Copyrights are bought, sold and exploited via licensing fees and royalties. But new technologies that enable a diffusion of authorship and ready reproduction are wreaking havoc with traditional copyright protection. Music is by no means the only creative field struggling with copyright problems. The US film industry is still engaged in negotiation over videotape copying of films, and the computer software industry has been plagued by copyright difficulties since its beginnings.

The United States government has provided a means of copyrighting music since passage of the Copyright Act of 1909. In 1971, an amendment to the Act provided for copyrighting of 'sound recordings'. Four years later, the 1976 Copyright Act provided copyright protection for both published and unpublished sound recordings.

The 1976 Copyright Act defines sound recordings as:

> works that result from the fixation of a series of musical, spoken, or other sounds, but not including the sounds accompanying a motion picture or other audiovisual work, regardless of the nature of the material objects, such as disks, tapes, or other phonorecords, in which they are embodied. (US Copyright Act, 1976)

The biggest and most recent controversy over copyright concerns home taping of records and compact discs. Though beginning in the mid- and late 1970s, when the recording industry's sales slumped, it has taken on altogether new meanings with the development of digital recording.

The late 1970s found US record companies no longer enjoying steady, predictable sales. Home taping shared the blame with a depressed economy and a stagnant musical climate. The cassette had become a widespread high-fidelity means of taping records, radio shows, music from all sources. Concerned that home taping was cutting into record sales, the recording industry began advertising home taping as theft, and pursued the US Congress to amend copyright laws. Home taping, the industry reasoned, is copyright infringement.

Little came of these lobbying efforts, however. In the early 1980s, several home electronics manufacturers began marketing dubbing cassette decks, which enable cassette duplication with just one machine. The recording industry (in the form of the Recording Industry Association of America, Inc., the RIAA) again unsuccessfully lobbied Congress, this time for a tax on dubbing decks. The reasoning was the same as with home taping, but the industry went slightly further in their demands. They originally called for a tax on both single and dubbing cassette decks, with money collected to be distributed to recording artists. The pay scale the industry suggested virtually mirrored the top record charts, since presumably those artists with the highest record sales would also have their recordings copied most.

A bill was presented before the US House of Representatives in 1985 (HR 2911, 1985) that proposed a tax on blank tape and tape recorders. Known as the Home Audio Recording Act, the bill included a penny per minute tax on blank tape, a tax of ten per cent of the retail cost on tape recorders, and a tax of 25 per cent of the retail cost on dubbing tape decks. Money collected was to be divided among record companies and distributed to copyright owners, but no mechanism of distribution was established. Although the law was to exempt individuals taping their own records, amateur musicians, and others who were purchasing tape recorders for their own musical use, there was no mention of how subsequent use would be determined at the time of purchase. The bill, though at one time tenuously connected to the Parents' Music Resource Center record rating issue, did not pass Congress.

The *Washington Post* reported (Harrington, 1986) that the RIAA was moving its headquarters to Washington, DC, to more effectively lobby Congress for home taping bills and to pursue another legislative avenue, source licensing for film and television music. Source licensing is primarily concerned with residual payments for composers whose music is broadcast on television. BMI and ASCAP are currently involved in litigation over source licensing in an effort to increase such income.

The recording industry's next lobbying effort came in the wake of the development of Digital Audio Tape (DAT). Regarded as the ultimate in home taping, DAT works on the same principles as the compact disc. Sound is sampled and reproduced digitally, with no distortion from copy to copy. In other words, dubbing a record or CD onto DAT does not produce a copy, it produces a clone, an exact replica. The threat to the recording industry is thus greater with DAT. Presumably some home tapers were discouraged by the noise and hiss added to each copy generation. DAT produces no noise and hiss. And, since CDs are digitally recorded to begin with, DAT would be the perfect medium for copying CDs.

The problem was one the computer software industry faced from the start – protecting a product that is simultaneously creative and unique yet by definition copyable. Ultimately, some computer software began including copy protection devices which would cause a programme to self-destruct or prevent copying. The recording industry opted for a similar solution for DAT by lobbying Congress for a trade bill that would force DAT manufacturers to include anti-copying devices in their machines. The anti-copying mechanism would read information from a CD, and respond to a message to lock a DAT deck out of record mode. Though successfully demonstrated in prototypes, the mechanism is expensive and produces a noticeable difference in sound when compared to machines without the anti-copying mechanism. DAT manufacturers are (at best) reluctant to raise the cost of an already expensive device, and feel that the record companies should take the initiative in preventing copying; after all, they are the ones providing the software. By October 1990 DAT decks were available in the US for around $800, and digital codes are embedded in pre-recorded DAT tapes that enable only one digital-to-digital copy from a tape. However, this code does not prevent multiple analogue-digital or analogue-analogue copying. Currently, the market for pre-recorded DAT tapes in the US is very small.

The dilemma faced by the recording industry is based primarily on the copying and piracy of CDs, perhaps the industry's saviour from its mid-'70s doldrums, and not records, because CDs are virtually perfect copies of the master tape. The industry was slow to switch over to compact disc, but since the mid-'80s CD sales have boomed and record companies quickly capitalised on the CD market. Part of the reason for their initial sluggishness in releasing CDs lay in the large capital cost of manufacturing CDs. Now that manufacturing costs are falling, the industry is immediately faced with copying and pirating problems. Record companies are also concerned that consumers will prefer DAT over CD since they can record on DAT. Technology to record sound on blank CDs is currently available, though very expensive and within reach only of the largest audio mastering facilities. The cost of CD-R (Compact Disc Recording) technology will, however, most likely fall as other such technology has. It is also likely that consumers will prefer a format that fits existing hardware. DAT is becoming a pro-audio technology in the US, in part because US consumers are accustomed to purchasing products that include extensive graphics and artwork – DAT tapes are too small to provide adequate space for graphics.

The evolution of copyright and royalty issues concomitant with the development of DAT augured for an apparent parallel to the home taping acts of the 1970s. It seemed doubtful that legislation regarding a home taping tax or an anti-copying mechanism for DAT would pass the US legislature, in the case of the former because of the difficulty establishing the taxing and distribution process, in the case of the latter because the current administration and Congress seem to favour a private sector compromise.

On 10 July 1991 United Press International (UPI) reported just that sort of compromise, and the stage was set for a landmark agreement between the recording industry and the consumer electronics industry. The agreement provided 'for the two industries to jointly request Congress to adopt a set of copyright laws that would codify [their] pact' (UPI, 1991). The agreement found immediate approval among publishers, record labels, BMI and ASCAP, industry associations, and many musicians. It was introduced in the US Senate as 'The Audio Home Recording Act of 1991', in the fall of 1991, and introduction to the House of Representatives swiftly followed. According to an article in *Billboard* magazine, the legislation calls for 'a 2% royalty on the wholesale price of recorders (with an $8 cap and a $1 minimum) and a 3% royalty on the wholesale price of blank tape' (Holland, 1991). The bottom line, as reported in the *New York Times*, is that:

> Record companies will get about 38 percent of the royalty pool, performers will get about 26 percent, and songwriters and music publishers will each get about 17 percent. The American Federation of Musicians will get 1.75 percent and the American Federation of Television and Radio Artists will get about 1 percent. (Shapiro, 1991)

How these moneys will be distributed is unclear, although involvement of the US Copyright Office has been mentioned in the legislation. Interestingly, the Audio Home Recording Act of 1991 (which was passed in 1992) includes a provision for Congress to amend the law as needed in light of the development of new technologies.

SOUND AND COPYRIGHT

Despite the publicity surrounding home taping and copyright legislation, little has been made public about a pending US (and, indeed, international) copyright problem – the ownership of sound. Modern synthesizers have enabled creation of unique sounds, and some of the programmers and musicians who create the sounds are keeping close watch on copyright matters. The issues can be roughly divided into two categories and are currently the scene of great debate in the US.

First, there is the issue of digital sampling of sound. Musicians involved in the recording of popular music have a habit of referring to sounds created by other musicians. For instance, during a recording session, a drummer may ask the engineer if he could get a 'Phil Collins' type of drum sound. As one engineer said:

> For me the most pressure comes when an artist or producer says 'I want this sort of sound' and I have to give it to them or else they'll get someone else who will. It's especially tough if it's something another artist has done because then there's no excuse. He got it so why can't you? Like one time I got a call from this guy the day before his session and he said, 'I want the drums to sound like the drums on the Elton John album.' That night I got hold of the album and listened to it at home and figured out ways to do it. (Kealy, 1974, p. 136)

Equipment manufacturers design effects units with the thought that they should make it easy to reproduce 'hit' sounds. But an even easier method of reproducing those hit sounds is to sample them. Synthesizers such as the Ensoniq Mirage, Kurzweil 250, Fairlight, Akai S900, and many others, permit recording of sound events and subsequent manipulation and playback via a keyboard. Thus a musician can sample the drum sounds from a Led Zeppelin record, for instance, assign the bass drum to one key of the keyboard, the snare drum to another, cymbals to another, and so on. This of course does not mean that the musician can then *play* drums like John Bonham of Led Zeppelin – but he can *sound* like John Bonham, and that is of crucial importance.

The second category that US copyright legislators are struggling over is the copying of synthesized sounds by means other than sampling. Much of the problem revolves around the programming industry's selling of sounds. As with the computer software industry, there is little to prevent someone from purchasing a set of sounds and copying them at will. And there is little to prevent someone from hearing a sound on a recording and programming that sound themselves with their own synthesizer.

The point is almost moot in fact, since many of the most popular recordings use sounds that are created by the manufacturer, and consumers get them built into the synthesizer. They are, in computer software terms, public domain sounds. That is, they are free to be copied. A problem arises, however, because once they are used on a recording, it could be argued that the copyright notice on the record covers the sounds.

Two forms of copyright can be filed for a published (i.e. publicly released) recording in the US; a 'circle C' which denotes a musical copyright, and a 'circle P' which denotes copyright of the sound recording. As synthesist and programmer Bryan Bell said, 'The circle P copyright is for the whole record album. The musical copyright is 8 bars or whatever it is. The circle P is for anything that's on there for any amount of time. Sounds included' (Bell, 1987).

The solution to these problems is by no means simple. For one thing, sampling and synthesis are intimately connected to concepts of authorship and authenticity. Public reaction to the introduction of the RCA Electronic Music Synthesizer in 1955 set the terms of the debate between synthesis and acoustic instruments:

> Although crude-sounding, the results nevertheless came near to the actual qualities of the instruments, near enough to make them almost credible. As for the 'new' sounds, that will have to be left to the creative musician rather than to the engineer to exploit ... the synthesizer ... could be made to reproduce the sound characteristics not only of an orchestra, but of its concert hall as well. There would be no need for the recording director to tour churches, auditoriums and theaters in quest of the 'perfect' acoustical setup ... More important, the primary function of such a mechanism should not be to *imitate* the quality of existing sounds, but to create and experiment with new sound ... the synthesizer may some day offer remarkable opportunities to the composer – provided he has the patience and skill to manouevre his way around the complicated [electronics]. (Lawrence, 1955)

The author was being quite open-minded. Musicians' unions had quite a different reaction, stemming from the fear that eventually there would be no need for the performer. Frederick Dorian (1942, p. 342) foresaw the problem and wrote, 'We have only to think of the possibility of an apparatus that will permit the composer to transmit his music directly into a recording medium without the help of the middleman interpreter.'

The debate centres on whether there is a need for live performers or not. In popular music, the synthesizer quickly gained acceptance in progressive rock, but in traditional rock forms it is still frowned upon. The synthesizer is inherently dishonest, the argument goes, because it imitates acoustic instruments and therefore presumably does not require the skill necessary to play an acoustic instrument. Brian Blain, the British Musicians' Union publicity and promotion officer, gave the typical unionist perspective:

> the Union does seek to limit the use of synthesizers where they would be used to deprive orchestras of work ... However, I think it is to the Union's credit that we see the essential difference between that use of the synthesizer where it is clearly taking work away from 'conventional' musicians and its use in a self-contained band where there would not normally be any question of another conventional musician being used ... It is hopeless to look for a totally consistent view but I must say that I see a big difference between a synthesizer in a band, which at least requires a musician to play it, and a machine which takes the place of a musician. (Frith, 1986)

The drum synthesizer is particularly frowned on by rock and roll fans since it not only produces drum sounds, but can play rhythm patterns on its own.

The debate has shifted somewhat since about 1985, from duplication of acoustic instrument sounds to duplication of sounds in general. This may be due to the widespread use of synthesizers for electronic sounds and the public's quick acceptance of those sounds.

To couch the debate in terms of performance, however, is inappropriate. A performer of some kind or other is needed no matter the instrument. Even a sequencer or recorder needs someone to operate it. A more appropriate site for the debate is within the terms of the value of sound.

Bryan Bell has worked with many musicians, from Herbie Hancock to Neil Young. He founded a service called Synthbank, which exists to publish sounds. It is 'a consortium of professional programmers provid[ing] consulting services ... a publisher of commercial sounds that can actually be bought and sold' (Bell, 1987). Synthbank, according to Bell, was 'started to protect the authorship of the intellectual property and programming of sound' (Bell, 1987). By regarding sound as intellectual property, the question of musical copyright takes on different dimensions. In effect, sound itself can be regarded as a creative work, apart from music.

Though Bell began it several years ago, Synthbank is only now beginning operation. Part of it is located in the Performing Artists Network (PAN), a database and computer bulletin board service for those in the music industry. Via PAN, Synthbank users can upload and download sounds by calling the database from their computer.

The reason it took Synthbank some time to get off the ground is because copyright difficulties prevented its operation. The US Copyright Office simply did not provide a means for copyrighting sound apart from music. The Copyright Office does make a provision for copyrighting sounds on their Form SR. One paragraph states: 'Use Form SR for copyright registration of published or unpublished sound recordings ... briefly describe the type of sounds fixed in the recording. For example: "Sound Effects"; "Bird Calls"; "Crowd Noises".'

Sound recordings are defined as 'works that result from the fixation of a series of musical, spoken, or other sounds' (Form SR, 1976). But the main problem is one of notation – how to submit a sound for copyright. Bell related his brush with copyright law:

> The copyright has taken us over two years to get ... Because they just went through a whole bunch of rewording in the law, in the grey area of the law, at considerable expense to try to get this more clearly identified in terms of commercial property ... it's been a major hassle ... I've been back and forth with the copyright office and my

> lawyer's office, about 15 times. We just sent in a final application but we have not received confirmation of its acceptance yet, but as far as the dialogue between my attorneys and the senior examiner, we've gotten everything in that we were supposed to ... it'll be an acceptance of how to copyright. It'll be what format they have decided on as satisfactory, from that standpoint, it'll be a precedent ... It's just a matter of whether they classify it as a sound recording or a computer program. It's a clarification of what kind of intellectual property it is. It's a matter of whether it's backed up by source code or what kind of file ... Once it's done that will give us the ability to copyright sound ... We've been holding back on sounds because we've been working on this thing. (Bell, 1987)

As a sound publisher, Bell must place financial value on synthesizer programs and samples. His solution is pragmatic:

> Placing a value on the sound is, whether or not it's saleable, if it's unique or not unique. As far as the actual commercial value of a sound, I pretty much affix that to the instrument. You know, something like a Casio sound or a DX7 sound is about a dollar, say. A Chroma sound or an Oberheim is about two dollars. But when you get into the high end samplers like a piano for a Fairlight, that would be $200 ... it's more in terms of what the user is going to get out of it. If the user can get 32 DX7 sounds for 32 dollars that is a fair market value. Someone who has a Fairlight [and] is making a professional recording can pay $200 for the sample. So we are trying to attach the service to the value it has to the user. When it gets down to samples, it's the amount of time it took to make the samples. (Bell, 1987)

According to Bell, response to Synthbank from musicians has been excellent. And Synthbank provides a payment structure for programmers, without discriminating between professional programmers and amateurs.

The legal problems remain, however, regardless of the change in copyright law that Bell foresees. Just as nothing stops the consumer from copying a record onto cassette, nothing prevents someone buying a sound from Synthbank from copying it for a friend. Though a useful distinction can be made between someone who copies a sound and then uses it for a published recording (the distinction between copying and pirating) the difficulty of determining copyright infringement is tremendous. One would expect an enormous amount of litigation. Bell said,

> The point is that if a sound is made unrecognizable to an expert witness, [there will be] no case. If they play the record and play the sample and a jury can't tell the difference [there will be] no case ... [there will be much litigation] but Columbia [Records] has 250

> lawyers on call at all times, so some joker ripping off sounds to do McDonald's commercials will get sued. Synthbank was actually the devil's advocate for the consumer, saying let's protect the artist before the record companies do, and pay a royalty on sounds and distribute them to everybody and fairly, but pay the author. As far as I know I pay the highest rate. (Bell, 1987)

One can expect the record companies to become involved immediately. In general, the 'circle P' copyright is owned by the record company; will record companies claim ownership of sounds and samples?

The solution of having a jury decide whether copyright infringement of a sound has occurred is not as simple as it seems. First, in the case of infringement of a piece of music, court cases can take days and weeks. Second, it is hard to imagine that sound could be the only determinant of infringement. For instance, if an infringement of the sound of a car crash was claimed, and the sound of the two car crashes in question did sound alike but were taken from different accidents, would there be infringement? If Led Zeppelin's drum sound were sampled, and the frequencies between 700 Hz and 1 kHz removed by equalisation, would that be infringement? And one has to wonder about implications of precedent in other areas; what might happen to impersonators such as Rich Little? What of intent to infringe? What of prior access? And with the difficulty in determining authorship on modern pop records, how would one determine who is responsible for an infringement?

The constant use of sampling in rap music has resulted in the creation of sample clearance houses similar to Bell's Synthbank. For a fee, sample clearance houses trace copyright owners of samples used in to-be-released recordings. Most often they are hired by record companies wishing to avoid litigation or expensive settlements, and sometimes they are hired by artists themselves. Their use has greatly increased since Gilbert O'Sullivan's 1991 suit against Biz Markie in which a US federal judge ruled that Markie's song 'Alone Again' infringed copyright and recommended criminal prosecution.

Sampling has created resentment among some musicians, as the following, excerpted from a *Wall Street Journal* article, illustrates:

> Frank Doyle, a New York engineer, recently plugged into his sampler the sound of Madonna screaming 'hey' on her song 'Like A Virgin', raised it an octave and dropped the new sound into a few parts of a coming song by Jamie Bernstein. He took a horn blast from a James Brown song and turned it into a lush, mellow tone for a Japanese singer's love ballad. 'I didn't feel at all like I was ripping James Brown off,' he says.
>
> That's not the way James Brown sees it. 'Anything they take off my record is mine,' says the soul-music pioneer ... 'Is it all right if I

take some paint off your house and put it on mine? Can I take a button off your shirt and put it on mine? Can I take a toenail off your foot – is that all right with you?' (Miller, 1987)

Frank Zappa, who features sampled sounds prominently on his recent recordings, included the following statement on his *Jazz From Hell* LP: 'Unauthorized reproduction/sampling is a violation of applicable laws and subject to criminal prosecution.'

Most musicians alter beyond recognition the sounds that they sample. Sampling is a means of easily acquiring raw sound material, and shaping it is part of the creative process. A description of a recent concert performance using a sophisticated sampler illustrates sampling's potential:

> I recently attended a concert ... and I was fairly skeptical ... and it totally floored me, it was beautiful. Very wonderful music. A couple of days later [the composer] revealed that the entire piece was constructed from twelve samples, such as a ship's mast creaking, a breaking twig, water running, you get the idea. All these sorts of bizarre mundane sounds, [he] put these sounds on hard disk and wrote a program to select which ones you want. (Junglieb, 1987)

Sampling technology is far from perfect, and creating samples requires a great deal of effort. It is not as simple as recording a sound, because samplers are not of sufficient quality to perfectly reproduce a sound that is fed into them. Instead, several sound parameters (frequency, equalisation, etc.) must be altered so that what one puts in is the same as what one gets out. Stanley Junglieb described it best by saying: 'sampling is pretty easy, but it has its inherent problems. It's pretty easy to plug in a mic or a guitar. The hard part comes in deciding what to do about control of sound. That has been discouraging to a lot of people. You shouldn't have to think about mapping, about envelope shape.'

Visual editing systems which allow the user to see the waveshape and amplitude envelope help one sample, but are still quite costly and time-consuming. Tom Curley, who operates a small studio in New York and considers himself a 'sampling freak', concurred:

> How do you put a value on [samples]? Because I don't know if you've ever tried to make a sample, but making one is a real pain in the ass. Everybody thinks, oh, sample, oh, I just play a note and that's it. It's a lot harder than that, because of the vagaries of the machine once you get in and once you get out. Before the sample goes in you have to screw it all up and do all sorts of crazy equalization things to it in order for it to come out right. Then you've got to go in and set all your parameters and your envelopes so that it is appropriate to that instrument. In the case of the [Ensoniq] Mirage, you have to take multi-samples. If you want to get a piano,

> you can't just hit a note and that's the sample, you have to take several samples because the sound is only good for an octave or so, so for every note you have to take 5–7 samples. In the case of the Mirage, you have to take two samples for every note, you have to take a sample when you hit it soft and a sample when you hit it hard. And then you have to get the synthesizer to adjust the mix of those samples so that the velocity is like when you hit a piano and the envelope has to be like when you hit a piano. And that goes for all the other instruments. (Curley, 1987)

A further difficulty with sampling is the relationship of the keyboard to the sampled instrument or sound, especially when the sample is of an acoustic instrument. It is one thing to play a sampled piano – the piano itself is a keyboard instrument – but to play a sampled guitar on a keyboard is very difficult. The guitar, for one thing, is set up quite differently from a keyboard. Its strings are tuned in fifths, whereas a keyboard is a linear scale. Though a sound can be sampled, the performance characteristics of a particular instrument must be attended to by the performer if the sample is to resemble the acoustic instrument. Curley explained:

> [Sampling] is definitely opening up a new world for coming up with new sounds. But initially most people will buy a sampler because they think they're going to have any instrument that they want. And you do. It's just not as easy as it sounds. The next thing that I find very interesting is as a keyboard player, I can play different instruments, because you can put up a saxophone sound and it sounds like a saxophone only if you play it like a saxophone. A keyboard tends to play everything like a piano. And it comes out sounding totally strange; like I've learned when to take a breath when I play the trumpet, could a trumpeter hold a note that long? Would a trumpeter do that kind of a trill? Well, obviously he couldn't play a block chord. Like with a violin, you can have a wonderful violin sample, but then you begin to think with a violin player, sometimes he plays it short with a pizzicato, sometimes he plays it long with a slow attack time with a nice long release time, sometimes they play with a quick release time. You have to change your instrument so that you have immediate control over all those paramenters, so that you can then play like a violinist. (Curley, 1987)

Performance characteristics are therefore vital to sampling, and it is doubtful that copyright legislation could cope with them. It would be absurd to believe a performance style could be copyrighted, but it is not inconceivable that litigation based on style infringement could come to trial.

What is most interesting about the issue of sampling and copyright is its insertion into questions of labour, income and control. Copyright in the music industry has traditionally been associated with income, since royalties are paid on the basis of copyright ownership. It has also been a means of control, since copyright owners can determine the uses to which a song is put. The administration of copyright, royalty and control is performed by a music publisher. Until the advent of Synthbank, however, there was no such thing as a sound publisher. Copyright of sound was not an issue until sound could be marketed. And now that there is an administrator of sound copyright, and sample clearance houses, an entirely new branch of the music industry will grow.

NOTATION

In 1959, *Billboard* magazine reported the introduction of a Congressional bill to modify copyright law to cover electronic sounds. The bill was requested by 'a composer of the new-type sounds who has contributed to a movie soundtrack, but has no way of copyrighting his music, since it has no conventional notation to deposit with the Copyright Office' (*Billboard*, 1959). The bill did not pass, though the Copyright Office now requires a recording of a piece of music if a notated lead sheet is not available.

What the bill points out is the change in musical notation following the evolution of recording. Prior to written notation, music was memorised by musicians, the same way that epic poems were memorised and recited. It is no coincidence that epic poems and oral history were sung, set to music. Folk music, popular music, is based on memory.

Notation externalised musical memory, as writing is a form of external memory. However, written notation is not a medium of hearing, but of sight. As composer André Kostelanetz once remarked, 'Music is not what you play but what people hear' (Eisenberg, 1987, p. 57). The notes on a page represent music, not sound. Chris Cutler (1985, pp. 95–6) argues that the development of notation brought about the division between composer and performer. Eisenberg (1987, p. 13) writes: 'Perfect preservation is a matter not simply of technology, but of ontology as well. A defect of preservation is a defect of reification, and this is the trouble with clefs and quavers. They aren't music; they just represent it. The music itself is sound.'

Recording presented a means of notating sound. Cutler (1985, p. 96) writes that recording '"remembered" actual performances; more importantly, it could equally well "remember" any sound that could be made, whatever its source. Thus, through the medium of recording, all sound became capable of musical organization and therefore the proper matter of music creation.'

Cutler goes on to say that recording enables the 'reunification of composer and performer'. In brief, that often accounts for the desire to record, since one is able to perform one's own composition. Eisenberg

(1987, pp. 128–9) writes: 'What are the causes of this impulse to create records? ... Marks on paper can be misinterpreted ... When the composer is the performer, what the recording records is nothing less than the composer's intentions ...'

Recording enables those who cannot read music to none the less make music. The popular music artist can often be counted among those who do not have formal musical training, cannot read notes, but can play. This use of recording was highlighted early on:

> Gordon Parks [composes] with a couple of tape recorders and a grand piano. Parks cannot write a note of music ... [he] composes directly on tape, using two or even three recorders to develop counter themes, harmony and orchestral structure. Tape also serves as note-taker for his musical ideas. He files these work tapes, and refers to them when he needs ideas. 'Otherwise, I'd never be able to remember or use many of the themes that occur to me,' says the composer ... After he completes the composition, it is scored by a professional musician. (Lowe, 1955)

Written notation, then, is removed from sound – it is music transferred into the realm of sight. Analogue recording returns music to its base in sound, but denies sight. Although one can see the grooves on a record or the iron oxide particles on magnetic tape, one can interpret them visually only with the greatest difficulty.

Digital recording combines sound and sight. By breaking music down into computer bits, it makes it possible to represent the music in either of two ways – by analysing the notes or the sound, as reconstructed from the bits. Computer programmes exist that allow a digital recording to be created in several ways, by writing notes or by performing a piece. They can then switch between playing the piece or printing it out as a score. Composer Steve Reich uses an Apple Macintosh computer for scoring:

> a Macintosh ... is now my way of notating music. I am finishing with writing out my scores. A copyist would send me to the cleaners for thousands of dollars. I am now liberated thank you, and the next piece I am writing for the San Francisco Symphony will pay for this Macintosh plus about ten times over it ... The pencil and paper has been replaced by the mouse and keyboard. (Reich, 1987)

Although Reich does not use them, programmes exist that create a score from a piece composed on a sequencer.

Digital recording also allows detailed analysis of sound waveforms. Computer programmes like SoundDesigner let the user portray the waveform of a sampled sound on a computer screen, then modify it visually and hear the results.

Probably the single most striking feature of digital recording is its ability to interpolate bits. If a bit is missing, a microprocessor can substitute another bit by interpolating between the ones before and after the missing bit. In other words, sound, a continuous phenomenon, is converted into discrete steps. The steps can then be modified aurally or visually, by man or machine, and converted back into a continuous sound wave.

It is precisely such aural and visual control over sound that is creating copyright problems. Not only has the representation of music changed, but the representation of sound has been altered too. Is sound a wave created by differences in air pressure, or is it a series of bits, or a series of instructions for a synthesizer? Copyright lawyers will have to decide, as Bryan Bell said, because if sound is to be copyrighted the means of representing sound must be made uniform.

COPYRIGHT AND CONTRADICTIONS

The inherent problem with copyrighting music and sound lies in the nature of recording. The moment of musical production is extended beyond its origin by recording, and therefore control over the music and sound is surrendered.

Copyright law, as Simon Frith points out, was conceived within the 'terms of nineteenth-century Western conventions', and is not well-suited to coping with twentieth-century technology (Frith, 1987, p. 12). The definition of 'fixing' music has changed dramatically. Frith writes:

> In the days before recording, 'fixing' music could only mean scoring it. The author of a song was the author of its sheet music, which frequently meant that the first person to transcribe a folk song or blues became its author and that a ragtime improvisation was credited to the first listener who could write it down. (*ibid.*, p. 13)

Dick Hebdige has described reggae and hip hop cultures which pursue a folk/oral tradition but use modern technology to do so:

> At the centre of the hip hop culture was audio tape and raw vinyl. The radio was only important as a source of sounds to be taped ... The hip hoppers 'stole' music off air and cut it up. Then they broke it down into its component parts and remixed it on tape. By doing this they were breaking the law of copyright. But the cut 'n' mix attitude was that no one owns a rhythm or a sound. You just borrow it, use it and give it back to the people in a slightly different form. To use the language of Jamaican reggae and dub, you just *version* it. And anyone can do a 'version.' All you need is a cassette tape recorder, a cassette, a pair of hands and ears and some imagination. The heart of hip hop is in the cassette recorder, the drum machine, the Walkman and the ... ghetto blasters. These are the machines that can be used to take the sounds out on to the streets and the vacant lots, and into the parks ... By taping bits off air and recycling it,

> [they] were setting up a direct line to their culture heroes ... And anyway, who *invented* music in the first place? Who ever *owned* sound and speech? (Hebdige, 1987, p. 141)

The mix of technology and folk culture causes problems when viewed from within the music industry, but as Hebdige correctly asks, who owns sound, music and rhythm?

Since sampling allows easy recombination of sounds, authorship becomes ever more confusing. American rap groups, for instance, or the British group Art of Noise, use snatches of sound from various sources. Reggae groups use backing tracks dozens of times for different songs. These forms of 'versioning' are widespread. How should copyright be established in these cases? This is not a new problem. Wallis and Malm (1984) note that in many third world countries musicians record backing tracks that are used by producers for overdubbing singers and other instrumentalists. David Toop (1984, p. 111) suggests that part of the reason for use of backing tracks is economic. 'Versions are obviously a convenient way of making records,' Toop writes, 'as most of the ideas have already been worked out in the original.'

The following description of a song by New York rap group Grandmaster Flash and the Furious Five illustrates the confusion surrounding copyright and authorship:

> [Grandmaster] Flash's concept was to turn the turntable on itself, making it a musical instrument in its own right. He did this by rubbing the needle against the groove, instead of allowing the needle to play the record normally ... The result was Jimi Hendrix's alien sound with a basic James Brown beat ... Study Grandmaster's 'The Adventures of Grandmaster Flash on the Wheels of Steel' to understand how the masters do it. It begins with 'You say one for the trouble,' the opening phrase of Spoonie Gee's 'Monster Jam,' broken down to 'You say' repeated seven times, setting the tone for a record that uses the music and vocals of Queen's 'Another One Bites the Dust,' the Sugar Hill Gang's '8th Wonder,' Grandmaster Flash and the Furious Five's 'Birthday Party,' and Chic's 'Good Times' as musical pawns that Flash manipulates at whim. He repeats 'Flash is bad' from Blondie's 'Rapture' three times, turning singer Deborah Harry's dispassion into total adoration. (George, 1985, pp. 6–7)

It's interesting that digital sampling evolved at around the same time that city kids like Grandmaster Flash and Afrika Bambaataa were creating sampled effects with turntables. Multitracking, overdubbing, and versioning confuse copyright issues almost as much as sampling.

Currently, artists who sample employ a 'four-second' rule, and ask questions such as, 'Is the sample melodically essential to both the original and new work? Is it readily recognizable in its new context? Is it crucial to the financial success of both the original and the new work (Aaron, 1989, p. 23)? Such questions will no doubt become a kind of test should litigants ever come to trial for a case of copyright infringement via sampling. However, the emphasis has been on *melodic* infringement, and one must wonder what may happen when cases of *rhythmic* infringement come up.

At present most artists will print a credit for a sample on a recording's accompanying insert or jacket, or will negotiate for a license (as was the case with MC Hammer and Rick James for Hammer's 'Can't Touch This'.) At present, though, the US recording industry is generally unprepared for such negotiations, and, as mentioned earlier, engages sample clearance houses to perform such tasks. Since, traditionally, licensing has been granted for full cover versions of songs, for which full mechanical royalties are paid, there does not exist a mechanism for payment of a percentage of mechanical royalties to pay for a sample. However, as negotiation for licenses for samples has become rather commonplace, it is but a matter of time until a fee structure will emerge.

Current copyright controversies, whether they involve sampling, piracy or other forms of infringement, must be viewed as part of the recording industry's exploitation of all income-generating means at its disposal. Simultaneously, the breakup of the Soviet Union, the westernisation of Eastern Europe, and similar occurrences on a smaller scale throughout the world mean that broader exploitation of copyright is possible. This has not escaped the attention of the US government and recording industry. For example, the International Intellectual Property Alliance (IIPA) claimed that 'Taiwan, Poland, and the Philippines top the list of countries whose inadequate copyright laws cause huge losses for the US copyright industries' (Kelly, 1992). The IIPA enlisted the aid of US Trade Representative Carla Hills and asked her to negotiate with those, and other, countries, to 'end their allegedly unfair trade practices'. Hills is to decide whether or not to 'retaliate' against those countries. Similarly, the IIPA asked the US government to intervene in trade negotiations with China to ask that 'it offer US record companies full international-level copyright protection' (Holland, 1992).

It is particularly noteworthy that even the Audio Home Recording Act is viewed by the RIAA as an international agreement. Jason Berman, the association's president, hopes that 'the royalty bill – if passed – will create waves that ... will alter copyright protection throughout the European Community, Japan, Latin America, and Canada' (Berman, 1991). The association has also been involved in GATT talks.

Interestingly, a similar situation occurred in magazine publishing in the mid-1800s, as Pauly (1988) found. Nathaniel Parker Willis began publishing the *Corsair* in 1839, reprinting popular articles from England

and Europe, without permission or payment. Willis's action was in response to a British law that did not grant copyright protection to American authors, and thus deprived him of royalties for his own writing. Pauly notes that it was 'improvements in transportation technology' that made Willis's piracy possible, since steamship travel made access easy to new material from abroad. Similarly, new technologies make access to new sound material easy, and make reproduction of that material easy as well.

Still, the copyright situation in the US itself is quite unstable. The contradictions in copyright law must be worked out before it can cope with new technology. A recent decision by the US copyright office to treat 'colourised' versions of black-and-white films as 'derivative works' if they show 'a minimum amount of individual, creative, human authorship' (AP Wire Service, 1987) may set a precedent for music copyrighting. Probably the best illustration of the difficulties that will be encountered during litigation over sound and/or music infringement comes from the 'Stars on 45' recording, as described by Frith:

> The earliest great mastermix, a series of Beatles songs segued with fine imagination over a shifting disco beat could not be released in its original form because it breached copyright. A cover [version] of the mix was released though – for his Stars on 45 version Jaap Eggermont hired studio musicians to *reproduce* the sound of the Beatles. The latter duly got their mechanical royalties as composers; the deejay whose idea/beat/sequence was exactly copied was entitled to nothing at all. (Frith, 1987, p. 18)

And nothing illustrates the evolution of recording better than the current copyright struggle. When first invented, recording was thought of as a means of sound transmission, primarily via telephone lines. It was in essence an adjunct to the telephone and telegraph, meant to enable later decoding of very rapid messages. An auxiliary use was for storing sound. Since the late nineteenth century, the emphasis has shifted to the retrieving of sound, and development has focused on facilitating retrieval. In an analysis of the history of copyright, Ronald Bettig notes that

> The dominant trends in the development of US copyright law and judicial interpretations were the extension of the duration of copyright protection, the application to new forms of artistic and literary creativity and expression, and the concentration of intellectual property in the hands of increasingly larger corporate entities ...
>
> With ... technological developments, authors and artists found new outlets for their creativity, while publishers and other owners of the means of communication and dissemination found new ways to make a profit. (Bettig, 1990)

Such trends continue to this day. Even though it appears that sampling allows artists to 'reclaim' or 'recontextualise' sound, it must be remembered that sampling is a *production* method and not a means of distribution. So long as the structure of the US music industry, the US legal system and us copyright law, which support corporate ownership of copyright, remains intact, dissemination of sampled material will remain problematic. The use of digital recorders, compact discs, DAT, hard disk drives and the forthcoming recordable CD is based not only on fidelity and mass storage, but on rapid recovery of sound as well. Recording without playback is, for all intents and purposes, senseless, and it is *playback* that is, in the final analysis, problematic for copyright owners.

REFERENCES

Aaron, C. (1989), 'Gettin' Paid' *Village Voice Rock & Roll Quarterly*, Fall, pp. 22–6.

A. P. Wire Service (1987), report, 21 June.

Bell, B. (1987), telephone interview with the author, 9 June.

Berman, J. (1991), 'International Copyright Battle Persists', *Billboard*, 21 December, p. 12.

Bettig, R. (1990), 'Critical Perspectives on the History and Philosophy of Copyright', paper presented at Association for Education in Journalism and Mass Communication annual conference, 5 August, Minneapolis, Minn., USA.

Billboard (1959), 'Bill to Copyright New Electronic Sounds Offered', 16 March, p. 1.

Copyright Act of the United States of America (1976), 17 USC 101.

Curley, T. (1987), telephone interview with the author, 5 June.

Cutler, C. (1985), *File Under Popular*, London: November Books.

Dorian, F. (1942), *The History of Music in Performance*, New York: W. W. Norton & Co., Inc.

Eisenberg, E. (1987), *The Recording Angel*, New York: McGraw-Hill Book Company.

Form SR (1976), US Copyright Office.

Frith, S. (1986), 'Art Versus Technology: The Strange Case of Popular Music', *Media, Culture and Society*, 8, London: Sage, p. 264.

—— (1987), 'Copyright and the Music Business,' unpublished manuscript.

George, N. (1985), *Fresh*, New York: Random House/Sarah Lazin Books.

H. R. 2911 (1985), 'Home Audio Recording Act,' US House of Representatives.

Harrington, R. (1986), 'RIAA Moving to Washington', *Washington Post*, 8 September, p. C2.

Hebdige, D. (1987), *Cut 'n' Mix*, New York: Methuen.

Holland, B. (1991), 'Senators Hear Foes Agree On Taping Royalty', *Billboard*, 9 November, p. 85.

—— (1992) 'China Hears US Pleas: Protect Copyrights', *Billboard*, 25 January, p. 6.

Junglieb, S. (1987), 'telephone interview with the author, 8 June.

Kealy, E. (1974), *The Real Rock Revolution: Sound Mixers, Social Inequality, and the Aesthetics of Popular Music Production*, Evanston, Ill.: Northwestern University, Ph.D. dissertation.

Kelly, D. (1992), 'Scant Copyright Laws in Taiwan, Poland, Philippines Pinch US', *Billboard*, 7 March, p. 6.

Lawrence, H. (1955), 'About Music – The Composing Machine', *Audio*, April, pp. 10–11.

Lowe, J. (1955), 'Tape Recorder Spurs New Interests For Audio-Minded Home Owners', *Musical America*, March, p. 21.
Miller, M. (1987), 'High Tech Alteration of Sights and Sounds Divides the Arts World', *Wall Street Journal*, 1 September, p. 1.
Pauly, J. (1988), 'Nathaniel Parker Willis', *Dictionary of Literary Biography: American Magazine Journalists*, S. Riley, ed., Detroit: Gale Research Co., pp. 349–56.
Reich, S. (1987), telephone interview with the author, 5 January.
Shapiro, E. (1991), 'Accord on Digital Taping Faces Hurdle in Congress', *New York Times*, 12 July, p. C3.
Toop, D. (1984), *Rap Attack*, London: Pluto Press.
UPI (10 July, 1991) 'Agreement Nears On Digital Recording'.
Wallis, R. and Malm, K. (1984), *Big Sounds From Small Peoples*, New York: Pendragon Press.

5

Bette Midler and the Piracy of Identity

JANE M. GAINES

The 1989 California sound-alike decision favouring Bette Midler over Ford Motor Company's advertising agency Young and Rubicam has left legal commentators wondering less about performance rights than what might be called persona rights. *Midler* v. *Ford Motor Co.* veered abruptly away from case law which had historically refused to grant either trademark or copyright protection to a vocal performer's rendition of a song. But such 'refusal to protect' is not necessarily negative in my analysis. What is so significant about the *Midler* shift? After a number of performers including Shirley Booth and Nancy Sinatra had been unsuccessful in their attempts to make a proprietal claim on an identifiable vocal style, *Midler* reversed the trend. The Ninth Circuit Court, overruling the trial court, concluded that Midler's brassy belting of the 1972 hit 'Do You Wanna Dance?' was hers alone. In hiring a singer to imitate the Midler style in a Mercury Sable television commercial, Young and Rubicam was 'pirating an identity', said Judge Noonan. In other words, the *Midler* court found a way around the apparent unprotectability of vocal style. Why this decision now?

As I see it, *Midler* falls in line with the politics of the Reagan Era in the US, not just because it closed a copyright loophole, but because of the way it shifted emphasis from performance to identity, as I will show. It also was heard in the midst of what might be termed a cultural heyday for television sound-alikes (and consequently appeals for injunctions).

In the late 1980s, Bobby Darin's son Dodd sued MacDonald's over the 'Mac Tonight' campaign, which recalled the beat and tone of his father's hit rendition of 'Mack the Knife'. Patti Page sued over American Savings and Loan's recreation of her version of 'Old Cape Cod', and Rodney Dangerfield took on Park-Ins International for simulating his voice. The successful sound-alike list goes on to include Oldsmobile's imitation of Arlo Guthrie's 'The City of New Orleans', Close-up toothpaste's reworking of Linda Ronstadt's style in its 'Get Closer', and Heinz catsup's version of Carly Simon's 'Anticipation'.

My rule is that case law builds up around ambiguity in the law. A rise in sound-alike litigation is an indicator that US copyright law is being rocked back and forth, but not that it shouldn't be jostled. On the contrary, back and forth movement is basic to intellectual property law. This is the pattern I have discussed as the double movement of copyright law – from protection to refusal to protect, or from restriction to circulation (Gaines, 1991, p. 8). Let me cast the sides in the sound-alike case in these terms, with the celebrity talent on the protection-restriction side and the advertising agencies on the circulation-unprotected side, which I also discuss here as the 'creativity = availability' side of the debates.

On the circulation side, then, are the advertising agencies, which have defended their use of sound-alikes by arguing that television viewers respond positively to familiarity, that invariably one popular musical sound will remind us of another. Not surprisingly, the agencies take the position that sound-alikeness is inevitable, that there is no way around this re-use of signs. I would suggest, however, that we should not be fooled by this argument (even though it may correspond with semioticians' explanation of how popular culture works) because, after all, it *is* the argument especially designed to take advantage of a copyright loophole. And this is a loophole that is best explained as an acoustic space which in US copyright law cannot be occupied in such a way that other uses of it are prohibited. So that, for example, the Fifth Dimension could not prohibit others from singing 'Up, Up, and Away' in the style they popularised, although the composer of the song could prohibit use and prosecute singers who performed it without a license (*Davis* v. *Trans World Airlines*, 1969). Conflict stems from the fact that musical performances are not designated 'works of authorship' in the same way that the musical compositions performed and even the concrete sound recordings of these performances are 'works' under the US Copyright Law of 1976 (Gaines, 1991, pp. 50, 129). Ad agencies (until *Midler*, that is) have used this 'free' acoustic space in which vocal style 'imitation' is allowed, taking advantage of the absence of legal stipulation regarding sound stylistics.

To better understand the reasoning behind the 'availability of style' position, now encoded in the Copyright Act of 1976, let me return to the precedential case within which this position has been most fully rehearsed. In *Sinatra* v. *Goodyear Tire and Rubber* (1970), the court refused to acknowledge a property right in Nancy Sinatra's style of singing. Sinatra had claimed that in using a sound-alike to imitate her mode of singing the 1968 hit 'These Boots are Made for Walkin'' in television and radio commercials, Goodyear had appropriated her distinctive performance style. She asked for a permanent injunction and damages, charging Goodyear and their advertising agency Young and Rubicam with unfair competition. Citing the 1962 *Lahr* v. *Adell Chemical Co.* as precedent,

Sinatra argued that she had acquired a secondary meaning in her vocal performance, analogous to actor Bert Lahr's successful claim of property interest in his 'unique' and 'peculiar' vocal characteristics. But on the question of secondary meaning in 'style of singing', the court decided that Sinatra's singing style was an unprotectable 'expression'. On this basis, Nancy Sinatra lost to Goodyear Tire.

While the lay person in the culture might object to the outcome of *Sinatra* on the basis of unfairness to an artist whose creative product was appropriated without her permission, there are deeper issues here for intellectual property doctrine, issues which made the case an important precedent for almost twenty years. In legal literature, *Sinatra* has been significant for the way it staved off copyright collision. In the words of the court, a copyright in singing style might 'clash' with a copyright in the musical composition itself. Although the larger legal issue was the problem of Federal pre-emption (the court wishing to uphold the principle that states could not protect that which Federal copyright left unprotected), this dilemma got expressed in other terms. The court imagined a nightmare tangle of secured rights with which future singers seeking to perform a rendition of 'These Boots are Made for Walkin'' would have to contend. In addition to the permission of the composer Lee Hazelwood, these artists would also have to secure the consent of Nancy Sinatra whose performance would seem to have left a proprietal deposit on the musical composition. Unlike Sinatra who sought damages and an injunction against the use of 'her song', Bette Midler did not seek damages for Ford Motor's use of 'Do You Wanna Dance?' After all Ford, like Midler earlier, had obtained a license for use of the song from composer Bobby Freeman and Clockus Music, a song which had been previously recorded by eight different groups (Callagy and Aieta, 1989, p. 14). But, after *Midler*, the question for critics of the case becomes: Will the next singer who wants to perform 'Do You Wanna Dance?' have to ask Bette Midler for permission?

And this question is oriented less toward fairness to a particular artist than fairness to future artists. The *Sinatra* decision, in its resistance to protection for performance style, then, has become aligned in legal literature with a position which might be summarised as 'creativity = availability'. That is, supporters of the decision held the position that the creative options of artists would be severely limited if performers could claim that a distinctive, identifiable mode of attacking one's material – whether song or theatrical piece – could not be borrowed. This has been a particular fear with regard to popular music (as used in commercial projects) and commentators voiced the concern that popular forms were especially 'derivative' and eclectic. Popular artists, the implication was, could not be expected to create anew if the circulating performance signs they needed to use were entangled with the rights of other artists.

The dilemma of performance rights is an old one in US copyright law, and I want to digress here in order to fill this out, attempting in my discussion to make visible that which is always in danger of disappearing: the performer's interpretation. The US Copyright Law Amendments in 1856 and 1859 made allowance for copywritten musical and theatrical works as performed, and the 1909 Copyright Law Act extended that allowance to works reproduced mechanically (the phonograph record and the piano roll). But although this early law took note of performance, it was really concerned with protecting written works (the musical score and the theatrical script) as they were activated on stage and in concert (Nimmer, 1985, p. 214). This has meant that the creative 'work' that actors and musicians performed on that notated 'work' has historically been unseen by copyright law. It is as though the interpretive labour which always tends to evaporate for audiences as soon as it is apprehended has never been solid enough for copyright law to recognise.

One of the very first comprehensive discussions of performing artists and European copyright law describes the dilemma of the interpretive artist somewhat differently. For Robert Homburg, it is the simultaneity of creation and execution that makes the performing artist's contribution so difficult to discern (Homburg, 1934, p. 9). Following this line of thought, the interpretive artist also leaves something on the work which can't ultimately be removed from it. (Although it has not been clear whether artistic style is a copyrightable 'work of authorship' on top of another work in the manner of a 'derivative' work which is grounded in an 'underlying' work) (Nimmer, 1985, pp. 19–24). For those who have argued for seeing style as artistic property, the argument is that this secondary 'something' contributed to the work is unlike the contribution the skilled labourer makes to the construction of an implement or a monument. That is, the skilled labourer employed on a 'work for hire' basis leaves his or her contribution in the created object in exchange for a wage. In contrast, the freelance interpretive labourer produces a work that can be exchanged again whenever another artist wants to use the style he or she elaborated (Hombug, 1934, pp. 9–10).

Performing artists enthusiastically greeted the perfection of mechanical means for recording and storing their musical and theatrical acts, expecting that these new devices would concretise their artistry. The radio, the phonograph, and the motion picture, were understood as producing a 'materialisation' of an artistic interpretation, making the value of the performer's contribution more manifest (Homburg, 1934, pp. 11–15). To some degree, this has been the case with actors (and some musicians) whose commercial television and radio 'work' earns them royalties with every replay of their performance, the very repetition writes stylistic 'difference' into the memory of viewers and listeners.

And yet at the same time that mechanical reproduction would seem to have produced interpretive performance as a commodity value, it has also worked to erase it. If, for instance, the fee of the musical recording artist, paid at the time the recording was produced, is included in the price of record, tape or disk, replaying the recording at home reduces the cost of the performative labour (per play). So that while stylistic 'difference' is reinscribed in the memories of fans, the work that produced it is increasingly distanced from them. This system of compensation for musical performing artists currently operative in the US and the UK, imperfect though it is, is brought into sharp relief when compared with the history of Soviet law regarding performances broadcast on radio. There, a 'freedom of the microphone' law historically took the position that re-recording and re-broadcasting an artist's performance did not involve any supplementary labour and therefore that the artist could not claim compensation for the mechanically produced 'performance' (Homburg, 1934, p. 17).

But finally this question of the mechanical stand-in brings us to the problem which becomes doubled in *Midler*. If mechanical reproduction made it possible to substitute a recording for live musical and theatrical performance (rendering musicians and actors 'redundant'), technologies of duplication also made it possible to substitute one performer or musician for another, particularly in the 'blind' medium of radio (Arnheim, 1936). This technical capability gave rise to the kind of conflicts which occasioned the earliest of the sound-alike cases, *Gardella* v *Log Cabin Products, Inc.* (1937) where Italian actress Tess Gardella, the 'voice' of Aunt Jemima, filed suit against the maple syrup company for using a radio jingle imitating the 'characterisation' embodied in the vocal style she had perfected. And later, the issue arose regarding the exclusivity of the instrumental 'sound' of the popular American bands directed by Glenn Miller, Artie Shaw, and Guy Lombardo. In these cases, New York courts held that while the musical compositions themselves, and recordings of the actual orchestras, should be treated as exclusive property, the arrangements of the music were not copyrightable. Meaning that another orchestra could recreate the Glenn Miller sound in *The Glenn Miller Story* sound-track album or Time-Life Records could make new recordings of a contemporary band playing in the Artie Shaw style for an album of swing era hits. But the outcome of the Lombardo case prefigures *Midler*. There, although a television advertisement had recreated the orchestra leader's playing style, it was in the appropriation of his persona as 'Mr New Year's Eve' that the court drew the line. Musical style was not property, personal identity was (McCarthy, 1988, Sec. 4.14).

The pattern in these cases confirms the fact that courts make a distinction between duplication and imitation, the former a sound-alikeness produced by machine and the later a sound-alikeness originating in the human body (Goldstein and Kessler, 1962, p. 822). But courts have never had trouble with the live performance of sound-alikeness, the comic voice imitations of Rich Little or even the many post-1960s proliferations of rock band imitations of the Beatles 'sound'. Even in the recent dispute in which Frank Sinatra tried to enjoin Sinatra sound-alike performer Nick Edonetti's nightclub act, Edonetti would have had a defence of his imitation based on the copyright provisions regarding parody. It is, however, at the point that the imitative performance is recorded on audio or videotape that it becomes a problem for courts. To state this in terms used in legal discourse, the problem is that there is no performance right in sound recording. Although in the Sound Recording Amendment of 1971, the US Congress saw record producers as 'authors' of sound recording, the impetus here was to curb piracy (duplication), not to protect musical performance from style 'imitation'. (D'Onofrio, 1981, pp. 170–1, 175). The question becomes, do gestures, timing and mannerisms become a copyrightable expression when fixed in tangible form in a sound recording? Some commentators say yes. *Midler* said neither no nor yes, but decided the popular singer's case on a completely different legal principle.

Midler also alerts us to the way new recording technologies extend an operative *cultural* principle regarding the production of musical and other sounds. This principle, characteristic of Western culture, one might call the principle of musical disembodiment, a phenomenon music theorist Susan McClary has described as the erasure of physicality in both the production and the reception of music. Western culture, she says, has historically attempted 'to mask the fact that actual people usually produce the sounds that constitute music.' New electronic technologies including the sound-enhancing disk and digital audio recording are the culmination of this ideal (McClary, 1991, p. 136).

And this is one way to see Nancy Sinatra, Shirley Booth, and now Bette Midler – as reenacting a return of the human performer to claim an electronically disembodied (incorrectly attributed) sound – to put the right body with the voice. But what I will be arguing is that the return of the human performer to the mediated voice is essentially a conservative move which confirms culture as private property over culture as shared domain. Here, in order to clarify my position, I need to distinguish personal rights (which can only be asserted by celebrities) from performance rights which ordinary actors and musicians have attempted to claim historically as a means of ensuring their livelihood. There is a point, however, when the one set of rights may impinge on the other, and to some degree, this is how the court in *Sinatra* framed that dispute – refusing to allow a popular singer's style to become restricted property, thereby leaving it available (theoretically) to other performers.

In the literature on copyright protection and performance, there is a tendency to characterise the courts' refusal to grant property status to some forms of expression (aesthetic styles, musical arrangements, vocal qualities) as a position which leaves these forms 'free' to performers. Not only is this 'availability' position aligned with 'creativity' as I have said, but it is associated with the public domain in which things are 'free to the people'. And here is where this position shows itself to be more an expression of *laissez-faire* capitalism than any utopian vision of equal access. It is more likely that popular signs (such as singing styles) are 'free' and available to advertising agencies and their corporate clients rather than 'free' to ordinary people and struggling performers. More often than not, however, these corporate creators argue *in the name of lesser performers*.

A case in point is singer Tom Waits's suit against Tracy-Locke Advertising Agency and Frito-Lay in which Waits won punitive damages. Here, Texan Steve Carter sang a jingle for Frito-Lay's 'Salsa Rio Dorito' corn chips, approximating the gravelly vocal style of Waits's 1976 *Nighthawks at the Diner* album and the delivery of his 1973 hit tune 'Step Right Up'. Plaintiff Waits successfully argued, citing *Midler* as precedent, that his voice, a 'tangible asset', had been appropriated. But what I want to call attention to here is the structure of the defence position which was aligned with artistic freedom. That is, Frito-Lay and Tracy-Locke essentially characterised their position as benefiting performers such as Carter, a Waits fan and former band member who once put together a stage act based on imitating the Waits style. As we would imagine, this is none other than the availability = creativity position that if the Waits style were owned exclusively, it wouldn't be 'free' for other singers such as Carter to draw on and to reinflect as parody or imitation, robbing such creative artists of their sonic materials.

But what is the significance of the fact that Steve Carter was unemployed at the time the court brief was written? Would the commercial availability of the Waits style make it possible for the musician to make a living as a vocal simulacrum of the celebrity? Did the outcome of the Waits dispute (which followed *Midler*) guarantee the rock star a personal monopoly that operated in restraint of trade in musical signs (King, 1985, p. 43)? Problematic as it is to try to think of living persons as well as intangible acoustic signs in market terms (despite the apparent success of US intellectual property law at doing this), market control is exactly what is at stake and this becomes clearer if we can see 'Bette Midler' less as a person than as a corporate entity needing to exert monopoly control. The discussion of 'value' in *Midler*, as the case diverges from *Sinatra*, makes this point.

First, a short summary of *Midler* v. *Ford Motor Co.* In this case, the singer took action against the automobile company and their advertising agency, claiming unfair competition, invasion of privacy, infringement of her right of publicity, and violation of California Code 3344 which protects the name, likeness, and voice of the living. Dismissing the unfair competition as well as the invasion of privacy claims, Circuit Court Judge Noonan focused on the value of Midler's voice to Ford Motor Company. What Ford sought, he said, was 'an attribute of Midler's identity. Its value was what the market would have paid for Midler to have sung the commercial in person.' In support of this line of argument, the judge offered the information that Ford had hired a singer (Ula Hedwig who earlier sang with Midler as a 'Harlette') who was given instructions to sing 'Do You Wanna Dance?' in Midler's style. In effect, the court reasoned, Ford saved the money they would have had to pay Midler to perform the song. But these disputes are not finally about Ford Motor's attempt to get out of paying fees and royalties to a superstar by substituting less expensive talent, because the emphasis in *Midler* is finally not on employment but on property.

The concern with the 'value' of Midler's vocal characteristics translates into an entitlement which owes something to the new California Code 990, section (b), also known as the 'Celebrity Rights Act', particularly in its reference to 'property rights' in the name, voice and likeness of the celebrity. Code 990 is a key indicator of a kind of legal muscle which was developed in the 1980s, toughness benefiting powerful financial interests, a significant change since *Sinatra.* But the reference to the new 1985 California Code 990 in *Midler* was somewhat odd since, as different from Code 3344 which pertains to the rights of the living, Code 990 deals with the entitlements of deceased celebrities (Brassel and Kulzick, 1985; Rohde, 1985). As it has evolved, this code enables the families of the famous – Clark Gable, John Wayne, and W. C. Fields – to guard the images of their ancestors. This celebrity image protection sometimes amounts to a right to monitor and censor popular imagery, and this is certainly one of its more reactionary implications (Gaines, 1991, pp. 229–30). But for our purposes, the significance of Code 990 is that a state code recognised the 'voice' as inheritable property, and while this state law may explicitly apply only to the dead, the 'property right' spirit of Code 990 is alive in *Midler* and would seem to have successfully supplanted *Sinatra* as precedent.

As I have argued elsewhere, the momentum behind Code 990, including the cases which paved the way for it, could be defined as a movement from a right of privacy to a right of publicity (Gaines, 1991, pp. 181–2, 194–5). Over the last fifty years, the principles which established the right to be let alone (to not have one's privacy invaded) seem to have metamorphosed into the opposite – the right to exclusive use of one's name, voice and likeness. And the right of publicity, fifty years ago a suspect right, has become an effective remedy in commercial disputes. Thus it is no surprise that it would inevitably be recruited into performance right case law (Levine, 1980). What is interesting about the arguments for commercial exclusivity (requisite to entering into competition) is that one still hears the personal privacy argument in the property argument. And this ambiguity is there in *Midler* where Judge Noonan described his analysis of the case as an 'invasion of "proprietary" interest in identity'. So the slippage between 'invasion of privacy' and 'invasion of property', effects a double claim-staking, borrowing two cultural ideals that vied for ascendancy: personhood and property. Although elsewhere I have argued that personhood and property come from the same Lockean root in Anglo-American culture, here I want to look at something additional (Gaines, 1991, pp. 63–5). I want to ask how the idea of 'natural' attributes is at odds with a concept of 'constructed' ones in *Midler* as well as in the discourse around the case. From there, I want to go on to consider where 'performance' fits in relation to this duality. Does it come down on the side of natural endowment or on the side of labour?

Midler is characteristic of all sound-alike cases in that it argues for the particularity, the individuality, the recognisability of a popular singer's vocal style. Where it is slightly different (where this performer succeeded) is in its attachment of 'voice' to 'identity'. And it is where voice is attached to identity that *Midler* also straddles the fence. *Midler* called upon all of the ambiguity of 'identity' to make the case that the singer's 'voice' (an 'attribute of identity' in the judge's terms) is *both* private and part of a public persona. Further evidence of the attempt in *Midler* to have it both ways (appealing to natural attributes as well as constructed ones) was Judge Noonan's comparison between the voice and the face. ('The voice is as distinctive and personal as a face.') But in his choice of words the judge made implicit reference to trademark doctrine's test of protectability – the 'distinctiveness' of a word or image (Miller and Davis, 1983, p. 162). In intellectual property doctrine 'distinctive' calls up associations with popular public recognition, the construction of popularity, the work of promotion which produces one sign as distinguishable from other competing signs. Surely, then, any notion of voice as 'distinctive' is at odds with an understanding of it as 'personal', which, in its association with the face, takes on connotations of physiological 'givens', natural traits rather than commercial signifiers of recognition.

The comparison between voice and face in *Midler* reminds us that historically in sound-alike cases, plaintiffs have attempted to argue for seeing look-alike cases as precedent, presumably because in the cases involving Woody Allen, Jacqueline Onassis and others, plaintiffs have successfully argued that commercial uses of celebrity doubles should be enjoined. In these cases the argument has been that the face is inviolate, the deepest indicator of individuality and the clearest marker of personhood. If the face is synonymous with selfhood, then to appropriate another's face is to steal that most personal sign in Western culture – the 'I'. It is also to set up a chain of confusion as to who is whom which, most importantly, complicates the determination of what *belongs* to whom. The face (like the mark of the handwritten signature), is the guarantee of property. Midler's case gains much from this comparison, a specious comparison which does nothing more than borrow the proprietal mechanism of the face. And to suggest how this works, I would refer to Deleuze and Guattari who have described the process by which Western culture makes everything over in the image of 'Man' as the 'faceification' of the world (Deleuze and Guattari, 1988, p. 181). We have here, then, nothing more nor less than the 'faceification' of the voice, a deeply conservative move in its return to an outmoded humanism.

The tendency over the last thirty years in sound-alike actions as well as look-alike cases, has been to argue for distinctiveness, and the successes of the plaintiffs in the majority of cases has hinged on their ability to argue that their definitive difference (from other voices and faces) was either inherent or produced. The inconsistency of this will stand out sharply to cultural-studies scholars familiar with the literature on stars as social constructions (Dyer, 1979). What interests me in particular is the way that arguments about the 'work'of the celebrity have appeared erratically in these cases, although the issue of 'work' has been raised fairly often in the discourses around the cases. For instance, Leonard Marks, discussing *Midler*, argued that plaintiffs in sound-alike actions should have historically been able to make stronger cases than plaintiffs in look-alike actions because, while the physical appearance of a person is a 'mere birthright', the singer 'devotes his energies to achieving a commercially successful and distinctive "voice"' (Marks, 1988, p. 2). This statement is somewhat misleading because until *Midler* (with the exception of *Lahr)*, plaintiffs in sound-alike cases have had no success at all whereas plaintiffs in look-alike cases from *Chaplin* v. *Amador* (1928) on, have enjoyed relatively favourable outcomes as a whole. Marks also ignores the possibility that a popular stage or screen performer often labours to produce a signature character and a public 'face'. The point about the work of vocal production is an important one, but case law in this area reflects the conflictedness of a culture which cannot decide whether personal 'identity' means physical features or cultivated self.

What has become clear to me from my study of intellectual property rulings in the light of the construction of social meaning is that social realities solidify around key points of law, reminding me of the way commonsense knowledge operates (Gaines, 1991, pp. 14–15). What we might call aesthetic theory according to intellectual property doctrine would show us theories abut 'what is sound' and 'what constitutes likeness and similarity', knowledge culled from a reading of precedents. This body of knowledge might be called 'the world according to copyright and trademark law'. It is a special ontology of things derived from preexisting rulings: 'Voices are ephemeral'. 'Likenesses don't have to resemble, but must not confuse viewers.' 'Imitation alone doesn't constitute an infringement.' 'A cultural sign must be "distinctive" in order to attain property status.' And finally, 'intangible things may be protected property, but these intangibles must still be "fixed".'

And 'fixation', as one would suspect, is a key issue in sound-alike cases where the impermanence of the acoustic sign presents difficulties for legal doctrine. What has happened in sound-alike cases is that because of the perceived need to leave some aspects of performance unprotected ('free'), the 'fixed/unfixed' dichotomy in Federal copyright law has been used to serve this end. Historically 'fixation' has had the function of separating the ephemeral 'performed' theatrical play or musical composition from the copywritten record of it – whether in script, videotape or phonorecord form. The fixed/unfixed dichotomy originally worked to the advantage of musical composers who used the 'limbo' of ephemerality to the ends of exclusivity. If their work was neither recorded nor published as a score, no matter how many times it was performed, they could still keep it out of the mandatory circulation decreed as early as the 1909 copyright act. An 'unfixed' work, although not protected by Federal copyright laws, has been a work secured for its author, that is, 'secured' by common law (Goldstein and Kessler, 1962, pp. 827–32).

But note the entirely different function that the fixed/unfixed dichotomy has had in sound-alike cases where the 'unfixedness' of the voice is the rationale given for not treating it as protectable property. So that a legal concept which protected musical composers had the opposite effect when applied to vocal performers. For instance, in *Shirley Booth* v. *Colgate-Palmolive Co.*, the comic acress was not able to claim property in her style of speaking (simulated in an advertisement for the detergent Burst) because, as the court argued, the 'voice does not function as a trademark or tradename'. Judge Noonan in *Midler* reiterated this: 'A voice is not copyrightable. The sounds are not "fixed".' And yet he went on to conclude that the voice, however unfixed, was Midler's property. So the lack of material 'fixedness' in these cases is really an alibi for keeping some signs 'free' while others are tied up. So what happens in *Midler* is that there is deference to the availability side of the available-unavailable dialectic at the same time that the decision in *Midler* produced a result which is the reverse of the outcome which the 'voice is not copyrightable' principle is supposed to produce. *Midler* sides with restriction and unavailability. And it does so by playing an ace: 'identity'. ('To impersonate her voice is to pirate her identity.')

So it seems that I am still sceptical of the 'identity = property' outcome in *Midler*, and supportive of the 'availability' position of *Sinatra*, but only by default. To some degree it is the argument from within legal studies against the monopoly on performance signs that persuades me. Then again, I am not fooled. As a calculatedly popular rock star, 'Bette Midler' is after all an industry masquerading as a person.

REFERENCES

Allen v. *National Video, Inc.*, 610 F. Supp. (SNDY, 1985).

Arnheim, R., Trans. Ludwig, M. and Read, H. (1936), *Radio*, New York: Arno.

Auslander, P. (1991), 'Intellectual Property Meets the Cyborg: Performance and the Cultural Politics of Technology', unpublished paper.

Booth v. *Colgate-Palmolive*, 362 F. Supp. 343 (SDNY 1983).

Brassel, R. and Kulzick, K (1985), 'Life After Death for the California Celebrity', *Los Angeles Lawyer*, pp. 12–15.

Callagy, R. M. and Aieta, M. (1989), 'Rights in Persona and Style of Performance', *Practicing Law Institute.*

Chaplin v. *Amador*, 93 Cal. App. 358 (1928).

D'Onofrio, S. J. (1981), 'In Support of Performance Rights in Sound Recording', *UCLA Law Review*, 29, pp. 168–98.

Davis v. *Trans World Airlines*, 297 F. Supp. 1145 (1969).

Deleuze, G. and Guattari, F., trans. Massumi, B. (1988), *A Thousand Plateaus: Capitalism and Schizophrenia*, Minneapolis: University of Minnesota Press.

Dyer, R. (1979), *Stars*, London: British Film Institute.

Gaines, J. M. (1991), *Contested Culture: The Image, the Voice, and the Law*, Chapel Hill and London: University of North Carolina Press.

Gardella v. *Log Cabin Products, Inc.*, 89 F. 2d 871 (2d Cir. 1937).

Goldstein, R. and Kessler, A. (1962), 'The Twilight Zone: Meandering in the Area of Performers' Rights', UCLA *Law Review*, 9, pp. 819–61.

Hodgson, C. L. (1975), 'Intellectual Property – Performer's Style', *Denver Law Journal*, 52, 561–94.

Homburg, R., trans. Speiser, M. J. (1934), *Legal Rights of Performing Artists*, New York: Baker and Voorhis.

Kent, F. (1988), 'New Tune in Using "Sound-Alikes"', *New York Law Journal*, 22 July, 3, col. 1.

King, B. (1985) 'Articulating Stardom', *Screen*, pp. 27–50.

Lahr v. *Adell Chemical Co.*, 300 F. 2d 256 (1962).

Levine, M. (1980), 'Right of Publicity as a Means of Protecting performance Style', *Loyola Law Review*, 14, pp. 129–63.

Liebig, A. (1969), 'Style and Performance', *Bulletin of the Copyright Society of America*, 17, pp. 40–7.

Lombardo v. *Doyle, Dane & Bernbach, Inc.*, 58 AD2d 620, 396 NYS2d 661 (1977).

Lugosi v. *Universal Pictures, Inc.*, 160 Cal. Rptr. 323 (1979).

McCarthy, T. J. (1988), *Rights of Publicity and Privacy*, New York: Clark Boardman.

McClary, S. (1991), *Feminine Endings*, Minneapolis: University of Minnesota Press.

Marks, L. (1988), *The New York Law Journal*, 5 October, p. 1.

Midler v. *Ford Motor Co.*, 849 F. 2d 460 (1981), 463.

Miller v. *Universal Pictures*, 214 NYS 2d 645 (1960).
Miller, A. M. and Davis, M. (1983), 'Intellectual Property: Patents, Trademarks, and Copyright', St Paul; West Publishing Company.
Nimmer, M. (1985), *Cases and Materials on Copyright and Other Aspects of Entertainment Litigation – Including Unfair Competition, Defamation and Privacy*, 3rd edn, St Paul: West publishing Co.
Onassis v. *Christian Dior-New York, Inc.*, 122 Misc. 2d 603 (1984).
Rohde, S. F. (1985), 'Dracula: Still Undead', *California Lawyer*, pp. 53–5.
Shaw v. *Time-Life*, 38 N.Y.2d 210 (1975).
Sinatra v. *Goodyear Tire & Rubber Co.*, 435 F.2d 722 (1970).

6

Making It Visible: The 1990 Public Inquiry into Australian Music Copyrights[1]

MARCUS BREEN

When Australian Labor Party Government Minister, Senator Nick Bolkus, announced on 15 February 1990 that the Prices Surveillance Authority (PSA) would conduct an inquiry into the prices of recorded music, the previously somnolent executives of the major record companies went into virtual paroxysms. The unrelenting opposition to the federal government's request for an inquiry that began with that announcement early in 1990 continued until after the PSA handed down its report *Inquiry Into the Prices of Sound Recordings (IPSR)* on 18 December 1990. By then it was clear what the record companies' outrage had been about. Amongst other things, the PSA recommended radical changes to the 1968 Copyright Act, to allow parallel importing of recordings. Indeed, when the federal government agreed to introduce a version of the inquiry's recommendations on 10 June 1992, the struggle over Australian copyright law had been won by the reformers. As well as this reform victory the inquiry offered an important side benefit, namely an inquiry process that exposed the entire structure and operations of the Australian music industry to public scrutiny.

The PSA inquiry was a watershed in Australian music history, separating the status quo assumptions about copyright from the need to realign them with an Australia keen to compete within the global trade network. Until the inquiry, the recorded music industry had been relatively unregulated by a range of clauses within the 1968 Copyright Act. The inquiry was a challenge to the prevailing free market structure that was upheld by the Act. As the title of this chapter suggests, the inquiry revealed the otherwise private and relatively invisible hand of copyright law in regulating the interests of the major record companies in Australia by controlling and maintaining their monopoly over product distribution. Following the economist, Kenneth E. Train, it is possible to see the major record companies' faith in the 'invisible hand of competition', as expressed in the 1968 Copyright Act, in contrast to the 'visible hand' of government intervention and regulation acting 'to ensure socially desirable outcomes' (1991).

Specialist legal commentators valorise copyright as a primary organising mechanism for defining property rights, which are expressed as a balance between ownership and incentive or creativity and competition (Ricketson, 1991; Ryan, 1991). Another less frequently encountered view suggests that 'the form of law reproduces the requirements of capitalism, in the area of cultural production' (Barker, 1992). These views suggest that copyright law needs to be contested more fully, both as a site for interventionary reform and to challenge the restricted way in which the debate circulates, where it is too frequently a territory dominated by lawyers rather than social scientists or policy makers.

PUBLIC OUTRAGE – PRIVATE POWER

When the Minister for Consumer Affairs, Senator Nick Bolkus, announced the terms of reference for the inquiry, it was the culmination of tempestuous activity within the music and cultural industries in Australia. Music retailers who imported to Australia from the US and UK current releases for sale, had been under surveillance for some time. Specialist retailers – most of which catered for fans – believed that their importation of current releases that were also being imported and released in Australia by the major record companies was innocuous. In contrast, the majors said the existing clauses of the 1968 Copyright Act gave them an exclusive right to import recordings, most frequently from their parent companies, and it was their perogative to grant those rights to other importers. WEA (Australia) was especially aggressive in claiming their exclusive distribution rights against the small numbers of imported recordings. Frequently during the years just prior to 1990, retailers would be charged under the 1968 Copyright Act of illegally (parallel) importing recordings for which they had no licence.

In another part of the Australian cultural industries, a long awaited public inquiry was being held into the book publishing industry by the PSA. The *Inquiry into Book Prices Final Report* was published by the PSA on 19 December 1989. This inquiry, which also investigated the parallel importing provisions of the 1968 Copyright Act, provided the incentive the specialist music retailers needed. Working together as the Australian Record Sellers Association, the organisation lobbied federal government ministers and the PSA, suggesting that, like the book publishing industry, the recorded music industry should be the focus of an inquiry into the restrictive, anti-competitive import licensing arrangements that occurred because of the Copyright Act. Historically, it was also possible to align the inquiry with the gradual development of a national culture and the need for a copyright law that reflected an independent nation's place in the world (Lahore and Griffith, 1974, p. 1). Equally relevant was the tradition of public inquiries in Australia that forms a basis for Australian socio-political style (Breen, 1993).

If these arguments were not convincing enough, then the federal government had the 1988 Copyright Law Review Committee's report *The Importation Provisions of the 1968 Copyright Act.* This committee was established in 1983 by the Federal Labor Party government to discuss and review the copyright issues that kept a private coterie of lawyers and bureaucrats well paid. The committee had recommended a relaxation of aspects of the Act, in particular parallel importing (1988, p. 3). More telling was the committee's conclusion that 'a number of inefficiencies ... probably exist because of the protected position of the exclusive licensees' (1988, p. 243). The government needed little encouragement to call a PSA investigation of the music industry, with such findings in its back pocket. Perhaps there was even more incentive for the government to act because the history of Australian copyright law had been painfully slow and emasculated by the traditionalists who wanted to get the law right rather than address 'the wider economic and social issues' (Ricketson, 1992, pp. 17, 18).

Senator Bolkus opened the door for a full inquiry with the terms of reference he announced in parliament in February. He asked the PSA to conduct an inquiry into: 'competition and efficiency, the 1968 Copyright Act, piracy, the effect of current industry structure and pricing practices on the development of Australian music, profitability and employment, the introduction of new technologies' (*IPSR*, 1990, p. xi).

The PSA recommendations confirmed the majors' worst fears when they appeared in December. They were:

1. After considering the possible consequences of allowing parallel imports of records, the Authority is convinced that such structural reform is the logical and preferable policy solution to the problem of high prices. It is therefore recommended that sections 37, 38, 102 and 103 of the Copyright Act be repealed in relation to parallel imports from countries providing comparable levels of protection over the reproduction of musical works and sound recordings. Proclamation of legislative amendments giving effect to this recommendation should be delayed for 12 months to allow the industry time to implement necessary contractual rearrangements.
2. As a very much second best solution to some of the current problems (principally availability) in the record market, the Authority considers that it would be sensible to reform the importation provisions for musical works and sound recordings so that they were in line with the reforms adopted for books; and that the effects should be reviewed in three years (as proposed for books).

3. In the event that the repeal of the importation provisions was not implemented, the Authority recommends declaration of the six major record companies – BMG, CBS, EMI, Festival, Polygram and WEA – under The Prices Surveillance Act 1983.[2]
4. The Authority recommends the adoption of better targeted policies to protect more effectively against the piracy of records:
   – the amendment of section 135 of the Copyright Act to cover pirate sound recordings, where the copyright owner has given notice to the customs service regarding the expected time and place of importation;
   – in relation to the importation and distribution of pirate sound recordings, the amendment of sections 37, 38, 103 of the Copyright Act to bring their knowledge requirements into line with those of sections 36 and 101;
   – the raising of maximum penalties under section 133 to an unlimited fine and two years imprisonment.
5. The Authority recommends that the Government consider favourably the possibility of legislation for a performers' levy based on sales and used to fund directly the development of Australian artists.
6. The authority recommends that the Government reconsider the creation of a performers' copyright comparable to that provided for the makers of sound recordings.
7. The Authority recommends the removal of the tariff on imported polycarbonate as an appropriate way to assist local CD manufacturing.
8. The Authority recommends that the Government consider the establishment of an 'Industry Council' representing all parties involved in the industry (PSA News release, 18 Dec. 1990).

When the recommendations were handed down, the opponents of the inquiry launched a double-pronged campaign to discredit the PSA, while moving to stop the introduction of the recommendations. The campaign lasted throughout 1991 and spluttered into 1992.

The debates achieved a high public profile, especially in the print media, after Midnight Oil's lead singer Peter Garrett prophesied the death of the Australian music industry as a result of the proposed changes to the 1968 Copyright Act. Garrett's public prominence guaranteed that the PSA recommendations would be noticed, which, after all, was what his presence as an agenda-setting pop star was about. His comments were typically catchy: 'Why should this government try to dismantle a successful industry which is working well, employs large numbers of people, and which earns export income for the country, by removing the very mechanisms which allow it to exist?' Professor Allan Fels, Chairman of the PSA refused to let such comments go unchallenged: 'In the run-up to a

Cabinet decision on records, the record industry is encouraging its closely associated supporters to manufacture every conceivable scare story'. In the meantime the *Financial Review* ran articles in support of the PSA recommendations under headlines like 'Rich rock stars fighting to retain the consumer rip-off'.

The outcome of Garrett's involvement in the fight was increased public confusion, which led to questions like: Why was Garrett supporting the high price-setting activities of the (foreign owned) major record companies, and not supporting consumers in seeking lower prices for recordings? There were two real questions to ask. Would changes to the Copyright Act to allow for parallel importing lower prices? And in so doing, would Australian artists be threatened with imports of (their) cheap records from overseas for which they would receive no royalties under existing copyright agreements?

This would happen if recordings by the band had been released and failed to sell in a foreign country. The recordings would be deleted from the company's catalogue, denying copyright royalty payments to the song writers. These 'deletions' or 'cut-outs' (piling up unsold in warehouses) could be bulk purchased in that country by an Australian importer and sold in Australia at prices below those being charged in Australia for the same locally released product, for which copyright payments are made.

Garrett was correct to argue this case, but his methodology was flawed. He did not appreciate the extent to which the public was antagonistic to the major record companies, or more precisely, to the unreasonably high prices they charged for CDs. He also failed to understand that the PSA's intervention into the record industry was not only about the repeal of 'one of the buttresses of the industry – copyright protection from parallel importing', but the reform of an entire system in which he was entrenched as a star. His comments focused the debate but failed to carry the opposition and he removed himself from public view, apparently distressed at the negative response to his normally effective media management.

Negotiations continued on the sticking point of the parallel import changes to the Copyright Act, with a resolution announced in *A Letter to Australian Musicians* from Australian Council of Trade Unions Secretary, Bill Kelty, on 25 October 1991: 'The ACTU is proposing that the Australian product be protected from importation by legislative means to ensure no possible avenue exists which could disadvantage musicians and the Australian product when sections 102 and 103 (of the Copyright Act) are repealed.' The 1968 Copyright Act was to be used to enhance opportunities for consumers by allowing for parallel importation and therefore price competition, while maintaining the interests of Australian artists in stopping the importation of cut outs. With that arrangement in place the debate diminished and the recommendations slowly rolled into Cabinet.

The ultimate outcome of the inquiry was realised on 10 June 1992, when the Australian Treasurer, John Dawkins, and the Attorney General, Michael Duffy, announced that: 'the Federal government has decided to open up the Australian market to imported records of foreign performers in two years' time.' The Government passed all but the recommendation covering a performer's copyright, which would be formulated by the music industry council and then presented for government consideration. The phased introduction of the changes was a compromise – a reform rather than an immediate breach with the established legislative order.

In the following pages I will use the PSA inquiry to explain the regulatory structure and networks in the recorded music industry in Australia. In doing so I will make explicit the structural characteristics of the recorded music industry, where a system of external regulatory organisations combine and compete with internal regulators in an extensive network of relations brought about by the 1968 Copyright Act. In undertaking this task the process of making visible the agency of regulation can be strengthened and brought into the public domain, rather than hidden amongst the exclusive trappings of the law and its keepers.

COPYRIGHT LAW AS REGULATION?

The task of explaining regulation and how regulatory frameworks operate is more necessary than ever in the deregulatory context of the late 1980s and early 1990s. It is even more important given the 'informational asymmetry' that permeates the subject through the blatant anti-regulatory stance of vested interests who have most to gain by relying on the invisible hand of the market (Train, 1991, p. 314).

In the first instance, the following model of the Australian system of copyright and regulation fulfils the call made by Tunstall about media organisations: 'Where there is specific promotion of entertainment that reflects national culture it is likely to come through understandings within media organisations that certain elements of society should be served. Such understanding are rarely made explicit' (1974, p. 189). By making regulation and regulatory frameworks explicit, the linkages between local, national and international media and communications organisations are more comprehensible. With the increasing convergence of the media, it is no longer appropriate to *not* see the recorded music industry essentially linked to radio, film and entertainment in general. It is a convergence brought about by 'fractionalisation of the media', where 'multi-media packaging' encourages global firms to exploit all media 'synergistically' (Golding, 1991, p. 3). In this convergence context, regulation is increasingly important if only for the purpose of organising an effective market.

The convergence has been brought about by:

1. Uneven technological developments such as satellite and trans-border communications, smart cards, digital compact cassette, digital audio tape, digital audio broadcasting, and cable delivery systems; some yet to be experienced in Australia, with unknown outcomes and potential to influence the public. Recognition of the need for regulations to assist these changes is increasingly the focus of public policy worldwide and in Australia (e.g. the formation of Austel to oversee changes in telecommunications, the introduction of the new act in 1992 for broadcasting).
2. Recent corporate ownership transactions (e.g. Time Inc. purchasing Warners, Sony purchasing CBS Records, Matsushita purchasing MCA). Creation and ownership of the new technology will increasingly be in the hands of the large hardware manufacturers like Sony and Matsushita, which now also have the ability to provide the (musical/entertainment) software through their ownership of record and music publishing companies and their control of music catalogues through copyright.

Ownership is power. Regulation is aimed at controlling that power, both the current and developing delivery systems and the broadcast creative material. As Armstrong has said, the convergence of technology to offer new, improved services creates difficulties where these new services 'leap the existing legislative boundaries' (Armstrong, 1991, p. 43).

Law is the means whereby the power over the hardware and the software (the intellectual property) is controlled. Law is the ultimate regulator. The notion of 'legal decision-making as an agency in the cultural field', reinforces the role of law (Saunders, 1989, p. 20). The prevailing characteristics of regulators are those organisations or agencies which exist by law and in turn derive their power from the law.

The 'dual nature of law' sees it act 'both as a means of policy expression and implementation and as a form of control on government policy making and administration' (Arup, 1990, p. 5). According to James Michael, this 'instrumentalist' or 'utilitarian' view of the law is important because the implications of the law are often not understood (1988). In the Australian context, statutory institutions or agencies such as the Prices Surveillance Authority and the Australian Broadcasting Tribunal have an established function to interpret and implement government law and policy. More important still is the function of the regulations in determining the detail of the relationships between producers, consumers and governments. Regulation for example, can be viewed as a form of legalised, executive-sanctioned intervention, where the terms are virtually synonymous and laced with the inadequacy of political science rhetoric (*ibid.*). The interchangeableness of the terms was illustrated by

Tony Sheehan, Minister for Finance in the Kirner Labor government in Victoria, in 1990.

> The facts of economic life are that the markets don't have a very good record, and that economic dogmatism of the left or right doesn't have a very good record in terms of outcomes. *You have to work out where you want regulation, where you don't want regulation, the markets you want to intervene in, those that you don't want to intervene in, where government should intervene and where it shouldn't.* (my emphasis, Dixon, 1991, p. 16)

The unpopularity of intervention and regulation of the 'free market', with the attendant 'Big Brother' scenarios, has served to muddy already murky waters. This is especially the case in the cultural domain, where commentators engage in a polemic for and against regulation, often without understanding the linkages across legal and regulatory domains that are undefined and in need of explication.

> ... in characteristically Australian fashion the three industries usually connected with [popular] culture – book publishing, music and film production – have been *distorted out of recognition by legislation or subsidies, usually in the name of cultural arrogance.* There is no real evidence that any of this government-induced *distortion* of the market playing field has helped more than hindered the relevant industry. (*Financial Review*, 21 December 1990, p. 8, my emphasis)

'Distortion' here appears to refer to a form of economic regulation, although the real point of this comment is to maintain the mythology of the effectiveness of the market place in cultural industries. The quotation also serves to show how animated emotions become when ignorance about regulation though legal and government involvement overwhelms better informed notions of regulatory systems and their function. Even the Industry Commission, which prefers the 'winding back of regulation', recognises that: 'over the years, the range of interventions has increased in Australia as regulations have been introduced to further a wide range of economic and social objectives' (*Annual Report*, 1989–90, p. 79). Nevertheless, much of the debate about regulation is troubled by the absence of 'a theory of regulatory policy' which encourages frequent attempts to play market analysis off against regulation (Blankart, 1990, p. 211).

The nature of the relationship between government, policy and property rights as a political discourse has been put succinctly by Price and Simowitz:

> When government regulates it redefines existing property rights. Property rights guarantee an individual that he or she can use an item largely independent of the will or interference of others. When government policymakers establish regulations prohibiting property holders from using their property as freely as they have in the past,

these policymakers are, in essence, reducing existing property rights. (1986)

A REGULATORY MODEL

I want to describe the structure which gives regulation its cogency within the recorded music industry in Australia in relation to the agency of law, policy and executive power. I am aware however, of Armstrong's implied warning on implementing 'essential parts' of communication policy within a model or paradigm, when it is not possible to match the policies 'to reality and the attempted enforcement of the purported rules' (1990, p. 1). The risk of creating a reductionist model is extensive in any exercise, but this potential flaw should not stop the important efforts that need to be made in analysing the media and related regulatory spheres.

Possible regulatory systems within the recorded music industry are:

- three (or four) interdependent systems of regulation;
- several co-existing, relatively contradictory regulatory systems;
- three (or four) mutually exclusive systems.

The following discussion will show that the first of these models describes the system of regulation that applies to the Australian recorded music industry. Identified as units, the regulatory groups that operate within various sectors of the Australian recorded music industry to form the interdependent systems are:

1. Internal regulators, who operate exclusively within the domain defined by the law, in this case the 1968 Copyright Act. They are internal in the sense that their primary relationship to the recorded music industry exists under the general powers bestowed in the Copyright Act, which are then applied specifically to music copyrights. (It is precisely for this reason – the application of specific laws from a general law – that this area is so complicated). The following organisations operate within the local recorded music industry as internal regulators: Australasian Mechanical Copyright Owners Society (AMCOS), Australian Record Industry Association (ARIA), Phonographic Performance Company of Australia Ltd (PPCA), Australian Performing Rights Association (APRA), Australian Music Publishers Association Ltd (AMPAL) Worldwide Register of Copyrights (WROC).
2. Legal-external regulators, who are the established agencies that set the general regulatory domain in which the internal regulators and all other agencies operate. They are, Parliament, Copyright Tribunal, Courts (especially the Federal Court).
3. Statutory-external regulators, who exist outside of the everyday relationships that apply within a specific industry, but act as regulators in an interventionary sense. They are the Prices Surveillance

Authority, Australian Broadcasting Tribunal, Trade Practices Commission, Industries Commission.

4. Internal self-regulators, who include new government initiated and funded organisations established in the late 1980s, such as Ausmusic, Victorian Rock Foundation, The Push, Western Australian Rock Music Industry Association. They are not included in the following discussion. By definition internal regulators are *not* self-regulatory, where self-regulation involves corporate, institutional and public participation in consensual decision making, or as it was defined in *The Role and Functions of the Australian Broadcasting Tribunal* (1988): 'self regulation is the product of consultation between industry, the Tribunal and the public by which the rules so developed are applied by industry itself with accountability to the Tribunal.'

INDUSTRY AND INTERNAL REGULATORS

The organised production of cultural or material goods like records, cassettes or CDs often precedes regulatory relationships until such time as public interest, policy and politics merge to create or find the appropriate agency to enact a régime. An industry comes into play when the component producers exist in relation to and together with a supervening regulator which provides coherence for those otherwise disparate and or competing producers. The supervening groups within the industry are the internal regulators. Blankart suggests, more forcefully, that the nature of regulation makes sense only when it is understood in relation to 'interest group activity' (Blankart, 1990, p. 221). In my model the interest groups are the internal regulators. Furthermore, when the regulatory régimes and systems exist as an extension of the activities of the interest groups an industry formally exists, due to its relation to the regulators of law, executive and policy. This internal 'regulatory régime' defines the activities of groups of like-minded producers with shared economic (and, in relation to the recoded music industry, cultural) goals. The economic goals are market share and profit. The cultural goals are more difficult to categorise, but include an aesthetic environment for music tied to the promotion of an entertainment and leisure lifestyle.

The recorded music industry derives its coherence from its internal regulators, whose purpose is generally defined by their power under the 1968 Copyright Act. These internal regulators exist specifically to 'police' their industry, which they define themselves, but in relation to copyright law. The internal regulators in the recorded music industry are AMCOS, ARIA, PCA, APRA, AMPAL. These 'industry groups' create the sense of an industry – an order or coherence. They work from within their industry to oversee the activities of individuals and organisations that use industry products. In this sense they are 'discretionary administrative regulators', who rely on 'regulatory law' for their power (Michael, 1988, p. 49). In cases involving copyright, Parliament, the law and the Constitution provides the ultimate power to the internal regulators.

THE MAIN GAME – INTERNAL REGULATORS AND COPYRIGHT

Internal regulators and regulatory law in the recorded music industry are most prominent in the area of copyright. 'In technical and practical terms the industry is about the creation of what is generally taken to be two copyrights. Firstly, there is the copyright of the musical work or song, which generates publishing income, and secondly, there is a copyright in the master record, which generates recording income. (ACTU submission, 1990, p. 2) These copyrights involve the issuing of licences for the reproduction of music, the broadcast and performance of that recorded music, and the collection of royalties or copyright fees by copyright collection agencies. The issuing of licences and the collection and distribution of royalties under the copyright law is the real motivating basis for the recoded music industry.

Put more starkly, according to Peter Garrett, copyrights 'provide the actual basis for all your [writer/musician] earning capacity and they also provide the basis for industry investment itself over time' (Garrett, 1991). A less generous view of copyright sees it as a privileged, yet fundamental legal and structural mechanism within cultural production, where legal agency holds sway. But its function within the territories of law and culture make it considerably more complicated to deal with than an isolated economic or industrial interpretation suggests. Franco Fabbri points to its linkages across socio-cultural domains and its role in maintaining an economic status-quo: 'copyright may (or must) be seen as the area where ideologies of art, of individual rights and collective freedom, and of intellectual work and property are re-encoded to support the existing system of production' (1991, p. 114). The role of copyright outlined here suggests that it traverses areas of creative endeavour, which are then reduced, or in Fabbri's terms, 're-encoded' to minimise challenges to the established economic order.

Australia has no universal system of copyright registration. Copyright protection is free and automatic, but the law provides for no automatic enforcement of copyrights. Creators have well-established rights under the 1968 Copyright Act, but only when they formally claim those rights. It is generally recognised that these intellectual property rights cannot be administered by the individual creators. This recognition encourages the loss of power over copyright of creators who hand over their responsibilities to agencies. The Australian copyright collection agencies, which are directly involved in setting copyright fee rates and collecting the fees within the music industry, are ARIA, AMCOS, AMPAL, PPCA, APRA. While aria may dispute its inclusion in this list, because it is not strictly a copyright collection agency, it established and controls the PPCA, which is a copyright agency. ARIA's role as the trade association for record companies sees it take on copyright enforcement roles, for example, the pursuit of music piracy cases for record companies. By so doing it becomes the key internal regulator for the Australian record industry, deriving its legitimacy from the law of copyright. The copyright agencies collect fees from radio stations, live music venues and other licensed users of recorded music. These are the internal regulators, mentioned above. Record companies and music publishing companies also collect, if they do not transfer copyright licensing and collecting functions to the specialist agencies. This is unlikely because it is considered administratively prohibitive to duplicate the activities of the agencies. Other players involved with copyright include the Copyright Agency Limited (CAL), which may be involved in discussions about copyright issues, although its primary function is to represent authors and publishers in collecting photocopying fees. At yet another level, the Australian Copyright Council does not act as a collection agency but as a further internal and voluntary regulator within the creative domain, providing free legal advice on copyright as well as acting on a consultancy basis for individuals or organisations requiring copyright advice. WROC is a new player in the copyright domain, offering a form of private registration of copyright to all creative artists. The register of copyrights WROC keeps is insured through Lloyds of London and that insurance enables artists to enforce claims to their rights.

THE COPYRIGHT REGULATION SYSTEM AT WORK

The role of the internal regulators and the nature of copyright is multifaceted. AMCOS publicity material explains that copyright in relation to musical works involves several rights of ownership and control. The rights are:

- the right to reproduce the work in a material form;
- the right to publish the work;
- the right to perform the work in public;
- the right to broadcast the work;
- the right to broadcast the work by cable;
- the right to adapt the work.

The mechanical right whereby a work may be reproduced onto a disc or audio-tape is gained by requesting permission from AMCOS. This organisation both collects and distributes 'royalties on mechanical reproductions where it would be impossible, impractical, uneconomical or uneconomic for individual members to do so. We act as a central clearing house for users, enabling the recording of music to be authorised swiftly, efficiently and economically – without the need to enter into the labyrinth of copyright clearance' (AMCOS guide, 1990).

ARIA has a slightly different role, more in line with that of an internal administrator. It acts as 'an advocate for the industry domestically and internationally'; 'as a licensor and enforcer of copyrights'; 'as a focus for industry opinion and the dissemination of industry information' (ARIA brochure, 1990). Of special significance for ARIA are its anti-piracy activities, which it believes go to the foundations of defending the music industry structure. The notion of 'defence' can be taken as a further signifier for the internal regulatory function of ARIA. Its publicity statement says:

> ARIA's strenuous and ceaseless anti-piracy operations are directed internally but utilise the services of highly competent and experienced lawyers and investigators, who work closely and effectively with Federal and State law enforcement agencies to ensure the continued protection of sound recordings against unauthorised duplication and commercial sale. This has resulted in a great many heavily publicised 'raids' on copyright infringers ('pirates') and the seizure and destruction of large numbers of counterfeit and pirated tape cassettes. (*ibid.*)

While this claim explains the ARIA line on regulation of copyright in relation to piracy it evades more difficult copyright issues. Publishing income, for example, is payable by a record company to the owner of the copyright in the song for the right to reproduce that song on record. It is a sum set in arrangement between ARIA, AMCOS and AMPAL. It is set at a fixed percentage of the recommended retail price of the recording, which was 7.28 per cent when the agreement was last made on 4 April, 1990 (ACTU submission, 1990, p. 4). Interestingly, there are cases where a conflict of interests appears to override the collection agencies' stated role to collect royalties for their members. The agencies act for the holders of copyright, who are both the creators of music and the record and publishing companies. Those interests are often mutually exclusive and at odds with one another. So, for example, while ARIA acts for copyright holders, it must also act for the record companies. It therefore acts to minimise the statutory fee paid to copyright holders, in order to maximise record company profits. The figure for 'statutory royalty' paid to copyright holders is really not very high. Arguments to increase it and thereby benefit musicians and composers are given little or no credibility within record companies because they threaten record company profits and surplus operating revenue. For example, the mechanical copyright fee stayed at 5 per cent from 1912 to 1979. The *Report of the Inquiry by the Copyright Tribunal into the Royalty Payable in Respect of Records Generally* described this rate as 'not equitable' (1980 p. xiv).

APRA is involved in collecting (copyright) licence fees paid by venues, television and radio stations for the right to publicly perform musical works. The collected money is allocated between songwriter and publisher members of APRA (ACTU submission, p. 4). At the same time, income can be paid by broadcasters directly to the record companies who control the copyright in the master recordings for the right to broadcast those records. So the record companies can circumvent the role of APRA as an internal regulator and act as regulators on the radio stations if they so wish. This is unlikely, given the role of APRA.

A further internal regulatory function derives from the relationship between the record companies and radio and television stations, whereby the provision of recordings and videos for promotional purposes is linked to copyright law and the requirement to pay royalty fees for broadcast. In 1969 the PPCA was established by the Australian-based record companies 'to act as their agent for the purposes of issuing licences to cover the broadcasting and public performance of sound recordings protected by the Australian Copyright Act 1968' (PPCA brochure, 1990). The PPCA's licence fees from radio and television stations and public places (such as supermarkets) generates an income relative to the potential size of the audience. The fees are distributed to the Musicians' Union and Actors' Equity to fund activities and to record company members who disburse them to artists and other licensors. The PPCA has been and still is a controversial organisation, largely because of its close association with ARIA and its very private nature. Indeed, its somewhat opportunistic foundation after the introduction of the Copyright Act 1968, and the PPCA's efforts to enfore its claim to mechanical royalties from commercial radio led to the refusal by the broadcasters to put songs from 'a small number of very large companies mostly representing giant overseas interests ' on air during 1970 (*B&T*, 7 May 1990, p. 1). One outcome of the lengthy dispute was a move by Macquarie Broadcasting Services and the Major Network to form a record company that would not have to pay fees for broadcast and which would 'be set up in the interests of local talent' (*B&T*, 19 March 1970, p. 7, 6 August 1970, p. 1). The issue was resolved, but points to the history of disputes that plague copyright. The PPCA and APRA licensing arrangements help consolidate the system of copyright regulation of music into every avenue of reproduction and broadcast. The PPCA notes in its publicity material that:

> In granting sound recording copyright, Parliament recognised the skill and investment which goes into performing and recording music on the high quality recordings available today. Therefore, where a public performance of a sound recording protected by The Act takes place it is necessary for the person or company who

> authorised the playing of the sound recording to hold a licence from both PPCA and APRA. (PPCA brochure, 1990)

While this is commendable, it is important to note that the internal regulators use the 1968 Copyright Act to generate income only within the confines of established record and publishing company relations. Critics of the agencies note that they are not keen to act for performers. 'Performers have no copyright in their performances and thus have no entitlements or rights in relation to subsequent uses or broadcasts of their performances' (ACTU submission, p. 7). Mr J. Martin Emerson, the president of the American Federation of Musicians said: 'the myth that musicians, singers and other performing artists benefit when their work is used by others for profit is only that – a myth (cited in ACTU submission, p. 7). That American view of the lowly status with which performers are held is also reflected in the behaviour of English radio stations. Always keen to maximise their audiences, in recent years they have made effective use of 'golden oldies' formats, while minimising their royalty payments. The 'oldies' radio format (known in Australia as 'classic hits radio') draws its strength from the past successes of pop and rock music hits being offered up as steady fare for contemporary radio audiences. By drawing their selections from compilation albums imported from the Continent, rather than from the original albums or re-releases from the UK, 'oldies' radio stations in the UK avoid paying the Phonographic Performance Limited radio performance fees (the UK equivalent of the PPCA). Instead, they pay their performance fees to IFPI – the international equivalent of PPL and PPCA – whose royalty rates are lower (Barnard, 1991, p. 9).

The collection of fees by the internal regulators for record labels and music publishers is a major feature of the recorded music industry and an activity that excites most industry workers. Evidence of the importance of copyright across the music industry appeared in the summary of a submission made by Austrade and the Australian Trade Commission to the (former) Industries Assistance Commission and summarised in the *International Trade in Services Report* (IAC, 1989). The statement also indicated the way in which copyright arbitrarily spills over into other areas of cultural production as well as the difficulties associated with media convergence. With particular reference to popular music, the report noted:

> the failure to maintain a strong regime of copyright laws; particularly as a result of not changing the laws to keep up with technological advances which affect the reproduction and dissemination of copyright; sound recordings; the practice of hiring recordings (generally compact discs) to consumers who then make permanent copy without any recompense to the copyright owners; the maximum royalty that can be received by copyright owners from commercial

> and public broadcasters; the lack of protection to the copyright owners for sound recordings which are transmitted by diffusion systems (wires or optical cables rather than electromagnetic radiation); the rapid growth in piracy of sound recordings and the inadequate extent of enforcement of copyright laws; and the subjecting of sound recordings to sales tax of 20 per cent, whilst analagous products, such as books, are sales tax free. (*ibid*, p. 333)

The regulatory régime that forms the glue for this statement is the law of copyright. The highly interpretive area of international, federal and state copyright law, makes it necessary to note the importance of the internal regulatory system which increasingly sees 'private interests asserting their rights under state copyright laws' (Grabowsky and Braithwaite, 1987, p. 178). The result of this tendency is that 'private law', such as contract, is an increasingly important part of copyright and regulation (Michael, 1988, p. 3).

It is also necessary to note that Austrade, by making its submission to the Industries Assistance Commission, (now the Industries Commission – IC) was appealing to a statutory regulator that was not a recognised part of the internal regulatory copyright network, although the IAC conducted an investigation of the music industry and published its report *The Music Recording Industry in Australia* in 1978. Those IAC recommendations against regulation of the industry, in particular against the Australian Broadcasting Tribunal's Australian music content quota, brought the IAC into the regulatory territory in much the same way as Austrade, the PSA, or the TPC, as statutory regulators can move into a regulatory relationship with the music industry or almost any other industry at any time (Breen, 1990). Austrade, for its part, as a statutory authority/government department, can be seen as intervening as a statutory-external regulator in an effort to enhance the introduction of regulatory codes of behaviour within the copyright network system. By appealing to the IAC (for recommendations and action), Austrade itself would be legitimising the regulatory statutory-external nature of the IAC against the internal regulatory régime. The dialogue between the internal regulators and the statutory-external regulators will not always be welcomed, especially by the internal regulators. We shall see that the PSA inquiry was a good example of this dialogue between the internal regulators (of copyright) and a statutory regulator.

The internal regulators of copyright were challenged long before the PSA inquiry. The 1968 Copyright Act called for 'an inquiry in relation to the royalty or minimum royalty payable in respect of records' (62). The Act also established the Copyright Tribunal. The Tribunal is a special regulator within the internal schema, intervening, not as a matter of course, but when disputes over royalty payments and copyright matters need settling. Its task is to respond to applications from the owners of copyright for recordings and the maker of the record or the broadcaster and determine 'the amount that it considers to be equitable remuneration to the owner of the copyright for the making of the recording' (*ibid.*). This makes the Tribunal a regulator in the more conventional sense of the word, intervening in disputes from outside the everyday workings of copyright relations. Because the Tribunal has the sole function of addressing the legal refinements of copyright, it can be seen as a highly specific, legal-external regulator, yet operating strictly within the internal system. The Copyright Law Review Committee also operates within the system to refine the law. The debates that have taken place during committee sessions would, at times, suggest that it is seen as more of an external regulator than part of the copyright network, as copyright collection agencies argue against any liberalising of copyright law. These participants in the copyright system add to the difficulty of comprehending and analysing how copyright works on a national and music industry level.

GLOBAL PROBLEMS WITH COPYRIGHT AND MUSIC

Serious deficiencies in copyright law exist around the world. As technology changes and converges, the role of international copyright regulations and regulators grows less clear. For their part, the role of internal regulators or collection agencies like AMCOS, ARIA, AMPAL, APRA and PPCA are changing. Historically, at an international level, music publishing agencies collected the rights that accrued from the reproduction of sheet music. This was followed by the formation of the agencies to collect performing rights fees and grant these rights in a lump sum. Current concerns over intellectual property rights are a major issue, with satellite and cable communication making obsolete the conventional record player and radio means of consumption of popular music. Computer software is considerably more prominent in this respect, while photocopying has created major problems for music publishers. The German Federal Republic (prior to reunification) enacted a regulation that prohibits photocopying of sheet music (Juranek, 1989). Discussing the difficulties in enforcing copyright in such specific areas, Juranek provides a useful comment on the function of regulators, where law is once again the agency whereby a regulatory structure comes into play.

> Legal prohibition alone serves no purpose. If a law cannot be enforced that law is worthless. In certain fields of music, publishers must licence photocopying. *Only collective administration of reprographic reproduction rights, as in the case of the performing and transmission rights, is appropriate here.* (*ibid.*, my emphasis)

The Berne Convention and the Universal Copyright Convention both attempt to define some of the problems associated with copyright and the collection of fees, but are incapable of keeping up with the international, technological and economic variables (Porter, 1991). Existing collection agencies will no longer be able to enforce their rights and new organisations will have to be formed (Besen and Kirby, 1989, p. v).

International hit records give copyright and internal regulators greater relevance than they would have otherwise, because each country makes agreements for the collection and distribution of royalties to the country of origin. The large amounts of money that are returned to corporations and individuals who own copyright are a huge incentive to manage financial activities appropriately. Although the recorded music industry is a high turnover and high profit industry (in 1990, worldwide sales were estimated to be worth US $24 billion, *MBI* November 1991, p. 10), copyright conditions that pertain to it are based on international agreements, that are then interpreted at a national level on the basis of each country's law. *The International Convention for the Protection of Performers, Producers of Phonograms and Broadcasting Organisations* (known as the Rome Convention) sets out minimum rights for performers. But examination of Appendix 6 of the Copyright Law Review Committee's 1987 *Report on Performers' Protection* shows that countries interpret their responsibilities very broadly, while some simply disregard their obligations under the convention. Analysis of any regulation, such as the Rome Convention, the Berne Convention and GATT make the entire system more difficult to comprehend and interpret for such reasons.

In general, the special difficulties involving copyright and the recorded music industry involve logistical factors such as: large volumes of money created quickly, producing accounting and revenue assessing vagaries; and international hits in territories which have eccentric laws regarding copyright, collection and licencing agencies. In the case of Eastern Europe, no signatures to trade/copyright treaties have meant that few records at all are sent from the west, because no royalty payments are made that can be collected. The non-recognition of eastern currency is also important.

In this context it is relevant to consider calls for increased worldwide regulation at a general level, not just in the area of copyright and related GATT debates. The claim from McQuail and Suine that '... the degree to which pressures have grown for a coherent policy for media, certainly at national and possibly also at international level', reflects the level of anxiety governments and public institutions have when confronted with corporate media giants and the immensity of their potential profits and the use to which they put those profits around the globe (1986, p. 5). The ability of internally regulated corporations and interest groups to act outside the control of legal or statutory (interventionist) regulators is a cause for concern. This is nothing new, and was considered at an international level in May 1986, at the World Intellectual Property Organisation's International Forum on the Collective Administration of Copyrights and Neighbouring Rights. One of the questions discussed went to the core of the model I am using: 'What supervision, if any, should governments exercise over associations or other entities, particularly if they are in a near-monopolistic position and if they represent also persons from whom they have not received the power of representation?' (Besen and Kirby, *1987,* p. 1)

Linking copyright functions automatically to government or some other legal or statutory regulatory body has universal appeal. The call for 'supervision' is relevant in the recorded music industry where a recent trend has seen large record companies expanding into and controlling music publishing in an increasingly monopolistic manner.

THE PSA – OUTSIDE LOOKING IN

Regulation must have authority to exist. The concept of the public interest in liberal democracies makes specific demands of governments. Regulation to reduce or stop unfair practices in the public interest is a virtual necessity. In some cases, the almost automatic calls for intervention from various sectors of the community 'regard government regulation as the last line of defence against unscrupulous or otherwise predatory corporate conduct' (Grabowsky and Braithwaite, 1987, p. 1). This is an aspect of the ideological background to the role of external regulators, both legal and statutory, in relation to the recorded music industry in Australia. (Contrast this with the US 'threat' to introduce trade sanctions against Australia when the PSA announced a review of the computer software copyright laws in 1992, and the liberalisation of the monopoly control over importing. The threat was sanctioned by the US Omnibus Trade Act (section 301), after pressure was put on the US government by the International Property Alliance, representing vested software interests, who began lobbying when the music industry inquiry was under way.) (Dobbie, 1992, p. 30, *VMB*, 1992, p. 1)

In terms of my model, the internal regulators fulfil a role, ordering, moderating and giving coherence to the industry from within – via membership – as well as reinforcing that industry by policing the activities of people and organisations outside the membership, primarily through licensing arrangements. ARIA's claim to 'work closely with state and federal law enforcement agencies to ensure continued protection of sound recordings' (cited above) indicates something of the relationship between internal and external, legal and statutory regulators.

But the lack of public accountability of the big six has led to serious breakdowns in competitive market behaviour and a commensurate lack of concern for the public interest. (The 'big six' and their parent companies are: Thorn-EMI (EMI), the Sony Corporation (Sony Music), Time-Warner Inc. (Warners/East-West), Bertelsmann Music Group (BMG), N. V. Philips (Polygram) and the only Australian established company, owned by News Corporation, Festival Records.) Strident claims about the record industry have been made in the debate over the PSA recommendations. For example, PSA chairman Professor Allan Fels described the record industry as a 'monopoly industry' on ABC radio, on 6 August 1990. Vertical intergration of the companies is a feature of this debate over their monopoly activities (Breen, 1992).

But the concern about the record industry is not restricted to its activities in Australia. Criticism of the major record companies made headlines in the US in 1990 when Fredric Dannen released *Hit Men*, his study of the rock music industry there (Dannen, 1990). The book detailed many of the activities of the record companies, in particular the use of independent publicists or pluggers who used dubious practices to achieve radio air play of new record releases. In reviewing the book in the *Financial Times*, Antony Thorncroft's conclusion was 'that music is too important to be left to the multi-national record companies' (28 September 1990, p. 16). Yet Thorncroft is caught like many critics, using the aesthetic criteria of music to analyse aspects of industry activity. This is a problem for cultural industries, where aspects of production and the industry appear to have very little to do with the actual pleasure that consumers derive from the product. The concern about the 'multinational record companies' and their inability to act in the best interests of Australian music was one of the reasons for the PSA inquiry.

INTERVENTION AT THE HEART

Returning to the starting point of the PSA inquiry, an examination of the inquiry guidelines shows that although, ostensibly, prices were being investigated, the industry as a whole was under scrutiny. The PSA inquiry was a distinct intervention into the otherwise unchallenged activities of the internal regulatory structures and networks of the recorded music industry. Its recommendations struck at the heart of the internal regulatory network. As a Commonwealth Statutory Authority, the PSA has a 'mandate' to act for the government of the day in the interests of both producers and consumers, to 'promote responsible behaviour by firms in both the private and public sectors' (*Price Probe*, Sept., 1989). This is what it attempted to do in its inquiry into the price of records, and in the context of Australia in the 1990s, the PSA's function as an institution is clear. This is despite public statements by the PSA, which attempt to underplay the interventionist and (external) regulatory role of the authority. For example: 'The statutory functions of the Authority are to conduct public inquiries and examine notices of proposed price increases from declared companies' (*ibid.*).

More recently, the PSA has tended towards a merger with the TPC, moving from its interest in direct price fixing, to take on a 'competition watchdog role' (Burton, 1991, p. 30). Professor Fels's comments about the monopoly activities of the major record companies represent an attempt not merely to control prices but to regulate corporate activities in Australia through the Trade Practices Act. At the policy level, the PSA has a specific brief. Chairman Fels, writing in *Price Probe*, the PSA newsletter, made the regulatory and policy function of the PSA clear: 'The PSA has an important role in the Accord's prices and incomes policy and in the process of microeconomic reform. It is constantly seeking to see that efficient and competitive outcomes strike a balance between producer and consumer interests.' (March 1990; the Accord was an agreement between the Federal Labor Government, ACTU and employer bodies.)

While the statement addresses the maintenance of 'a balance' in economic relations, which is a function of the PSA as an institution, that function exists through the PSA's role as a statutory regulator, a role it combines with an interventionary one to control prices in the interests of government policy. The PSA 'exercises its powers' under Section 17(3) of the Prices Surveillance Authority 1983. It acts under the direction of Federal Government Ministers (Treasurer and Consumer Affairs) and Parliament. The Trade Practices Commision and the Industries Commission conduct inquiries at various times for similar reasons. (In 1991 the TPC acted in a slightly different regulatory capacity to oversee the relationship between disputing parties in the case of video televison pay-for-play. In this case, the Polygram group of companies withdrew ABC-TV's licence to use Polygram, Phonogram or Polydor video products until the ABC had agreed to pay a negotiated fee. This followed an earlier dispute which began in 1987 and which was the subject of lengthy TPC hearings, and indicates that the TPC has a dispute-settling role which can be seen as an extension of its regulatory function.) (Stockbridge, 1989)

The linkages between regulators are important, and they became clearer when the PSA released its report *Inquiry Into the Prices of Sound Recordings*. As a statutory regulator, the PSA's recommendations were directed, in part, to the legal-external regulators, namely Parliament and the copyright laws. The first recommendation suggested that 'structural reform is the logical and preferred policy solution to the problem of high prices' and could be undertaken by changing the Copyright Act 'in relation to parallel imports from countries providing parallel levels of protection over the reproduction of musical works and sound recordings' (*IPSR* 1990, p. 160).

The linkages travel a considerable distance, connecting the local record companies with their internal regulators overseeing the copyright process (through international copyright provisions and overseas regulators) to the statutory-external regulator, namely the PSA, which makes legislative recommendations, to the legal-external regulators, namely the Government in Parliament, which receives the recommendations from the appropriate Minister, Cabinet and the Government of the day. The original PSA recommendation was part of a move to change the law to allow parallel importing; the ACTU/Kelty proposal introduced a further regulatory clause into the act to stop parallel importing of Australian performers, thereby giving the recommendations both a deregulatory and a re-regulatory function.

Other PSA recommendations shed further light on the far-sighted nature of the recommendations. The recommendation for a performer's copyright can be seen as a move that legitimises the law of copyright, but then suggests that its special powers be used to benefit those who are disadvantaged under existing copyright law. Set at about 6.25 per cent of the retail value of a recording – like the songwriter's copyright – the concept of a performer's copyright challenged the record companies profitability and the comfortable relationship the companies had with the copyright agencies by demanding that a new system of wealth distribution be introduced. It directed the attention of the internal regulators towards the large number of artists and performers who do not receive any rewards for their work because they do not own song writing or mechanical copyrights. The recommendation was aimed at the democratising and redistributive function of copyright law, which, in some ways, was turned on its head to provide power to the relatively powerless to claim economic benefits.

Two other PSA recommendations are worthy of mention here because they reflect the PSA's interest in creating a continuing, publicly beneficial regulatory structure for the Australian recorded music industry. Firstly, the Performers' Levy would be used 'to provide services to musicians (legal, financial, information and childcare) and performance programs' (*ibid.*, p. 171). In recommending the levy, the PSA said 'there would seem to be a strong case for more direct government involvement in the development of Australian artists' (*ibid.*, p. 171). This is a recommendation for a new methodology within the Australian recorded music industry, where government involvement is considered to be necessary for the good health of the industry. The recommendation for an Industry Council can be seen in similar terms. Its functions would include: the 'promotion of consultation and co-operation between industry parties; assistance in the development and the implementation of solutions to industry problems and the provision of advice to Government of appropriate policies to further develop the Australian music industry' (*ibid.*, p. 172). In the context of the intervention into the industry that the PSA inquiry represented, the Music Industry Council recommendation is recognition of the need for on-going, permanent regulation, in line with policy developments for the industry.

CONCLUSION

I have not described the entire model of the Australian recorded music industry, nor examined the PSA's inquiry into the price of recorded music in detail. I have described some of the systems and networks within the industry, using a model which other researchers could use to investigate particular systems and networks of control and regulation within other industries.

The relevance of copyright in intellectual property claims is of increasing importance, through the convergence of media ownership, technology and delivery systems. Intensive consumer demands for musical/entertainment software places incentives before corporations, enticing them to act as internal regulators for themselves, without considering the legal, social or cultural implications of their behaviour. The increasing likelihood that industries will use their own internal regulatory systems on a global scale, with less concern for the public interest at a local, national or international level is a major issue (Edelman, 1976, p. 23). The historical trend of businesses such as record companies to organise themselves to pursue their own interests cannot continue when the public's interests are denied. It is imperative that their activities be made visible in the interests of a more equitable distribution of wealth, rather than hiding behind the invisible hand of the market. Both legal and statutory external regulators must use the agency of the law and whatever other avenues are available to challenge the invisibility trend and support public and policy concerns. Opening up to public scrutiny the often self-contained internal regulatory systems of the music industry's copyright régimes, is a challenge that will not fade.

NOTES

1. The original research for this paper was undertaken with the Media Industries Research Group, funded jointly by Royal Melbourne Institute of Technology's Department of Social Science and Communication and the Centre for Internationl Research on Communication and Information Technologies (CIRCIT). This paper is based on *Copyright, Regulation and Power in the Australian Recorded Music Industry: A Model*, Institute for Culturl Policy Studies, occasional paper no. 13, Griffith University, Brisbane, 1992. Thanks to Richard Collins, Stuart Cunningham.
2. A declared company, if so nominated by the Prices Surveillance Authority under the Act, must inform the PSA of proposed price increases or new product prices. The Minister must approve all declarations and revocations.

REFERENCES

Armstrong, M. (1990), *Access to Decision-Making about Communications: Form and Substance in the Australian Experience,* Centre for International Research on Communication and Information Technologies (CIRCIT), December.

—— (1991), *Implementing Communications Policy: Who Makes the Decisions, and How.* CIRCIT, Melbourne, May.

Arup, C. J. (1990), 'Fitting Law to Innovation Policy', *Prometheus*, vol. 8, no. 1.

Australian Record Industry Association (ARIA) brochure, 1990

Barker, M., (1992), 'Review of *Contested Culture: The Image, the Voice and the Law', Media, Culture and Society*, pp. 492–4.

Barnard, S. (1991), 'Yesterday Once More', *Institute of Popular Music Newsletter*, no. 2, January, Liverpool.

Besen, S. M., and Kirby, S. N. (1989) *Compensating Creators of Intellectual Property: Collectives That Collect*, Santa Monica: Rand, May.

Blankart, C. B. (1990) 'Strategies of Regulatory Reform. An Economic Analysis with Some Remarks on Germany,' in *Deregulation or Re-regulation? Regulatory Reform in Europe and the United States*, ed. Giandomenica Majone, London: Printer Press, NY: St. Martins Press, pp. 211–22.

Breen, M. (1990), 'What Defence for *Australian Music on Radio*: Pop Music Quotas and National Identity', *Australian Studies*, no. 14, October, pp. 27–37.

—— (1992), 'Global Entertainment Corporations and a Nation's Music: The Inquiry Into the Prices of Sound Recordings', *Media Information Australia*, no. 64, May, pp. 31–41.

—— (1993), 'Interventions and Regulations in Australian Popular Music', in Bennett, T., Frith, S., Grossberg, L., Shepherd, J., Turner, G., *Rock and Popular Music: Politics, Policies and Institutions*, London: Routledge.

Broadcast and Television (*B&T*), (1970) 19 March, p. 7; 7 May, p. 1.

—— (1979), 6 August, p. 1.

Burton, T. (1991), 'Canberra Insider', *Sydney Morning Herald*, 24 August, p. 30.

The Copyright Act, Canberra: AGPS (1968).

Corones, S. (1992), 'Parallel Importing Computer Software: Consumer Welfare Considerations', *Australian Intellectual Property Journal*, vol. 3, no. 3, August, pp. 188–98.

Dannen, F. (1990), *Hit Men: Power Brokers and Fast Money inside the Music Business*, New York: Random House.

Dixon, R. (1991), *The Age*, 19 January, p. 16.

Dobbie, M. (1992), 'Copyright Move Angers US Lobbies', *Business Review Weekly*, 14 August, pp. 30–1.

Edelman, M. (1976), *The Symbolic Uses of Politics*, Urbana: University of Illinois Press.

Fabbri, F. (1991), 'Copyright: Dark Side of the Music Business' *Worldbeat*, no. 1, pp. 109–14.

Fels, A. (1991), 'Little pain and huge gains from lower record prices', *Sydney Morning Herald*, 12 August, p. 13.

Financial Review (1990), Editorial, 21 December, p. 8.

—— (1991), 7 August, p. 5.

Garrett, P. (1991), *PM* ABC Radio, 5 August.

Golding, B. (1991), 'FCB looks at multi media', *Broadcst and Television*, 20 September, p. 3.

Grabowsky, P., and Braithwaite, J. (1987), *Of Manners Gentle: Enforcement Strategies of Australian Business Regulatory Agencies*, Melbourne.

Industry Commission, *Annual Report* (1989–90), Canberra: Australian Government Publishing Service (AGPS).

Inquiry into Book Prices Final Report (1989), Melbourne: PSA.

Inquiry into the Prices of Sound Recordings (1990), Melbourne: PSA.

International Trade in Services Report (1989), Industries Assistance Commission, Canberra: AGPS, 30 June.

Juranek, J. (1989), 'Music Publishing at the Crossroads: Economic and Legal Problems of Music Publishing', in *Rights: Copyright and Related Rights in the Service of Creativity*, Spring.

Kingston, M. (1991), 'Popstars Misled in Import Row, says Fels', *The Age*, 13 August, p. 5.

Lahore, J. C., Griffith, P. B. C. (1974), *Copyright and the Arts in Australia*, Melbourne: Melbourne University Press.

McQuail, D., Suine, K. (1986), *New Media Politics: Comparative Perspectives in Western Europe*, London.

Michael, J. (1988), *The Regulation of Broadcasting by European Institutions: Conventions of Chaos?*, Programme on Information and Communication Technologies (PICT), policy paper no. 5.

—— (1990), 'Regulating Communications Media: From the Discretion of Sound Chaps to the Arguments of Lawyers', in *Public Communication: The New Imperatives. Future Directions in Media Research*, ed. Marjorie Ferguson, London: Sage, pp. 40–60.

Music Business International (*MBI*) (1991), November, p. 10.

Phonographic Performance Company of Australia, brochure, 1990.

Porter, V. (1991), *Beyond the Berne Convention: Copyright, Broadcasting and the Single European Market*, London: John Libbey.

Price, B., Simowitz, R. (1986), 'In Defence of Government Regulation', *Journal of Economic Issues*, vol. xx, no. 1, March.

Price Probe (1989), no. 1, September quarter.

—— (1990), no. 3, March quarter.

Prices Surveillance Authority news release (1990), *PSA Finds Records Prices Excessive: Recommends Structural Reforms/Removal of Import Restrictions*, 18 December, PR54/90. p. 6.

Report of the Inquiry by the Copyright Tribunal into the Royalty Payable in Respect of Records Generally (1980), Canberra: Australian Government Publishing Service.

Ricketson, S. (1991), *New Wine Into Old Bottles: Technological Change and Intellectual Property Rights*, Working Paper no. 5, Melbourne: Centre for International Research into Communication and Information Technology.

—— (1992), 'The Future of Australian Intellectual Property Law: Reform and Administration', *Australian Intellectual Property Journal*, vol. 3, no. 1, February, pp. 3–30.

Ryan, M. (1991), 'Copyright and Competition Policy – Conflict or Peaceful Coexistence?', *Intellectual Property Journal*, vol. 2, no. 4, November, pp. 207–20.

Saunders, D. (1989), *Legal Decisions and Cultural Theory*, Institute for Cultural Policy Studies, occasional paper, no. 6, Brisbane: Griffith University.

Stockbridge, S. (1989), 'The Pay-for Play Debate: Australian Television versus the Record Companies and the Myth of "Public Benefit"', in *Rock Music: Politics and Policy*, ed. Tony Bennett, Institute for Cultural Policy Studies, Brisbane: Griffith University.

Submission by the ACTU, Musicians Union of Australia and Actors Equity (1990), PSA Inquiry, Melbourne: Dwyer and Company, November.

Thorncroft, A. (1990), *Financial Times*, 28 September, p. 16.
Train, K. E. (1991), *Optimal Regulation: The Economic Theory of Natural Monopoly*, Cambridge, Mass.: MIT.
Tunstall, J. (1974), *Media Sociology*, London: Constable.
Video and Music Business (VMB), 27 March 1992, p. 1.

7

Copyright and Music in Japan: A Forced Grafting and its Consequences

TÔRU MITSUI

'Well, I tell you that Japan is a good place for me ... in the last statement quarter, the biggest cheque in there came from Japan,' said Jimmie Davis, former Governor of Louisiana and the alleged co-author of 'You Are My Sunshine'. He was referring to the Japanese royalties received for this song when I interviewed him in Baton Rouge in the summer of 1983 (Mitsui, 1988, p. 144). Japan can be such a beneficial country for overseas song writers, especially those from America and Europe.

The total royalty collections for the fiscal year 1988 (April 1988 to March 1989) calculated by the Japanese Society for the Rights of Authors, Composers and Publishers (JASRAC) amounted to over ¥ 43,100 million (approximately £188 million). The ratio of distribution for domestic and foreign copyright holders was roughly the same as in the preceding years – 70.7 per cent to 29.3 per cent with 122,903 items of music to 128,102 (JASRAC, 1989A, pp. 139–40). At the same time, royalty income from abroad – royalty collections made for JASRAC by foreign music copyright associations – was ¥195 million in 1988, accounting for merely 0.45 per cent of the total income for the year (JASRAC, 1989B, p. 14). The enormous imbalance reflected in these statistics, along with the numerous concerts in Tokyo by renowned artists from abroad, provides interesting material for discussing the Japanese music scene.

Karaoke, which has rapidly invaded other countries since the mid-1980s, also poses an interesting issue, which although typically Japanese, will possibly have international relevance. After winning the right to collect royalties from *karaoke* bars at the Japanese Supreme Court in March 1988, JASRAC's income significantly increased. This income included the royalty collection on 'videograms'. In the fiscal year of 1989, a quarter of JASRAC's collection of mechanical rights was accounted for by videograms, and over 80 per cent of JASRAC's videogram licenses were for *karaoke* video discs (Matsuoka, 1990, p. 3). Rental record shops, which are also probably unique to Japan, had seriously annoyed record companies when they appeared in 1980, but a copyright agreement with record shops was later concluded in 1985.

The technological advancement of household recording machines, is seriously affecting the record companies. This problem is universal among industrialised countries, but Japan seems to be particularly responsible, with its massive output of recording equipment. According to figures in the mid-1980s, some 40 per cent of the world's demand for audio recording machines and blank tapes was supplied by the Japanese industry, and 63 per cent of the machines produced in Japan were for export (Akutagawa, 1985, p. 266). It is no wonder that audio and visual home-taping was the central theme of the 34th general conference of the *Confédération Internationale des Sociétés d'Auteurs et Compositeurs* (CISAC) in Tokyo. For the first time, this conference was held in Asia in 1985, under the co-sponsorship of CISAC and JASRAC. At this time 95 per cent of the world's output of video tape recorders (VTRS) was Japanese, and 80 per cent of the Japanese-made machines were for export (Akutagawa, 1985, p. 266). More recently, in 1987, DAT, which boasts a recording sound considerably better than analogue tape, was placed on the market. DAT is equipped with a device which automatically limits the tape to one recording only when used to make a whole copy of a CD. But in July 1991, almost immediately after Sony began putting DAT on sale in the US, Sony was charged by four American music copyright agencies and one composer for infringement of copyright (*Yomiuri*, 12 July 1991).

These are some of the relatively prominent topics relating to music and copyright in Japan – the most industrially advanced country in Asia – a country with a fully developed copyright law. Nevertheless, such issues look less essential when one learns that Japanese people do not always respect the copyright laws, which were originally transplanted from the West with political concerns in mind, to a soil where social and moral conditions were basically different from Western countries. People still feel a certain awkwardness at the idea of making a business out of demanding payment, or having payment demanded according to one's legal rights, even when they fully understand its validity. Thus a historical investigation of the copyright laws in Japan, with a focus on music copyright, yields some insights into broader cultural problems. At the same time it enables one to presuppose how strenuous it would be for other Asian countries to institute copyright laws that would conform to predominant Western standards. Meanwhile, the lessons of the Japanese case might help them to establish legislation more effectively. At any rate, these countries are pressed by the US and other advanced countries to bring their copyright laws into line with international standards, especially in the field of music where 'piracy' is often strikingly conspicuous.[1]

The first substantial copyright law in Japan was established in 1899, a little less than a hundred years ago, and incorporated the then existing Publishing Act, Copyright Act and Scenario and Musical Composition Act. It was not brought about, however, by internal pressure from authors, composers or artists. In that year Japan signed the Berne Convention, and the act of entering into this international copyright treaty automatically involved Japan in its own domestic copyright law. The signing of the treaty was inevitable because it was virtually a requirement for having European countries and the US abolish their consular jurisdiction in Japan. The jurisdiction had amounted to an extra-territorial injunction, which was discriminatory and dishonourable to the Japanese government.

This exclusive jurisdiction, which covered not only diplomatic officials but also all citizens or subjects residing in Japan, was first included in a series of commercial treaties of 'amity' that the Tokugawa shogunate or feudalistic government had signed some forty years before (1858) with the US, Holland, Russia, Britain and France. The imposition of the unequal treaties was epochal – Western capitalism incorporated Japan into its worldwide market, at the same time subsuming Japan into modern international politics. China presents a similar case in point, with her incorporation as a result of losing the Opium War with Britain slightly preceding that of Japan. Then the giant step the invading capitalistic system took caused other East Asian countries to be absorbed into a subordinate role as well. One might be reminded that the 1850s was also a decade when newly discovered gold mines in California and Australia contributed substantially toward the global extension of the capitalistic market.

In the case of Japan, it all began when Commodore Perry and his fleet of formidable steamships abruptly appeared off the coast of Urawa in July 1853, threatening the shogunate with cannons to open Japan to foreign intercourse. The shogunate and the Japanese people were, as often described, 'aroused from their two-hundred year sleep', which had been undisturbed in the nursery of isolationism.

The following year, in March, the shogunate avoided armed intervention by signing, on Perry's second visit, an unequal treaty of 'amity' with the US, which had been pressing for trading opportunities. This was soon followed, from 1854 to 1855, by the signing of similar treaties with Britain, Russia and Holland. Under these treaties, which made the shogunate open up several ports, free trade transactions were not allowed, but Townsend Harris, who assumed charge as the newly established

American consulate general in 1856, forcefully negotiated with the shogunate, on the basis of the treaty of 'amity', for a commercial treaty of 'amity'. The new treaty was concluded, as mentioned above, in July 1858, only to be immediately followed by similar treaties with four countries, all signed in the same year. Granting consular jurisdiction to those countries was among the most demanding items regulated in the unequal treaties; others were the determination of tariff rates on mutual agreement without any autonomy for the shogunate, and granting those countries unilateral, most-favoured-nation treatment, under which any right given by the shogunate to one of the five countries automatically applied to them all (*Heibonsha*, 1985, vol. 1, p. 697). In the following years, the shogunate and the new Meiji government allowed eleven more European countries to sign similar commercial treaties, further consolidating Japan's subordinate position in international politics and economics (*Heibonsha*, 1985, vol. 15, p. 691).

It should be noted that this opening of Japan by the shogunate precipitated the Meiji Imperial Restoration (1867), which brought forth a constitutional monarchy in Japan. To put it simply, the restoration was triggered by the politically and economically harsh oppression and confusion caused by the signing of those unequal treaties by the shogunate – those from 1853 to 1858 were, in fact, executed without Imperial sanction.

In 1882, the Meiji government, more than a dozen years after the shogunate was overthrown, finally initiated painstaking negotiations with the pertinent countries for the abolition of consular jurisdiction and other legal rights. Japan first succeeded in signing a treaty of commerce and navigation with Britain in July 1894, which was a radical revision of the former commercial treaty of amity, restoring important legal rights. In the treaty, however, the Japanese government was compelled to state clearly that it 'promises to accede, before Great Britain abolishes consular jurisdiction in Japan, to the international treaty of alliance concerning proprietary rights to industries and protection of copyright' (JASRAC, 1990, vol. 1, p. 71).[2] The conclusion of this treaty with Britain, promulgated in August of the same year and put into operation in 1899, was promptly followed by similar treaties with the US and other countries, all of which were enforced in 1899. In the slightly delayed treaty with Germany in 1896, 'the international treaty of alliance concerning proprietary rights to industries and protection of copyright' was specifically replaced with 'the international Berne Convention concerning copyright' (JASRAC, 1990, vol. 1, p. 71). It was not until 1911 that the determination of tariff rates without any autonomy being granted to Japan, and unilateral most-favoured-nation treatments were finally abolished from those international treaties (Mori, 1978, p. 271).

Several years before, in 1885, Japan had been invited to attend the first conference for an international copyright convention, which was held in Berne. The translated version of the invitation letter written by the Swiss president (JASRAC, 1990, vol. 1, pp. 18–19) indicates that it was a circular or a letter identical to those sent to other countries. At any rate, the Japanese government seems to have been pleased to associate itself with European, 'civilised' countries. The participants were drawn from twelve countries – Japanese and American delegates attended in the capacity of observers. Kurokawa Seiichirô,[3] a councillor of the Japanese Legation in Italy, attended the Berne conference and wrote a full report on 10 December 1886, to Earl Inoue Kaoru, the Minister for Home Affairs; he included the details of the agreed items (Kurokawa, 1886). In April 1887 an excerpt from the German legislation, which concerned regulations on copyright (proclaimed on 11 June 1870), was translated into Japanese for use in the Ministry for Home Affairs (JASRAC, 1990, vol. 1, pp. 53–63). (This was two years before the promulgation of the Meiji Constitution which was modelled upon German constitutional monarchy and tinged with Japanese imperialism.)

In the documents collected by JASRAC, there is no record of Japan's attendance at the Berne conference being related to the signing of improved treaties of commerce with European countries and the US in 1894 and 1895, but the attendance might possibly have been a precursor to Japan's unavoidable accession to the Berne Convention. More directly, attendance at the conference contributed to an amendment of the existing Publishing Act, which served both for censorship of publications and for protecting publishers: it was in late 1887 that copyright, then called *hanken*, was dealt with as a separate issue from publishing (JASRAC, 1990, vol. 1, p. 41). The first Publishing Act under the Meiji government was established in 1869, two years after the Meiji Imperial Restoration, and was amended several times. In 1875 the term *hanken* was coined to signify copyright, but it was not until 1887 that copyright became 'independent' with the establishment of a Copyright Act, of a Publishing Act and a newly established Scenario and Musical Composition Act, which protected performance rights. It is not known how efficacious the new acts were, but, as to the Publishing Act before its division. there seem to have been about a dozen lawsuits over a six-year period for violation of its stipulations (JASRAC, 1990, vol. 1, p. 1). Then, in 1893, the Copyright Act was again revised.

In 1898, the year before the treaty was put into operation, Mizuno Rentarô, an official at the Ministry for Home Affairs, who took a doctorate with a dissertation on copyright, toured around Europe, 'primarily to make an investigation on the International convention for copyright protection to which Japan is to accede next year', and gave a lecture on the

Berne Convention at a gathering of a learned society (Mizuno, 1898). After giving a historical survey of copyright and before making a detailed explanation of the Berne Convention, he said, 'now in Europe all the countries which are considered civilised acceded to the convention. With those countries Japan will associate herself next year. While it will be disadvantageous, it will be an honour for us'. It was this jurisprudent who drafted the first modern copyright law in Japan, combining in the process all the three acts mentioned above and replacing the term *hanken* with *chosakuken*, which first appeared in an official report in 1886 (Kurata, 1983, p. 9). He accounted for the law as follows:

> In the treaties with Britain, France, Germany, Italy, Belgium and Switzerland, Japan declared her accession to the international convention for copyright protection in advance of having their consular jurisdiction abolished, making the accession a bargaining point for the abolition ... Our present copyright law is, however, not only inconsistent with the regulations of the convention, but does not give legal sanction to the convention. To begin with, the range of protection provided for in our present copyright law is quite limited, granting copyright only to writings, pictures, musical scores, scenarios and photographs. The range of copyright in the Berne Convention is extensive enough to include such art works as sculptures and maquettes, which we also should protect. Moreover, our present copyright law consists of three simple separate acts with regulations which are inevitably insufficient. Thus we propose to establish the following law after the model of the laws of European countries, especially those of Germany and Belgium, which are regarded as the most comprehensive, and with due consideration of our own social customs and other laws. (Mizuno, 1899, p. 91)

The idea of copyright which had developed in advanced capitalistic countries in Europe and the law which protected it were thus forcibly grafted in 1899 onto an Asian tree which had an 'underdeveloped' or different idea of copyright. An indication of this may be seen by the fact that in the mid-1930s even lawyers were unfamiliar with copyright law in Japan: a contemporary playwright reportedly commented that 'even among lawyers there were some who did not know the existence of copyright law and few of them, if they knew, would be able to give its outline' (Hiroshima, 1937, p. 334). The formation of JASRAC was also initiated by governmental officials with political considerations. (The fact that it was not until 1970 that a sweeping revision was made to the law should not be very surprising when one notes that the US, for the first time in sixty-seven years, did the same in 1976.)

Even if the accession to the Berne Convention was 'an honour for Japan', making herself associated with European, 'civilised' countries was decidedly 'disadvantageous', as Mizuno himself admitted. The Convention was, in the first place, established for the mutual advantage of European countries that were geographically adjacent to each other, and Japan was linguistically and culturally more clearly an outsider than the US whose representatives also attended the Convention as observers in 1886. Theoretically the Convention gave the Japanese copyright protection by other member nations, but the interest of the people in those countries in Japanese culture was so limited as to mean few requests for potential copyright permissions. Cultural exchanges were, much more than today, one-way, with a dominant influx from Europe, Japanese intelligentsia being keen on Westernisation.

We can, then, understand the apprehensions of Hatoyama Kazuo (who obtained the first doctorate in law in Japan and was a former Speaker of the House of Representatives) about Japan's accession to the Convention, expressed in an article published in early 1898. In a nutshell, his point was that 'the regulations to protect copyright would not only be detrimental to the interests of persons concerned, but, in its turn, hold sway on the advancement of Japanese culture and national development' (Hatoyama, 1898). (This repetitious lament is sustained throughout.) He shows first that he is mostly concerned with the provisions 5, 7 and 9 of the Convention which, respectively, protected translation right for ten years, made it possible for publishers and writers to prohibit translating their press articles, and similarly protected the authors of scenarios and musical compositions. Then he appeals to his readers:

> Japan has devoted herself, since her opening to foreign intercourse, to infusing into her mind new Western learning and thoughts either by reprinting or translating, striving for cultural advancement and accelerating national development. In fact, the advancement and development in the past decades have been remarkable, but, when compared to Western countries, there remains such a marked disparity in learning and thoughts between Japan and those countries that further infusion on a large scale is definitely wanted. And our dependable recourse for that purpose is still either to reprinting or translating. In this regard, I can't help deploring the incaution of our authorities who failed to give very careful consideration before acceding to the Convention.

And to justify his argument concerning unrestricted reprinting and translation, Hatoyama refers to the US practice of arbitrary reprinting, although with strong reservations about her supposed ignominy:

> The USA quickly reprints new and noted books published in Britain whose people share the same language, and sells them at much lower prices than the originals. Consequently, not only few original prints are imported to the USA from Britain, but cheap reprints

> published soon after the appearance of originals invade the London market, trampling upon originals. British authors and publishers can't tolerate such abuses and denounce the American publishers for their injustice ... Such acts are not entirely permissible from a humanitarian point of view, but the measure taken by the USA at the temporary cost of justice in favour of her cultural advancement and national development should not necessarily be censured in the present international situation.

It should be noted that in 1906, the US (which did not accede to the Berne Convention) and Japan concluded a special treaty concerning copyright protection, on which Mizuno commented in an article for a law journal (Mizuno, 1906). The treaty stipulated mutual freedom of translation in the second provision: 'a subject or citizen of either country can translate and publish without permission any book, booklet, and other written document, and also scenario and musical composition which a subject or citizen of either country published in his own country.'

The Japanese sense of 'disadvantageousness' expressed in the quotations above was internationally disclosed by Mizuno two years later, in 1908, at the conference to revise the Berne Convention held in Berlin. Mizuno had stated at the end of the article mentioned above, the necessity of having an escape clause in the Convention regarding translation; he also expressed his satisfaction with Japan's signing of the treaty which guaranteed mutual freedom of translation (1906, p. 99). He had been conscientious enough at the same time to say, 'I can't help feeling a pain as a scholar to advocate this view when I see it in the light of copyright theories', but he, as the Japanese representative, made a speech to explain the necessity of freedom of translation at the conference, which, incidentally, lasted for nearly a month. According to his detailed report (Mizuno, 1909), after giving the main reason for his proposal, which was basically an affable version of what was given by Hatoyama, Mizuno tried to explain that Japanese translations would not affect the sales of originals at all; he encouraged other countries to translate Japanese works freely, and referred to the increasing number of institutions for Oriental studies in various European cities. Then finally he strove to clarify that a Japanese translation should not be taken as a duplication because the language is entirely different from European languages (it had been proposed at the conference, among other things, to regard a piece of translation as a duplicate or reproduction of an original).

'The speech was greeted with a clapping of hands' (Mizuno, 1909, p. 104), but Japan's proposal was severely criticised by most of the representatives of other countries as a fundamental contradiction of the Convention, and two days later was turned down. In response, Japan proposed to make reservations to the amended Convention by withholding her accession to the revision concerning translation rights, which was more limiting than before, 'until the state of national affairs will be ripe enough' (p. 112), and the proposition was approved in the final analysis. At the same time Japan also withheld agreement to the provision concerning '*droit de représentation et d'exécution*' of scenarios and musical compositions, which dispensed with the system of giving a written specification on a music sheet to prohibit performance. Mizuno did not mention the issue in the report for an unknown reason, but the rationale for these reservations might have been the same as the one for translation. Twenty years later, in the anonymous official Japanese report on the Rome conference to revise the Berne Convention, it was inferred that:

> [the reservations] must have been made with a purpose to facilitate the development of Western music in Japan by increasing opportunities to perform Western compositions without required permission from composers. It would have especially been vexatious and complicated to get permission when the compositions were performed for musical education or at charity concerts ... (JASRAC, 1990, vol. 1, pp. 189–200)

These two issues were not the only ones that were disadvantageous to Japan, but the government refrained from making further reservations, as is stated in the official report on the signing of the Berlin revisions, on 13 November 1908: 'Needless to say, there are other regulations in the revised Convention which are unfavourable to our Imperial Government, but we feared that too many reservations would contradict the aim of the Convention ...' (JASRAC, 1990, vol. 1, pp. 114–16).

These reservations concerned the Berlin revisions, and Japan was to observe the former pertinent regulations. But it is questionable whether the government gave sufficient instructions about them to the people concerned. It is not clearly documented, as far as I can ascertain, whether publishers tried, before and even after 1908, to get permission from a European copyright holder, or paid the necessary fees for each and every translated version of a book published less than ten years before. Neither is it known if a public performance of a relatively new musical composition in Europe, with a written specification concerning performing right, was given only after dutifully obtaining permission from overseas. To begin with, was it practically feasible in those days for a promoter to spend an indeterminable length of time in overseas correspondence to get permission for the performance of some compositions at a prearranged concert? In other words, such anxieties as expressed by Hatoyama seem to have been unfounded. Needless to say, translating European writings published more than ten years before, was free of copyright, as was performing scenarios and musical compositions which had no written copyright specification. Thus Western culture must have been digested in

Japan rather freely, facilitating 'her cultural advancement and national development'. This might remind one of the relatively unrestricted use of American and Western music in present-day Asian countries, which has evidently contributed to the enrichment and vitality of their contemporary, especially popular, music, as in some African countries. It should be noted that such use might have often been regarded as piratical simply because many countries are not signatories to an international treaty.

Also dubious was Japanese observance of the domestic Copyright Law, given people's unawareness of the law, which was a byproduct necessitated by Japan's unavoidable accession to the Berne Convention; authors and composers, that is, were not, in the first place, acquainted with the idea of copyright. The first time that copyright attracted the attention of many people was in 1912, when legal proceedings were taken against a reproduction of the wax phonograph recordings of *naniwabushi* or *rôkyoku* by Tôchûken Kumoemon, a popular performer of the narrative chant. What would now be called a counterfeit was an effect of the development of phongraph recording. This new industry in Japan was just being established at the time and the existing Copyright Law proved unable to solve the problems that arose. It was ruled first at the Tokyo District Court in 1912 that vocals could be regarded as an object of copyright, and their mechanical reproduction without permission was an infringement of the Copyright Law (JASRAC, 1990, vol. 1, p. 146). But the sentence was reversed two years later at the Supreme Court: 'Though the act is unquestionably contrary to the idea of justice ... we cannot help but tolerate it without question at present when there are no regulations to control it' (JASRAC, 1990, vol. 1, p. 170). The case seems to have been much talked about, if primarily in legal circles, as is shown by the fact that some long arguments are found in legal periodicals (JASRAC, 1990, vol. 1, pp. 127–52) along with several newspaper articles (*Taishô*, 1986, vol. 1, pp. 521–2). It should also be remarked that the accusation was not made by Kumoemon, the performer himself, but by a Mr 'Wadaman' who had purchased the copyright of Kumoemon's collected work of *naniwabushi* (Araki, 1913, p. 127) and that Mr Richard 'Wadaman' was a German (*Taishô*, 1986, vol. 1, p. 522).

As a matter of course, the inadequacy of the Copyright Law in the face of newly developed phonograph records was fully realised by the people concerned, but it was again tradesmen in the business, not performers, who demanded amendment of the law, which was finally made in 1920 in the light of German Copyright Law (Hatoyama, 1920, pp. 170–1). As stated in a phonograph monthly, the decision made at the Supreme Court:

> gave a fatal blow to the phonograph makers ... A monkey which fell off a tree is the one and only phrase that precisely describes them ... It paved the way for people to snatch, at a swoop and, what was

> worse, under legal protection, the products which were painstakingly manufactured by others with a large investment. (Yokota, 1917, p. 156)

What was ultimately at stake was neither artistic creativity nor the accompanying monetary reward for composers or performers but business finance concerning what are now called neighbouring rights. And this tendency has continued until the present day when probably the most marked copyright issue remains illegal record renting, raised by the Japanese Phonograph Record Association (this organisation was renamed the Record Industry Association of Japan on 1 January 1992).

Copyright came into much brighter limelight about a dozen years later when what can be translated as 'the Plage sensation' was caused by a German named Dr Wilhelm Plage. He tried to be relentlessly exact in the collection of expensive internationl copyright fees as an agent in Japan of Bureau International de L'Edition Music-mecanique (BIEM) and, later, as an agent of Cartel de Sociétés d'Auteurs as well. This situation was clearly due to the fact that Japan, without due consideration, had overcome her reservations about the provision in the Berne Convention concerning performing rights in scenarios and musical compositions. (The provision concerning translation, however, was not acceded to.) The accession was made in 1928, when the conference for further amendments of the Convention was held in Rome, Japan having being pressured by Italy, according to the official Japanese report of the conference (JASRAC, 1990, vol.1, pp. 189–200). Consequently the Japanese Copyright Law was amended in 1931 just before Plage opened his office in Tokyo.

The decision to accede was a matter of national dignity – it was explained a few years later by an official investigator of 'the Plage sensation':

> the more reservations a country has in an international convention, the lower in rank it is looked upon. Unfortunately, Japan had been treated, because of the reservations mentioned above, as a nation of the second rank among the signatories to the convention. In the liberalistic spirit of the day Japan had increasingly been ashamed of the disgrace until she bravely discarded the reservations on 15 July, 1931, to become a nation of the first rank. (Hiroshima, 1937, p. 331)

But Japan held on fast to her reservations about translation rights, and that resolution might have caused her to give up the less substantial misgivings about musical presentation and performance rights, as is presumed by one of the JASRAC editors (JASRAC, 1990, vol. 1, p. 349). Thus any consideration for musicians' interests might well have been secondary. It is stated in the official report of the Rome conference that abandoning the reservations 'would not interfere with an expected development of Western music in Japan if we establish an appropriate civil regulation' (p. 191). But the concession was flatly criticised a few years later, in an article for a music monthly, as 'the result of the government's lack of understanding for musical circles, and [was] unquestionably a blunder' (Ishihara, 1934, p. 6). The article also pointed out the ignorance in music circles about the Convention:

> how much concern did our musical circles have in the issue of the revision of the amended Berne Convention when the Rome conference was held in 1928? How much when our Copyright Law was revised in 1931? I am afraid I have never heard of any campaign for the benefit of musical circles carried out by men of music on those occasions. Judging from the present condition, I can't help suspecting that a majority of the people in music circles didn't know the existence of the amended Berne Convention in the first place.

Incidentally, the unintentional revelation, in this quotation, of the supposedly customary practice of unrestricted performance of Western musical compositions is reinforced with the following newspaper article:

> Suddenly, Universal, a German music publisher, demanded a copyright fee for the performance of *Die Dreigroschenoper*, by the Tokyo Radio Orchestra with Konoé Hidemaro as the conductor, which was broadcast in the evening of 14 February – the station authorities were panic-stricken ... 'The demand was made through Mr. Hattori Ryûtarô, the Japanese agent of Universal ... This was the first time that any demand of the kind was made by a foreign company.' (*Yomiuri*, 18 March 1932; JASRAC, 1990, vol. 1, p. 287)

The radio station which broadcast this 1928 composition by Kurt Weill was NHK, the sole Japanese radio station at that time, and Japanese equivalent of the BBC.

Japanese acceptance of musical performance rights in the amended Berne Convention obviously prompted the European composers' associations to try to commission the Japanese composers' association to collect copyright fees in Japan for them. The association in Japan, however, found it unfeasible to do as requested and withheld a reply. 'The association was incapable because it was a study group consisting of only composers' was the reason predicated by the late composer Akutagawa Yasushi, who was the chief director of JASRAC in the 1980s (JASRAC, 1990, vol. 2, p. 90). The association was formed, according to a brief magazine article on composers and broadcasting copyright (Komatsu, 1932, p. 241), in 1928, with copyright protection as one of its purposes, and the chairman was not a composer, but Dr Mizuno Rentarô, the authority on copyright law (the membership increased from a little over a dozen in 1928 to sixty-five in 1932). Probably in the summer of 1931 – sometime after the revision of the Japanese Copyright Law – the European associations pressed for an answer, and 'told the association [in Japan] that, if the request is not complied with, they would choose a suitable third party and ask them to act as their agent'. This was anonymously reported in another music monthly in October, 1931 (JASRAC, 1990, vol. 1, p. 219). It is not known how the 'flurried' Japanese composers' association responded to the pressure, but it was undoubtedly negative, eventually causing Plage to serve as a copyright-fee collector.

It is not very easy to illustrate, due to the changes in the value of money, how expensive the fees demanded by this rigorous collector were; he had served as the German vice-consul in Japan after World War 1 before teaching German language at three different colleges (Shimbo, 1935, p. 321). The amount can be inferred, however, from the complaint made to a newspaper reporter by someone at Japanese Polydor – Plage 'collects no less than 12.5 per cent out of the wholesale price of each record. On top of that, ... he insists that the basis for the demand is applicable retroactively to the time when our company was founded. We have no choice but to go into bankruptcy!' (*Tokyo nichinichi shimbun*, 16 August 1933; collected in JASRAC, 1990, vol. 1, p. 289). Obviously, basic norms for copyright fees were not prescribed for Plage by the Cartel de Sociétés d'Auteurs. This fact can be judged from the procuration by the Cartel dated 1 August 1932, a translated version of which is collected in *Nihon chosakuken shi* (JASRAC, 1990, vol. 1, pp. 294–5), and more clearly from a statement in the telegram, sent presumably to the Japanese composers' association by the Cartel and translated in a music monthly, *Gekkan gakufu* (vol. 23, no. 11, November 1934; JASRAC 1990, vol. 1, p. 291): 'The Cartel commissioned Plage to set standards for the fees'. And the unusual amounts Plage charged for the use of musical compositions can be partly explained by item 12 in the procuration. The item stipulates that Plage is entitled to receive as much as 50 per cent of the total income in reward for his agency, but it also states that he should pay out of his pocket 'for everything needed to execute his duties perfectly', including expenses for travelling, superintendence, inspection and office work.

In parallel with many complaints, criticisms and protests expressed in print, Plage adamantly prohibited performances and threatened to charge sponsors, promoters and NHK. One example was the aborted performance, in 1940, of a part of *Madama Butterfly* by the opera troupe led by the well-known Miura Tamaki. The provisional disposition for interdicting them from performing the opera (1904) was ultimately made, through Plage, by Antonio Puccini, the heir of the composer. According to the survey conducted by the Ministry for Home Affairs in 1935, there were seventy-two lawsuits brought by Plage in the one year of 1931, out of which six were civil and sixty-five criminal (Omori, 1986, p. 223). A partially self-contradictory writer accuses Plage of 'resorting to a harsh measure' and 'demanding unreasonable fees' (Oji, 1937, p. 308), and concludes his article by assenting to the idea of Japan's withdrawal from the Berne Convention, which 'has been, so to speak, for the mutual benefit of European countries' (p. 310). The idea had been suggested publicly time after time (e.g. in an article whose title could be translated as 'Beware lest the fire set to our culture becomes disastrous', Katô, 1933). On the other hand, the writer admits that Plage helped open Japanese eyes to the notion of copyright and quotes a passage from a newspaper article he wrote in 1935: 'if Japanese persons concerned gain enlightenment from Mr. Plage's "activity" and have a great regard for copyright, I would suggest that something like a bronze statue of him should be erected' (*Tokyo Asahi*, 18 November, p. 308). The acknowledgement had also been expressed a year before, though implicitly, in another article for a music monthly (Ishihara, 1934, p. 6).

The Plage sensation finally died down when the Japanese government played their last card; they enacted a bill to exclude any agents who dealt with foreign copyright except the one they were to authorise, and JASRAC was formed after its enactment. The bill was modelled again on the German copyright law, according to Kunishio Kôichirô, who was involved in preparing its draft: '[the German regulation] was rather uncomplicated, and I thought it proper to apply' (his personal talk was recorded in JASRAC, 1990, vol. 2, p. 76). Then, as is stated in an anonymous article in the late May 1938 issue of *Ongaku shimbun*, 'the Ministry for Home Affairs established the tentatively named Japanese Federation for Copyright Protection as a result of their repeated discussions with the Modern Composers' Association and other cultural organisations ... to negotiate directly with foreign copyright associations ... and to drive out decisively such agents as Plage' (JASRAC, 1990, vol. 1, p. 338). The act was promulgated on 4 April 1939, and took effect on 15 December (Nakamura, 1940, p. 50), while JASRAC was authorised on 28 December, and began operating on 1 March 1940 (JASRAC, 1989A, p. 142).

JASRAC was thus born out of governmental anxiety about foreign pressure, and its *raison d'être* was, in the first place, to serve as an agent of foreign copyright organisations despite its nominal domesticity, namely, the Japanese Society for Rights of Authors (lyricists), Composers and Publishers (music publishers). JASRAC, then, was not formed to protect the copyrights of Japanese 'Authors, Composers and Publishers' themselves. The degree to which they were lacking a sense of copyright is illustrated dramatically by the speech made by Masuzawa Takemi, a music critic, on the day (18 November 1939) when JASRAC was formed and he was elected as its first chief director:

> now that such an organisation as this has just been formed, we have to work in accordance with the law. That is to say, we must pay

> copyright fees for the music composed by others. That's the situation we are in. To tell the truth, it was not until several years ago that this kind of idea ever came into my mind. Performers were simply unconcerned. They were careless in performing the compositions by others, including those by foreigners. They thought it was all right once they bought a music sheet, and took it easy. On the other hand, we had a different point of view concerning domestic compositions when Japanese composers were not well advanced. Composers themselves wanted to have their compositions performed as many times as possible, if not so eager as to pay money to performers in reward for their performance. Performers tried admiringly, in turn, to choose domestic compositions to promote the development of music writing in Japan. (Masuzawa, 1939, p. 41)

This view – of the chief director of JASRAC, also a permanent director of Tokyo Music Association – must have been shared by most of the JASRAC members, who numbered sixty-seven at the time when the Association was approved by the Minister for Home Affairs, on 20 December (JASRAC 1989A, p. 142). The Western, capitalistic conception of copyright, unavoidably implanted in an alien soil, had found it hard even to take root, let alone to flourish.

Be that as it may, JASRAC was obliged to suspend business immediately after it was established. To become a substantial agent of foreign copyright organisations, JASRAC promptly tried to negotiate with them through the ambassadors of Britain, France, Germany and Italy on 12 January 1940 (JASRAC, 1990, vol. 2, p. 79). But European countries were then too busy with a very grave issue – World War II had broken out four months before, and Germany was just invading Holland. Furthermore, after Japan participated in the war, the government banned phonograph records and performance of American and British music, defining it as 'a disclosure of nationalities characterised by frivolity, materialism and paying high regard to sensuality'. This quotation is from the 27 January 1943 issue of the official weekly published by the Public Information Section of the Cabinet, which lists many 'inappropriate' songs, including 'Valencia', 'My Blue Heaven', 'Londonderry'. 'Comin' thro' the Rye', 'Yankee Doodle', 'Annie Laurie', 'My Old Kentucky Home', 'Old Black Joe', 'Home on the Range', 'Ramona', 'Alexander's Rag Time Band', 'Blue Hawaii', and 'Aloha Oe'. Also in the list were numerous release numbers without their titles from several major record companies (JASRAC, 1990, vol. 2, pp. 97–102). Thus JASRAC's task was almost entirely pointless until the post-war period!

It was in 1947 that copyright again became the subject of talk among music circles, and, again, discussion concerned only foreign copyright. The emergence of copyright as an issue was caused, 'needless to say, by the notice from the occupation forces in which they prohibited us from using without permission any copyrighted foreign musical compositions', as reported in a music gazette (*Ongaku shimbun*, 1 August 1947; JASRAC, 1990, vol. 2, p. 108). An article on the post-war chronicle of copyright treaties states more explicitly that 'under the occupational policy of the Allied Powers, the General Headquarters took charge of foreign copyright, including that of the people of the USA, signatories to the Berne Convention, Latin-American countries ..., the USSR and China' (JASRAC, 1990, vol. 2, p. 153). Surprisingly enough, however, Japanese people did not have to pay any fees. 'You reported to the CIE [sic] of the occupation forces. Then you were not charged at all for the use of copyright ... They executed for you all the business concerning foreign copyright, though they were exacting in having us go through due formalities', recollected Kasuga Yoshizô, who was the chief director of JASRAC in the mid-1960s (JASRAC, 1990, vol. 2, p. 156).

The subsequent history of copyright and music in Japan does not need detailed examination. It developed, if awkwardly, more or less abreast with the continuous industrial and economic growth of Japan as an increasingly capitalistic country. As to domestic copyright, fees for music's use in broadcasting, films, records and publications were collected without much difficulty by JASRAC because major cultural and entertainment institutions were centralised in Tokyo. On the other hand, public performances of musical compositions outside Tokyo were usually given in disregard or without knowledge of copyright: 'Once you are off from Tokyo, things are preposterous ... People gave no heed [to it]' (Fujita, 1947, p. 109). But JASRAC persevered in their efforts in that regard, acting, for example, (as reported in several newspapers in 1959 and 1960) against a tourist company in Nagoya whose copyright infringement was intolerable (JASRAC, 1990, vol. 2, pp.178–9).

Composers themselves remained, however, as ignorant or indifferent as before, at least in the decade after the war. In 1970 Fujita Masato, chairman of the Authors' Union, recalled, as a witness at a small committee of the House of Representatives which examined a copyright bill:

> Private broadcasting stations started functioning in 1951. Then we realized a couple of years later that we hadn't received any fees for the use of our compositions when the records were played and broadcast. We composers were quite uninformed. We didn't have any knowledge of the Copyright Law, though it had been established in as early as 1899, or of how our compositions had been handled. (JASRAC, 1990, vol. 2, p. 226)

Such a situation must have arisen largely because each composer belonged exclusively to a record company which guaranteed him a fixed income. This system, in which a royalty basis did not function and composers were thus unconcerned about the extraneous idea of copyright, lasted until the late 1950s. Then composers became independent receivers of royalties, though some of them complained of the resulting lack of financial stability. The first Japanese music publisher, Suisei-sha, was also formed at the time, in 1959, though initially it dealt only with foreign compositions (JASRAC, 1990, vol. 2, p. 289).

With time, and in the natural course of events, composers were made more aware of copyright, which caused JASRAC to be more demanding. And in 1962 a copyright inquiry commission was constituted in the Ministry of Education in response to petitions for revising the Copyright Law presented by the Japanese Phonograph Record Association and JASRAC. The committee's proposals finally resulted in a radical revision of the Copyright Law as a whole in 1970. Internationally, Japan had restored herself as a signatory to the Berne Convention by signing the Japanese peace treaty in 1951. In the same year, JASRAC became the Japanese agent of ASCAP, which finally consented to serve as the agent of JASRAC in 1963 (the year when Sakamoto Kyû's 'Sukiyaki' made the charts in the US). Meanwhile, in 1956, in addition to the Berne Convention, Japan signed the Universal Copyright Convention. In the years after the entire revision of domestic law, Japan acceded to the Phonograms Convention in 1978 and the Rome Convention in 1989.

In Demitri Coryton's *Hits of the '60s: The Million Sellers*, which commendably mentions quite a few Japanese 'million sellers', 'Ozashiki Kouta' by the Mahina Stars and Matsuo Kazuko and 'Matsunoki Kouta' by Ninomiya Yukiko are accompanied by the comment: 'The composer is unknown, so under Japanese law ... royalties are paid to the Japanese Bureau of Justice until the writer [composer] is established' (Coryton, 1990, pp. 104, 131). Although one must take into consideration the conceivable oral tradition that might have been responsible for the anonymity of these parlour-entertainment songs, the fact that the composers are unknown can be taken as an indication of the existence of many less popular songs for which writers failed to claim authorship out of neglect or indifference. On the other hand, once every few years the discovery of the writer of a well-known song becomes a topic for the newspapers. Recently the identity of a female writer of two juvenile songs, 'Tulip' and 'Koinobori', both of which are familiar to almost all Japanese, was finally revealed, fifty-seven years afer the songs were published in an illustrated, educational collection (*Asahi*, 17 August 1989, p. 21).

The basic conception of copyright has become familiar in Japan mainly through newspaper coverage of copyright issues concerning records, tapes and computer programmes. But still the Japanese people do not take well to copyright, or more properly, to the idea of the individual right.

Generally speaking, to claim one's right is regarded as dishonourable or undignified, especially when the right involves money. A representative of BIEM got the impression, when he visited Japan in 1959, that Japanese composers readily backed down when their demand was not met (JASRAC, 1990 vol. 2, p. 186). This inclination might be illustrated in another way, by drawing on my own experience of writing – only about 30 per cent of Japanese editors of commercial periodicals inform a writer, in advance and of their own accord, of the amount paid for a commissioned article, whereas in Britain, as far as I know, almost all editors do. Making inquiries about the monetary reward in such a situation requires, on the part of a writer, some hesitant and disagreeable effort. It should also be noted that, in the case of book publication, publishers usually make a contract with an author, in contrast to Britain and other countries, *after* a book is printed (even though some of the stipulations presuppose signing in advance).

Significantly, before Westernisation there didn't exist any concept in Japan that equated with 'right' or '*droit*'. The word *kenri* or its abridgement, *ken*, as is used as a part of *chosakuken* (copyright), was coined as a term to translate 'right' into Japanese in the late nineteenth century (it was one of many Western words for which no fitting equivalents existed, such as 'society', 'individual', 'modern', and 'liberty' – such words as 'privacy' are used as loan words without being translated). And *kenri* (right), which was forged with much difficulty, as explained in a book on some important translated words (Yanabu, 1982, pp. 151–72), was a combination of *ken* (power, in the sense of control over others, authority, etc.) and *ri* (profit, advantage), giving unfavourable and more or less avaricious connotations to itself even in the present day, when it is used as a part of everyday language. To make things worse, the very idea of rights which has been at the centre of modern Western law, was transplanted to Japan. On the other hand, in Japan, the traditional idea of social order symbolised by the conception of *giri* is still alive and dominates to a considerable degree the way law and order should be. *Giri* signifies the moral principles derived from Confucianism which one should observe and put in practice in personal relations. Under this conception of *giri*:

> Social order is promoted by the way in which an obligee is socially pressured to conjecture the advantage and feelings of the obligors. The terms of the obligors would not be inquired into and the obligee should take whatever measures which he considers suitable. Therefore, to claim one's right is regarded only negatively, as an act that disturbs social order. (*Heibonsha*, 1985, vol. 5, p. 212)

Similarly, individualism, which involves the conception of individual right and is fundamentally related to Christianity, was implanted in Japan in the Meiji era and has only gradually been assimilated (and really only since the end of World War II). No matter how convincing the Western conception of individualism is in many circumstances, traditional collectivism has maintained a resolute persistence in Japan.

Akutagawa Yasushi, the chief director of JASRAC during the 1980s, was one of the witnesses at a meeting of the educational committee of the House of Councillors in 1984, at which he referred to the notion whereby copyright law and its acceptance is a barometer of the level of culture in a country (JASRAC, 1990, vol. 2, p. 253). This idea has since been cited repeatedly and has become strong justification of the copyright law for people who are in a position of influence. It has now turned out, however, through the present investigation, that these people sound as if they were governmental 'holdovers' from the Meiji era in their simplistic faith in Westernisation and capitalisation, or perhaps the cat's paws of their present-day equivalents in the US and Europe. But, as might be expected, it is not that they anyway have a wholehearted understanding of the copyright law. For example, recently the compiler of an admirable historial collection of Japanese popular songs on sixty-six CDs was sued for trying to include some recordings which were released more than fify years ago and were no longer under protection of the law. Eventually the court compelled the two parties to compromise instead of acquitting the compiler of the charge (Nakamura, 1991). In the world of the Japanese record industry, which is quite restricted, though financially prosperous, there seems to be more room for *giri* than *kenri* where domestic copyright is concerned.

Might it be impractical to suggest, now that the Copyright Law has been increasingly intertwined with international regulations, that the Japanese should reconsider the conception of copyright in the light of Japanese cultural traditions, and perhaps make a radical revision of the law? At any rate, not only the people in the East but also those in the West should be aware that the peculiar circumstance of Japan is to be shared in the course of time. Indeed, it is partly being shared now by other Asian countries, including 'a gigantic elephant finally awakened from a deep sleep' (Akutagawa, 1988, p. 273), namely China, which until recently had not found it necessary to implement an official copyright law.[4]

NOTES

1. Legal situations of copyright in many Asian countries were surveyed by one of the panelists at the symposium on copyright and popular music held by the Japanese Association for the Study of Popular Music in 1989 (Mitsui, 1990, pp. 24–31).
2. All the quotations in this chapter are translated from Japanese by the present author.
3. The names of Japanese people, in phonetic transcription, are written in the Japanese style of the family name preceding the given name throughout this chapter except the name of the present author below the chapter title.

4. China signed the Berne Convention on 15 October 1992, and the Universal Copyright Convention on 30 October 1992.

REFERENCES

All the Japanese titles are phonetically transcribed, as in the case of personal names, and translated in brackets when necessary.

Akutagawa, Yasushi (1985), '*Sangiin bunkyôiinkainiokeru sankonin iken*', ('A witness's comments at a meeting of the educational committee of the House of Councillors'), 4 June, JASRAC (1990), vol. 2, pp. 262–70.

— (1988), '*Sangiin bunkyô iinkainiokeru sankônin iken*' (' A witness's comments at a meeting of the educational committee of the House of Councillors'), 13 May, JASRAC (1990), vol. 2, pp. 271–6.

Araki, Toratarô (1913), '*Chikuonki heienbanno kokusojikenwo ronzu*' ('Comments on the indictment concerning phongraph discs'), *Hôritsu shimbun* (*Law gazette*), no. 837, 20 January, JASRAC (1990), vol. 1, pp. 127–30.

Asahi shimbun (Osaka). One of the major national newspapers in Japan.

Coryton, Demitri and Murrells, Joseph (1990), *Hits of the '60s: The Million Sellers*, London: B. T. Batsford.

Fujita, Masato (1947), '*Chosakushakara ensôkae chûmonchô* (2)' ('Requests from composers to performers (2)'), *Ongaku shimbun* (Music gazette), 1 August, JASRAC (1990), vol. 2, pp. 109–10.

Hatoyama, Ichirô (1920), '*Chosakukenhôchû kaisei hôritsuan*' ('Proposal for a partial amendment of Copyright Law'), presented at the forty-third Imperial Diet session, JASRAC (1990), vol. 1, pp. 169–71.

Hatoyama, Kazuo (1898), '*Bankoku hanken hogo dômei kameijô*no chûi' ('Notes on the accession to the international treaty of copyright protection'), *Taiyô*, vol. 4, no. 3, 5 February, JASRAC (1990), vol. 1, pp. 72–5.

Heibonsha (1985), *Heibonsha daihyakkajiten* (*Heibonsha encyclopedia*), 16 vols, Tokyo.

Hiroshima, Kazuo (1937), '*Plage senpû torishirabe nikki*' ('Diary on the investigation of the Plage sensation'), *Bungei shunjû*, vol. 15, no. 10, September, JASRAC (1990), vol. 1, pp. 331–7.

Ishihara, Ikio (1934), '*Chosakukenhô kaisei undôto gakudan*' ('Movement for copyright revision and music circles'), *Ongaku sekai* (*The world of music*), vol. 6, no. 5, May, JASRAC (1990), vol. 2, pp. 6–8.

JASRAC (1989A), *Nihon ongaku chosakuken kyôkai 50 nenshi* ('A fifty-year history of JASRAC'), Tokyo, 18 November.

— (1989B) *JASRAC* '89. Twenty-four page booklet in English, Tokyo.

— (1990), *Nihon chosakukenshi* (*A history of musical copyright in Japan*), 2 vols. A collection of historical documents, 20 March, Tokyo.

Katô, Eigo (1933), '*Wagakuni bunkano daikasaini sonaeyo*', *Ongaku hyôron* (*Music review*, vol. 2, no. 3, December, JASRAC (1990), vol. 1, pp. 304–5.

Komatsu Kôsuke (1932), 'Sakkyokukato hôsohosakuken' ('Composers and broadcasting copyright'), *Chôsa jihô* (*Research journal*), vol. 2, no. 24, December, JASRAC (1990), vol. 1, pp. 241–2.

Kurata, Yoshihiro (1983), *Chosakuken shiwa* (*Historical anecdotes of Copyright*), Tokyo: Sen'nin-sha.

Kurokawa, Seiichirô (1886), '*Berne jôyaku sôsetsu kaigi shusseki hôkoku*' ('Report on the conference to establish the Berne Convention'), JASRAC (1990), vol. 1, pp. 20–37.

Masuzawa, Takemi (1939), '*Chosakukenno mondai*' 'The copyright issue'),

Ongaku sekai (*The world of music*', vol. 2, no. 12, December, JASRAC (1990), vol. 2, pp. 41–2.

Matsuoka, Shimpei (1990), 'Bridge over troubled waters', an unpublished paper read by the managing director of JASRAC at the CISAC conference in Hong Kong, October.

Mitsui, Tôru (1988), 'Jimmie Davis: An Interview', in *Studies in Humanities*, College of Liberal Arts, Kanazawa University, vol. 25, no. 2, March. Two-thirds of the interview was reprinted in *Old Time Country* (Centre for the Study of Southern Culture, the University of Mississippi), vol. 7, no. 1, Spring 1990, pp. 4–13, and vol. 7, no. 2, Summer 1990, pp. 16–24.

— et al. (1990), *Chosakukento popular ongaku* (*Copyright and Popular Music*), JASPM Working Paper Seriess, no. 1, July, Tokyo.

Mizuno, Rentarô (1898), '*Bankoku hanken hogo dômeinitsuite*' ('On the international treaty of copyright protection'), published in *Kokka gakkai zasshi* (*Journal of National Academy*), vol. 12, nos. 141 and 142, 15 November and 15 December, JASRAC (1990), vol. 1, pp. 77–90.

— (1899), '*Chosakukenhô riyûsho*' ('Statement of reasons for Copyright Law'), JASRAC (1990), vol. 1, pp. 91–3.

— (1906), '*Chosakuken hogoni kansuru nichibei kyôyakunitsuite*' ('On the Japan-usa treaty of copyright protection'), *Hôgaku kyôkai zasshi* (*Journal of law association*), vol. 24, no. 6, June, JASRAC (1990), vol. 1, pp. 94–9.

— (1909), *Berlinniokeru chosakuken hogo bankoku kaigino jôkyo*' ('On the international conference on copyright protection in Berlin'), *Taiyô*, vol. 15, no. 6, February, JASRAC (1990), vol. 1, pp. 100–13.

Mori, Katsumi and Numata, Jirô, comps (1978), *Taigai kankeishi* (*A history of foreign relations*), Tokyo: Yamada-shuppan.

Nakamura, Tôyô (1991), Telephone interview, in late October, 1991, with Tôyô Nakamura, the owner of monthly *Music Magazine* and a widely-published writer of music.

Nakamura, Yoshihiko (1940), 'Shadanhôjin nihon chosakuken kyôkaino seiritsunitsuite' ('On the establishment of jasrac'), *Gekkan gakufu* (*Score monthly*), vol. 29, no. 2, February, JASRAC (1990), vol. 2, pp. 49–54.

Omori, Hitarô (1937), '*Plage senpûwa kokujokuteki senpûka*' ('Is the Plage sensation a disgrace to the nation?'), *Hôritsu shimbun*, 20 August, JASRAC (1990), vol. 1, pp. 306–10.

Omori, Seitarô (1986), *Nihonno yôgaku* (*Foreign music in Japan*), vol. 1, Tokyo: Shin'mon-shuppan.

Shimbo, Shinobu (1935), '*Plage hakasetowa donnaotokoka*' ('What kind of man is Dr Plage?'), *Hanashi*, vol. 3, no. 1, January, JASRAC (1990), vol. 1, pp. 321–7.

Taishô (1986), *Taishô news jiten* (*A collection of newspaper articles from the Taishô era*), Tokyo: Mainichi communications.

Yanabu, Akira (1982), *Hon'yakugo seiritsu jijô* (Tokyo: Iwanamishoten).

Yokota, Shôichi (1917), '*Chikuonkikaino shikatsu mondai*' ('Fatal issues concerning the phonograph industry'), *Chikuonki sekai* (*The world of phonographs*), vol. 4, no. 9, September, JASRAC (1990), vol. 1, pp. 153–60.

Yomiuri shimbun, one of the major national daily newspapers in Japan, Tokyo.

8

The Problem of Oral Copyright: The Case of Ghana

JOHN COLLINS

The idea of copyright first appeared in Europe of the sixteenth century in connection with the publishing of books – and in the eighteenth and nineteenth centuries was extended to technology and the fine arts. The first British copyright law as such was passed in 1842. This was followed by a sequence of international agreements such as the Berne Convention of 1886, the Universal Copyright Convention of 1952, the Rome Convention of 1961 and the Geneva Convention of 1971. All these agreements rest on Eurocentric assumptions that a specific art-work or intellectual idea is created by a single or restricted number of individuals who are therefore easily identifiable and that older artistic forms rooted in pre-industrial peasant society (i.e. folklore) can be regarded as public property as their authors are unidentifiable and anonymous. English law (on which much of Ghanaian law is based) also considers that there can be no copyright unless the work 'has been written down, recorded or otherwise reduced to material form'. (Anyidoho and Tsikata, 1988). This is a reflection of copyright's origin in book publishing.

In Europe, then, since the nineteenth century, when copyright really became effective, there has been a clear demarcation between folk music and culture on the one hand – i.e. 'dead' preindustrial art forms preserved in museums and archives – and popular or classical works that are composed by identifiable contemporary persons, on the other: i.e. between anonymous and therefore public folkloric works and individually authored and owned 'private' works. Thus the realms of the folk music archivist and the copyright official do not overlap. In many Third World countries, by contrast, there is a living folk tradition existing alongside private creativity. Therefore the realm of folklore and copyright do overlap. Indeed the very (European) concept of 'folklore' itself has to be reassessed in the Third World context. Moreover, in many Third World and African countries, many art and cultural works are not written down or materialised in any way, as they are part of a still dynamic oral tradition. Linked to this is the fact that non-European cultures have different norms appertaining to the 'creation' of works (e.g. to their collective creation, by composer, performer and even audience) and to the definition of music (e.g. the African emphasis on rhythm as well as melody).

In this paper I will examine the resulting problems of 'folkloric-copyright', particularly as they affect African (and specifically Ghanaian) music and dance. But the points made here could be extended to other areas of African or Ghanaian folklore and folk culture (poetry, drama, proverbs, etc.) and to the experiences of many other Third World Countries.

PROBLEM ONE – THE IDENTIFICATION OF ORAL WORKS FOR COPYRIGHT

There is a misconception that only literate or other materially recorded works (i.e. printed, scored, choreographed, taped, etc.) can generate royalties, and that as African folklore is oral, it can have no definite author or authors and therefore cannot be copyrighted. This notion favours the literate and industrial, at the expense of the illiterate and non – or pre-industrial. However, as noted by Anyidoho and Tsikata (1988), the author or authors of oral works can, in fact, 'often be pin-pointed'. They give the examples of the 'unwritten copyright' of Somali poetry and of the oral Ewe funeral poems of Akpalu and his predecessors and contemporary poet-cantors. They also mention the Ewe Haikotu drum clubs, in which the composer of the words and tune first works out the performance with the other members of the group in closed session, before presenting it to the public. Similar to this is the Eguamala dance-drumming of the Bendel State of Nigeria noted by Dr Fidelma Okwesa (1990), where the known composer and the group rehearse for two years in close secrecy before publicly performing the work – and subsequently can sell the whole work outright, as it is considered to be the private property of the group.

Two other examples I can mention here are the Ga Kpanlogo and Ewe BorBorBor neo-traditional dance-music styles that are often regarded in Ghana as anonymous folkloric works of the country. However, Kpanlogo was created around 1962 in Bukom Square by Otoo Lincoln together with drummers Okulay Foes and Ayitey Sugar, and dance from Frank Lane. It was Otoo Lincoln and his group who composed the songs. 'ABC Kpanlogo', 'Kpanlogo Alogodzan' and 'Ayine Momobiuye'. BorBorBor is Ewe recreational music that was created in Kpando around 1950 by the Kpando Konkoma Group (Konkoma is an earlyish form of highlife). One of the leaders of this Konkoma group was Francis Cudjoe Nuatro or 'FC', who wrote 'Mabia Dzogbe Nuye Se'.

PROBLEM TWO – THE DEFINITION OF 'FOLKLORE' IN THE AFRICAN CONTEXT

In a speech by Dr Mohammed Ben Abdullah at the Inauguration of the Folkloric Board of Trustees at the office of the National Commission on Culture on 12 September 1991, folklore was defined as all the 'literary, artistic and scientific works belonging to the cultural heritage of Ghana which were created, preserved and developed by ethnic communities of Ghana or by unidentified Ghanaian authors' (1991, p. 1).

This definition operates easily enough in the European situation of a dead folklore and a defunct oral tradition, but becomes exceedingly complex in the Ghanaian case of a living tradition. In fact, this is recognised in the 1989 WIPO report on the 'Protection of Expressions of Folklore', which notes that one of the major obstacles to creating an international agreement on the protection of folklore is the 'lack of appropriate sources for the identification ... of folklore to be protected' (1989, p. 11).

Just to demonstrate how difficult it is to define folklore, or to separate it from the contemporary composed performing arts of Ghana, the following is a list of just nine possible permutations that can occur – and I'm sure others could be added. To determine who owns what in this context is no easy matter.

1. Traditional music, dance, poetry, etc. created either communally or so long ago that it is beyond the reach of copyright; i.e. fifty years since the death of the composer(s). This is 'folklore' in the sense defined by Dr Abdullah above.
2. Modern neo-traditional genres (such as Kpanlogo, Akpalu, BorBorBor, etc.) where individuals or group authors can be identified and which fall within the copyright period; i.e. the composer(s) are still alive or the fifty years since their deaths has not elapsed.
3. Popular dance-music that draws heavily on traditional music and poetry. This includes all contemporary dance-bands, guitar-concert party bands and 'cultural' groups that employ traditional, modern or a combination of traditional and modern instruments to play music based on traditional highlife, adowa, aghadza and other folkloric rhythms, and/or use traditional melodies, poetry, proverbs, lullabies, children's songs, ceremonial songs, work-songs, war songs, funeral songs, etc.
4. Popular Ghanaian musics of dance and guitar bands etc. that utilise folkloric and/or popular music elements from other African countries, with or without a Ghanaian folkloric content. Examples include the local Ghanaian use of 'Congo Jazz', South African Kwela music, West Senegambian griot music, etc.
5. 'Serious' music that draws heavily on the traditional motifs mentioned

in 3.) above, but is composed, scored and orchestrated for symphonic orchestra.
6. 'Serious' scored orchestrated music that uses elements from the folklore of other African countries, with or without a Ghanaian component; such as pan-African compositions.
7. Commercial folkloric music used for cabarets and the tourist trade.
8. Governmental/para-statal/university traditionally-oriented dance ensembles who perform on stage and are professionally choreographed. This is the nearest Ghanaian equivalent to the preserved form of 'folklore' in Europe and the United States.
9. Music in which European folkloric elements are incorporated into Ghanaian procedures. An example is local Ghanaian gospel music that sometimes uses the melodies of European hymns and folksongs.

To emphasise the problem of defining folklore nationalistically I could also point to the history of Gahu and Gome musics which are normally regarded in Ghana as traditional Ghanaian genres. Gahu (or Agagu) which is associated with the Ewe people of the Volta Region, was actually created by the Egun-speaking people of Benin and subsequently brought to Ghana (via Nigeria) by Ewe fishermen around 1950. Gome (as Goombay) was originally a neo-African cult music of Jamaica, created there over 200 years ago by the Maroons (mainly of Akan descent). A Central African drumming technique was subsequently added and the music was introduced (in a sense returned home) to Africa (Sierre Leone) in 1800, from whence it spread throughout West Africa in the nineteenth and early twentieth centuries.

PROBLEM THREE – APPLYING EUROPEAN MUSICAL IDEOLOGY TO THE AFRICAN MUSICAL REALM

In the West, song composer royalties are divided so that 50 per cent is paid for the lyrics and 50 per cent for the music or melody. In African music rhythm is so important that royalties should be broken down into three components; lyrics (33 per cent), melody (33 per cent) and rhythm (33 per cent). This issue becomes even more complex when one considers that African music is usually polyrhythmic, i.e. uses multiple rhythms and cross melodies. I remember the question this raised at an international music conference held in Amsterdam in 1981. Two officials of an American copyright organisation became very excited about a snippet of the tune 'Somewhere Over the Rainbow' that they heard in one of Ebenezer Obey's Nigerian juju songs and demanded that the American composer should be compensated by the Nigerian one. I pointed out to them that they were only hearing one of several melodies that were going on simultaneously. There was also a juju refrain, a palm-wine music guitar riff, a Hawaian-style guitar, a touch of Fela's Afrobeat, not to mention the melody of Obey's own voice. So how were the various composers to be calculated? A further point on the topic of music composition should be made here. African music is usually associated with specific dances, and so in the African case royalty-accruing components should, in the name of creative equity, be divided into four: the lyrics, the melody, the rhythm and the dance-step – with the melody being further divided into the various contrapuntal or cross melodies and the polyrhythm into its multiple subrhythms.

This relates to a very important issue raised in Kofi Anyidoho's and Fui Tsikata's paper on copyright and oral literature (1988) concerning the difference in the concepts of a composer and a performer in Africa and in the West. In Europe and the States, these two roles are usually taken separately, whereas in Africa not only is the composer often the performer and vice versa, but, more importantly, performance is central to the meaning of composition (p. 5). To add to the confusion for a copyright administrator, in African performing arts the audiences often have a creative role too, as they chant, clap and perform dance-dialogues with the musicians. This is quite unlike the European (classical) musical tradition in which the audience sits motionless, contemplating the autonomous musical work, and only claps after the performance – not during it as in Africa. Anyidoho and Tsikata also point to the 'greater latitude for borrowing, adaption and improvisation' (p. 8) in Ghanaian performances than is usual in European classical concerts which are regulated by the score and the conductor's baton. This, again, poses a problem for the copyright administrator: how does one measure the degree (and value) of 'originality' or creativity in a continually *reworked* piece of music?

This issue of different artistic norms in Africa and the West cropped up in a recent High Court case between the pianist, Ray Ellis and the producer, Kwadwo Donkor (held in November 1990). Ellis claimed some of the composer royalties for the (already copyrighted) highlife tunes he played instrumentally on a record. However, as he had been paid as a session man by the producer, he lost the case. Ellis believed he was re-interpreting the songs and thus composing something new, and the case highlighted the 'grey area' between an arrangement and an adaptation. An arrangement is only a re-adjustment of, say, the key or orchestration of a tune, and, according to both the WIPO report and Ghana's PNDC Law 110, should accrue no royalties. An adaptation, however, is the creation of a fresh derivative of an original work, and so *can* gather royalties. In Ghana, with its traditional 'centrality of the performer' this neat European division between 'arrangements' and 'adaptations' is less clear. One answer to this is to divide the performance royalties into three equal portions: one third going to the composer/adapter, one third to the producer and one third to the performer/arranger. I believe that this is the procedure at the moment in Ghana for performing royalties and it seems to me to be the fairest system, although it does favour the performer as compared to the British system (where the norm is for the producer to receive twice as many royalty points as the performer). However, with so many grey areas between the role of composer, performer and even audience participation in Ghana, the whole question has to be looked into further.

PROBLEM FOUR – EXTENDING COPYRIGHT TO LIVING FOLKLORE

PNDC Law 110 vests works of Ghanaian anonymous folklore in the state for perpetuity, and prohibits their use without the permission of a government Secretary, who may charge a fee. In addition the 1989 WIPO report suggests it should be an offence to 'distort the expression of folklore' (p. 8): a point reiterated in Dr Abdullah's speech of 12 September 1991, concerning the distortion, mutilation and misinterpretation of folklore for the needs of the market (p. 2).

Although the idea of the Ghanaian government owning the copyright on folklore is a sensible one, in the light of the First World exploitations of Third World cultural traditions, the system of permissions and fees poses a problem for Ghanaians themselves. This was, indeed, noted in the 1989 WIPO report which talks of the need for a 'proper balance between protection against abuses of expressions of folklore ... and freedom and encouragement ... of their further development, dissemination and also adaption' (p. 4). The need for 'balance' was also mentioned in Dr Abdullah's speech (1991, p. 3), and Anyidoho and Tsikata warn that 'exaggerated claims of state ownership' could 'fossilise and stunt' the development of local oral traditions. (1988, p. 7). Unlike Europe and the States, as there is so much interaction between Ghanaian folkloric and popular genres, the 'stunting' could affect popular music, dance and drama as well. This would not only be a cultural disaster but also an economic one, for with the current Western interest in 'World Music', Ghanaian popular culture is a potentially renewable (cf. gold and diamonds) source of foreign exchange.

On the topic of the 'mutilation' or adulteration of folklore, the WIPO report suggests that the protection of folklore from distortion and commercialisation applies only 'beyond the country in which they originate' (1989, p. 10) and I also believe that to apply the policy *within* Ghana would have negative effects equivalent to those of a government or parastatal censorship mechanism. For example, Kpanlogo, which is today considered to be part of Ghana's cultural heritage, was for a time after its creation in the 1960s frowned upon by some members of the then Arts

Council – who, if they had the power to do so, might well have banned it as a 'distortion'. We could also consider the case of the black popular music of the United States that evolved out of African-American and, indeed, African folk music. If, at the turn of the century, the American government had had a policy of preventing the 'distortion' of their own folklore, I am sure that the Blues and Jazz would never have become that country's national music; for in their infancy they were called the 'Devil's Music' and were associated with low-class 'Boogie Houses', 'Jook Joints' and the red-light Storyville district of New Orleans.

The 1989 WIPO report also raises the question of how to handle similar folkloric genres existing in several countries (p. 11) and this is particularly pertinent to Africa where national borders do not always correspond to ethnic ones. Anyidoho and Tsikata also tackle this matter, and provide an example of the confusion that could arise if Ghana 'nationalises' a folklore, Dagarte, that also exists over its border. Burkina Faso has as much right as does Ghana to claim Dagarte folklore as its national cultural heritage (1983, p. 8). Similar examples are the Agbadza dance and music that is found in Ghana and Togo, and the Adowa dance and music that is found in Ghana and eastern Côte d'Ivoire. There are also traditional musical features and rhythms in Ghana (such as the bell pattern of Tigari) which are found dotted all over Africa – the sorting out of these folkloric overlaps will therefore involve copyright organisations from all over Africa.

Even if such border disputes could be resolved, to charge Ghanaians fees for the use of their own folklore could well damage the local popular performing arts based on this folklore. It would encourage, first, an ever-increasing adoption of foreign music by Ghanaian artists (who are already under the influence of the imported music of the 'spinners'), and, in order to dodge the folklore taxes, Ghanaian musicians would have a strong incentive to utilise African rhythms etc. , found outside Ghana, but which resemble Ghanaian ones (e.g. the Aghadza, Adowa, Tigari and Dagarte folklore).

To illustrate this problem we can imaginatively take the case of, say, Britain in Renaissance times, when, like present-day Ghana, there was a living folklore and an emerging area of art-works created by unknown individuals. If an alien entity had suddenly appeared in this Britain of 400 years ago, and persuaded the then King and Parliament to 'nationalise' and tax folkloric works, this would have been a calamity for subsequent British popular and classical music; particularly that of the Romantic composers, so much of whose works were based on local folklore. As a result, British composers might well have gone to other European countries where this law did not apply and helped those countries develop their national culture instead (or, maybe, given up on on music altogether).

I should stress that my argument that Ghanaians should not pay a fee or tax on their own folklore does not really go against the 1989 WIPO report, but rather updates and extends the report's concept of the free use of folklore in its 'traditional context' to the whole nation; for, as Anyidoho and Tsikata put it, the modern nation state of Ghana is a 'successor to and trustee of its pre-existing (i.e. traditional/folkloric) composite parts' (1988, p. 7). Indeed this whole notion of there being a vast gulf between the non-commercial traditional realm and the modern commercial one is another European ideological concept; for it is rooted in the fact that in Europe the folkloric tradition is dead (and safely stowed away in museums) and the popular arena is alive and commercial. The point is that this is not so in Ghana where because the traditional and oral is still very much alive it is therefore an integral part of both the non-commercial and commercial aspects of the modern nation state.

SOLUTIONS?

Any attempt to apply a folklore-copyright must begin from the principle of 'balance' emphasised in the WIPO report and by Dr Abdullah. In the Ghanaian case, for example, the 'distortion' of folklore should only be applied outside the country and not within it (except, of course, in the case of gross indecency, libel, etc.). As far as the fee system is concerned I would suggest the following structure.

1. *Ghanaians* For all Ghanaian performers, writers and artists in and outside Ghana, the fee to use Ghanaian folklore would be waived by the state. Nevertheless, folkloric elements used by Ghanaian artists should be clearly shown on their artistic products and failure to do so would be a fineable offence. This identification of the folkloric element in the commercial product of a Ghanaian composer or author would be a way of registering it for copyright purposes. This would bypass the tedious and complicated process of every Ghanaian artist having to register and seek permission from a government Secretary, before creating their work and putting it on the market.
2. *Other Africans* For non-Ghanaian Africans, a minimum nominal fee should be charged for their use of Ghanaian folklore commercially, so as to enhance inter- and pan-African artistic creativity. This interim measure would, I hope, lead to reciprocal agreements between African members of the OAU and regional sub-entities such as ECOWAS, so that eventually this nominal charge could be dropped altogether.
3. *Foreigners* Non-African foreigners who utilise Ghanaian folklore commercially should pay the Ghanaian state (via the Copyright Administration) that portion of the composer or author royalties that consists of Ghanaian folklore. This policy should be most

rigorously applied in the case of Western 'superstars'. The argument that the West would retaliate by demanding that Ghanaians should pay for their use of European and American folklore would not occur, as folklore in the West falls into the public domain and is therefore not the copyrightable property of Western states. The reason why WIPO suggests that anonymous folklore should be the property of Third World States, such as Ghana, is to prevent the undue exploitation of their arts and culture by First World nations, in the de facto socio-historical context of the separation of the world into rich and poor, north and south, developed and developing.

Because of the complex issues of copyright and 'folklore' in the international music market (and following the recent payment of $16,000 to Ghana by Paul Simon for his use of elements of the Yaa Amponsah highlife song on his *Rhythm of the Saints* album), the National Commission on Culture in Ghana decided in its wisdom to establish a National Folklore Board of Trustees – on which I have the honour of serving.

In the final part of this paper I would, therefore, like to turn to the ways this Board might help clarify and sort out folklore-copyright problems. Before proceeding to this, however, it must be born in mind that the 1989 WIPO report, on which some of Ghana's folkloric copyright norms are or will be based, concludes that an international convention on the protection of expressions of folklore was 'premature' (1989, p. 12). In short, given present disagreements about folklore definitions and boundaries, there can, as yet, be no global policy on folkloric copyright. Rather, each country or group of neighbouring countries, must adapt the recommendations of the WIPO report to their own particular social, cultural and historical circumstances. Because of Ghana's living oral traditions, for example, there is a constant interaction between folklore and the popular performing arts, and there is no clear demarcation between them as in the West. Indeed, if such a clear demarcation did ever develop it would indicate that the local folklore had become fossilised as it is in Europe where it has to be artificially preserved. The European definition of 'folklore' is therefore inapplicable to Ghana, and the first task for the Folkloric Board is to look carefully into the living nature of Ghanaian folklore.

It will, then, have the difficult task of collecting evidence concerning the uncertain and diffuse boundaries between anonymous folkloric works and identifiable individual or group-created works. To help the Board in this I make the following four recommendations:

1. The Board must include a number of active composers, authors and performers of both non-commercial and commercial works, to prevent an over-simplified or too abstract view of things being developed by the historians, lawyers and scholars who are the present Board members.

2. Advertisements should be placed in local newspapers and other media, asking the general public to come forward to give evidence concerning any works that hitherto have been considered anonymous folkloric works, but in fact were created by identifiable individuals or groups. A Post Office Box and a venue or venues for responses should be established to receive this information. University students doing arts research and National Service personnel could help document and sift this information. They could also interview or tape illiterate informants and even go to the regions to collect facts. The importance of drawing in the general public is that many details of the creation of folklore and its interactions with popular art and music have never been documented, and the public thus presents a largely untapped pool of knowledge of oral traditions. This input of information could ultimately help towards a history of Ghanaian folkloric and popular performing arts with the facts actually being produced by the 'folk' and the 'people' rather than just by intellectuals.
3. The Board should be involved in the collection, preservation and dissemination of all existing data on folkloric and indigenous popular arts, from the records and tapes to photographs, books, manuscripts, etc. This would include, for instance, documenting and copying the 12,000 tapes of traditional music collected by the University Institute of African Studies in the 1950s, which are now, due to lack of funds, sadly perishing. Universities, folkloric foundations, public and private archives, record companies, museums and radio stations in Ghana, the rest of Africa and throughout the world could also be contacted by the Folkloric Board, to provide copies of music, pictures, books, articles and university theses on both folkloric and folklore inspired local art works. Reciprocal or other working relations could also be initiated by the Board with the national, pan-African and international bodies.
4. The Folkloric Board should recommend to the Copyright Administration annual royalty lump-sums to be paid for identifiable originators of non-commercial neo-traditional performance styles (such as Kpanlogo, BorBorBor and some types of highlife) that have become popular and are now utilised commercially. This would prevent the unworkable situation of the originator(s) of such works making individual claims on the thousands of Ghanaians who have utilised their works.

The Copyright Administration is already collecting examples of contemporary recordings and works as evidence for royalty payments. This should be expanded into a major archive (music, books, photos, film etc.) concerning both 'folkloric' and 'popular' Ghanaian creations. This archive could have reciprocal relations with other archives in the country (such as GBC, the National Museum, the DuBois Centre, and other public and private collections). They could duplicate each other's works so as to decentralise Ghana's archival heritage (and thus prevent a re-occurrence of the loss through fire of unique film and video stock at Ghana Broadcasting several years ago). In fact, the folkloric/copyright archive itself could be decentralised on a regional basis – as has occurred with the Regional Community Centres; indeed, these two organisations could be linked at the regional level. A de-centralised archive would present no problem today, as modern technology (computers, fax, photocopying, video, networking, etc.) makes it easy to duplicate the material of a central archive. Each regional Folkloric/Copyright Centre could also act as a local gathering point for incoming copyright and archival information. As part of the Folkloric/Copyright Archive, the late Beattie Casely-Hayford's idea of a mobile unit with equipment to copy records (especially old 78s), photos and manuscripts is pertinent here. For much information is with the general public, who may be prepared to have materials taped, photographed or copied on the spot but are not willing or are too old or infirm, to travel. This mobile unit could be partially run by students on National Service, who could make on-the-spot interviews concerning copyright claims.

As already discussed, there should be no tax or censorship on any Ghanaians utilising what have been conclusively proven to be the country's genuine anonymous folkloric works whether for non-commercial or commercial purposes – even though these folkloric works will be vested in the state. The users of folklore would only have to register the folkloric content of his/her/their works on the marketed product itself. Within Ghana then, the role of the Folkloric Board would be rather like that of Parks and Gardens, creating an open free cultural space for the public, rather than a geographical one. Thus, just as a park provides an area within an urban setting for the enjoyment, recreation and creativity of the public, so Ghana's anonymous folkloric heritage would be held in trust by the state as a free gift from the past to present and future generations. Any form of fee and/or censorship on Ghanaian artists planning to use anonymous folklore would only stifle creativity, and could eventually result in a situation of cultural impoverishment, such as occurred during the 'socialist realist' period of Stalinist Russia.

Nevertheless, the Folkloric Board must have funds – and one source would be the previously mentioned charge to foreigners utilising Ghanaian folklore: in which case the royalties that would normally go to composer(s) would go to Ghana's Copyright Administration and thence to the Folkloric Board. Foreign 'superstars' would be charged a maximum fee; foreigners operating within Ghana or deemed beneficial to the country in some way, could appeal to the Board for fee reductions.

A second source of income for the Board would also come through the Copyright Administration. As it is generally recognised that folklore provides an important element in commercial Ghanaian popular music, a small portion of the total royalties collected annually or bi-annually by the Copyright Administration (for composers, performers and producers and to cover administrative running costs) could be earmarked for the Folkloric Board. One way this portion could be assessed is from the proportion of folkloric works performed on radio and TV. In a sense, this would be a back-to-front way of collecting folkloric royalties. Instead of taxing individual artists *before* they used folklore commercially (i.e. licensing its use), the tax or fee would be paid after the work was released in the market as part of the income paid to the Folkloric Board by the Copyright Administration on behalf of Ghanaian artists collectively (practically all of them are at one time or another inspired by or use folkloric elements in their works).

Similarly a small portion of the monies now being collected on imported blank cassettes (presently distributed to composer, performer, producers, Copyright Administration running costs and Customs) should go to the Folkloric Board, as many of the recordings that go on to these tapes will be indebted to folklore in some way or another. This procedure has, in fact, been operating in Sweden for a number of years; there a small tax added to imported (or locally produced) cassettes goes to the Swedish Folk Music Foundation, which was established in 1978.

A fourth way the Folkloric Board could obtain funds is by organising live shows that feature folkloric music, dance, drama, poetry, etc. (with free contributions from willing popular artists), and by itself releasing cassettes of anonymous folkloric and evergreen music on to the local markets. Both these fund-raising activities would have the added benefit of reintroducing forgotten or inaccessible folkloric works to the public.

NOTE

1. The original version of this paper was read at the 'National Workshop on Copyright' organised by the Ghanaian Copyright Commission in cooperation with WIPO at the Academy of African Music and Art , Kokrobike, Ghana, 9–11 October 1991.

REFERENCES

Abdullah, Mohammed B. (1991), Speech at the Inauguration of the Folkloric Board of Trustees, NCC Offices, 12 September.

Amegatcher, A. (1990), *Ghana Copyright News*, issue 2, December.

Anyidoho, Kofi (1983), 'The Haikotu Song and Dance Club of Whetta: A Communal Celebration of Individual Poetic Talent', in *Cross Rhythms*, Anyidoho *et al.* (eds), Bloomington, USA: African Folklore Publications.

Anyidoho, Kofi and Tsikata, Fui (1988), *Copyright and Oral Literature*.

Badasu, Ambrose (1988), 'Tribute to F. C. – Originator of BorBorBor', *Ghanaian Times*, 3 June, p. 4.
Collins, John (1983), 'The Man Who Made Traditional Music', *West Africa*, 19/26 December, p. 2946.
—— (1985a), *E. T. Mensah the King of Highlife*, London: Off the Record Press.
—— (1985b) *Music Makers of West Africa*, Washington DC: Three Continents Press.
—— (1985c), *African Pop Roots*, London: Foulshams.
Dekutsey, Wilson (1988), 'In Honour of Akpalu', *West Africa*, 21/27 November, pp. 2189–90
Kidenda, George (1990), 'Dissemination: The Copyright Issue', paper at the Audio-Visual Archives Conference, Falun, Sweden, July.
Malm, Krister (1988), 'The Swedish Folk Music Foundation', paper at the Audio-Visual Archives Conference, Oslo, Norway.
Okwesa, Fidelma (1990), 'The Problems of Collecting Data for Dance in Nigeria', paper at Audio-Visual Conference, Falun, Sweden, July.
Wallis, R. and Malm, K. (1984) *Big Sounds from Small Peoples*, London: Constable.
WIPO, (1989), General Introductory Course on Copyright and Neighbouring Rights: Protection of Expressions of Folklore.

Appendix 1

Copyright: The Dark Side of the Music Business

FRANCO FABBRI

Popular music studies have often pointed out the lack of reliable sources on music consumption, and thus concentrated on the most accessible data, related to the exchange of visible goods: records sales, or even simply charts. But a considerable part of the overall turnover of the music industry is based on the exchange of immaterial items: the rights to reproduce a musical 'work' or its performance. Relevant data are accessible to record companies', music publishers' and performing rights societies' executives, and (as far as they are concerned) to authors and (much less) to performers. But they are not public, even for research purposes. In a world where, for various reasons, the actual sales of phonograms become less and less important compared to the trade of rights, copyright stands as an unknown continent that music researchers *must* explore. A few figures will probably strengthen this assumption: according to an almost official source like Billboard's *This Business of Music – A Practical Guide to the Music Industry for Publishers, Writers, Record Companies, Producers, Artists, Agents* (p. 182),

> The greatest source of revenue in the music industry comes from public performance payments collected and distributed by ASCAP and BMI' [please note that this means *US* music industry, which is assumed to be *the* music industry all across the *Guide*]. In 1983, ASCAP alone collected some $198 million in performance fees from broadcasters and other sources. BMI's collection from such sources for the fiscal year ending June 30, 1984 was almost $125 million, and SESAC, a third licensing organisation, for 1983 collected about $5 million. The three organisations thus received an aggregate of some $328 million. This may be compared with 1976 collections of approximately $94 million for ASCAP, about $60 million for BMI, and over $3 million for SESAC, or a total of some $157 millions. Total collections thus more than doubled in the interval.

The introduction of copyright in various national legislations, and in international conventions, was an official acknowledgement of the 'new' role of the bourgeois artist (poet, writer, playwright, composer, fine artist) after the French Revolution (although in some cases much later on). Current laws and conventions are still shaped around that role; in music they reflect the idea of the score as the actual musical 'work'. Twentieth-century media like cinema, phonograms, radio and television are still subsidiary and peripheral to that nineteenth-century conception of art and communication (computer software still waits to be dealt with in copyright acts in many nations).

It is not surprising, then, that the very idea of 'intellectual property' is being threatened in the last decade of this century, by new technologies and by the new boundaries that these introduce between collective freedom and individual rights. The disputes about home taping, copycode and sampling, are in front of us, and present the music industry as the defender of long established collective and individual rights against abuse and exploitation.

An exploration of the inner mechanisms of record and music publishing would reveal a different reality. A number of composers and performers from Third World countries, a well known example, would probably not agree with the industry's self-projected image. However, a less frequently debated subject deserves even more attention. For decades, now, music publishers' involvement in actual publishing (i.e. printing) of popular music has been radically reduced. But popular music composers still do sign contracts with publishers, on assumptions that to a significant extent belong to the old age of 'Tin Pan Alley' publishing, and have very little to do with the actual service offered to composers in return of about half the income related to the 'work'.

In a few years, this will probably be the case of contemporary classical music too, as 'desktop music publishing' software becomes available to composers, who still have to depend on publishers for the very expensive process of score and parts reproduction. So, by the end of the century, the only task of a very large part of the music industry (and an equally significant part of its turnover) will be mediating about rights between authors and the media. But will both of these sides agree?

Let us now examine a few figures, drawn from the annual report of the '*Direzione della Sezione Musica*' of the Italian Performing Rights Society – Società Italiana degli Autori ed Editori (SIAE). In the following table the overall annual income of the Sezione Musica (the music division) is split according to the different sources (figures are in dollars).

We see from these figures that although the Italian record market compares very unfavourably with many others (including those of much smaller countries, like Holland, for example), copyright turnover is not far from the US figures mentioned above: if we deduct foreign rights (*Estero*) and mechanical rights (*Classe V*) we come to about $192.6

TABLE A1-1: Annual income of the Sezione Musica by source.

	1987	%	1988	%	Var.
CLASSE I (VENUE LICENSING)					
Balli	63,201,557	30.79	72,683,113	31.43	15.00
Concertini	5,432,057	2.65	6,921,690	2.99	27.42
Totale	68,633,614	33.43	79,604,803	34.42	15.99
CLASSE II (FILM RIGHTS)					
Film spettacolari	7,266,052	3.54	6,991,384	3.02	-3.78
Film pubblicitari	160,419	0.08	134,929	0.06	-15.89
Totale	7,426,471	3.62	7,126,312	3.08	-4.04
CLASSE III (BROADCASTING RIGHTS)					
Radiofonia					
Filodiffusione	37,244,913	18.4	44,387,773	19.19	19.18
Televisione					
Apparecchi radio	1,332,791	0.65	1,387,259	0.60	4.09
Apparecchi FD	1,363,952	0.66	1,356,660	0.59	-0.53
Apparecchi TV	3,458,246	1.68	3,826,901	1.65	10.66
Radio Private	1,815,414	0.88	1,744,499	0.75	-3.91
TV private locali	1,153,756	0.56	1,140,714	0.49	-1.13
TV private network	7,892,857	3,84	8,295,904	3.59	5.11
Totale	54,261,930	26.43	62,139,710	26.87	14.52
CLASSE IV (PERFORMING RIGHTS)					
Concerti	4,530,912	2.21	5,171,689	2.24	14.14
Riviste-Conc. Mus. Legg	11,707,936	5.70	14,134,842	6.11	20.73
Varieta	5,380,542	2.62	6,085,699	2.63	13.11
Bande	1,547,011	0.75	1,649,040	0.71	6.60
Strumenti meccanici	8,522,840	4.15	9,803,847	4,24	15.03
Totale	31,689,240	15.44	36,845,117	15.93	16.27
CLASSE V (MECHANCIAL RIGHTS)					
Dischi e nastri	19,478,163	9.49	22,730,914	9.83	16.70
Licenze centralizzate	1,626,342	0.79	2,297,446	0.99	41.26
Diritti di registr.	4,336,356	2.11	5,167,986	2.23	19.18
Produz. progr. RF–TV	27,235	0.01	32,026	0.01	17.59
Videocassette uso priv.	532,871	0.26	621,484	0.27	16.63
Totale	26,000,967	12.67	30,849,856	13.34	18.65
ESTERO (FOREIGN RIGHTS)					
Diritti di esecuzione	11,117,586	5.42	8,790,506	3.80	-20.93
Diritti di ripr. mecc.	6,153,510	3.00	5,923,447	2.56	-3.74
Totale Estero	17,271,096	8.41	14,713,953	6.36	-14.81
TOTALE	205,283,319	100.00	231,279,751	100.00	12.66

Note: Lire/$= 1,400
Source: '*Direzione della Seziona Musica*' of the Italian Performing Rights Society

million, which can be compared to the $328 million for the US in 1983. Even if we deduct some $15.6 million for performing and mechanical rights paid to foreign copyright owners, we still have the picture of a well established and profitable industry, much more adequate to 'the fifth most industrialised power' in the capitalist world than record sales figures would suggest. We can conclude that any account of an individual country's music industry based only on record sales figures is very inadequate, and cannot be in any way taken as an indicator of actual music consumption in that country.

If we take a closer look to some of the categories listed in the SIAE report, we find a few surprising figures: first of all, we notice that the largest slice of the annual turnover (34.42 per cent) comes from *Classe I*, specially from *Balli*, i.e. discos. If we add this to the figures from *Classe IV*, which is concerts and juke-boxes, we discover that slightly more than 50 per cent of the annual income comes from social modes of music consumption, the rest coming from more typically individualised modes of consumption, like buying a record, listening to radio and television, etc. Figures may be misleading in this case, as it is obviously easier for the music industry to control social gatherings than individual consumption, and also because of the particular state of confusion of broadcasting in Italy, which allows many of the commercial broadcasters to pay less than they should, or even nothing. However, these figures anyway indicate areas which can be considered safer for the industry's investments, and so can be used to explain production trends that would appear mysterious if we only considered record sales. Again, copyright figures show their importance as a tool for popular music research.

Unfortunately, as I mentioned, more detailed figures are not accessible: that is, the researcher cannot know how much money came to a copyright owner for a particular piece of music, unless she/he is one of them; so one of the most reliable indicators of the actual consumption of an individual piece is unavailable to researchers. We may sometimes be informed that this or that song is 'the most performed ever' ('Yesterday' being the most credited candidate, at least recently), but there is no way to verify even these rumours.

It must be said, also, that even when available, such figures wouldn't be very easy to understand, the total sum due to a copyright owner for an individual piece being the result of complex calculations, especially in the case of broadcasting. However, investigating the procedures used by performing rights societies to do these calculations (and these are public, and available) is another very interesting task for research. In fact, one can find in these apparently 'neutral' bureaucratic documents some of the most ideologically loaded assumptions on genre hierarchies, on music consumption, on the musicians' work, and so on.

Copyright may (or must) be seen as the area where the ideology of art, individual rights and collective freedom, intellectual work and property, and so on, is re-encoded to support the existing system of production. As such, it deserves the utmost attention.

NOTE

1. This paper was presented originally at the 4th IASPM Conference, Paris 1989 and was reprinted in *Worldbeat*, 1, 1991, pp. 109–14.

Appendix 2

Copyright in Germany[1]

SIMON FRITH

From 1949 until 1989 the German Democratic Republic (DDR) had, like other communist countries, a distinctive approach to musical copyright. This is worth recalling not just as an example of the problem of defining musical property in a non-capitalist society but also because it still has consequences for East German musicians' rights (and income).

Discussion of DDR law must start from the country's lack of a conception of civil society. The function of law, that is, was not to regulate 'free' dealings between individuals, but to maintain the state; individual rights were guaranteed, but only within state administrative procedures. Musicians had rights in their work, but only those rights assigned them by the state, which, in effect, held all copyrights for itself, determined licensing conditions and fees, and acted as the fee collection and distribution agency. This meant, of course, that copyright was defined and administered in the interests of the state, not of authors or composers. This was most obvious in the treatment of rights income from abroad. The state collected such hard currency for itself; authors could only claim (with some difficulty) a small proportion, to be paid in local currency (which explains why the more internationally experienced – and successful – authors, like Brecht, ensured that in international copyright terms they were registered as authors outside the DDR, in Austria or Switzerland). Even when the DDR signed the Berne Convention, and thus agreed to honour the copyrights of foreigners, the new state copyright agency still held the resulting fee income in a local, unconvertible currency account. As foreign works could only be imported via state companies and under state licenses, foreign rights holders had little option but to accept this condition.

For East German writers and composers themselves, there was, then, a kind of acknowledgement of their performing rights: they were entitled to pay, from the copyright agency, for radio, disco and live performances of their works. But although the system was supposedly based on a precise accounting of what songs were played where and when, it did not actually work like this. Broadcasting income, for example, was based only loosely on airplay and reflected, rather, political judgements and 'estimates'.

The disparities were an effect of two aspects of the DDR system. First, there was a significant gap between the bureaucratic account of the world and its messy reality. In practice, for example, a blind eye was turned to the 'illegal' import and public use of foreign records (for which no fee was paid), and the formal limit on the broadcasting of foreign records (no more than 40 per cent of music programming) was systematically breached. Performing rights fees were thus paid according to what *should* have been played on the radio, in the dance halls and youth clubs – the 'estimates'; favoured musicians could thus receive performance fees for music that had never actually been performed!

Second, state control of public musical expression (and in particular, of recording facilities) meant that the concept of 'authorship' was less significant than the practice of 'authorisation'. The right to be 'a musician' (to get an income from music) was determined by a state appointed board of musicians and composers, representatives of the state sponsored musicians' unions. The copyright agency might have sent out 'record sheets' to everyone involved in public music programming, but before any fees were paid out these sheets were checked to ensure that the listed composers were, indeed, officially registered. (It became common for young bands to hook up with a registered musicians somehow – as PA owner, for example; he or she could then be put down as lyricist!)

Favoured musicians – the composers of mainstream East German pop hits, say – could make a good living from these arrangements, particularly if (like the DDR's classical composers) their records were broadcast across Eastern Europe (there was a separate agency for regulating rights and collecting fees within the communist bloc). But this was more a reflection of state support than of market demand, and one effect was that no one in the DDR had any professional interest in musical copyright at all (the first Ph.D. thesis on the topic was, ironically, awarded in 1989). Not surprisingly, then, copyright did not feature in the negotiations leading to reunification, with consequences that, for many musicians, are still the cause of great bitterness.

For those (few) East German composers who had already registered their titles with GEMA, the West German performing rights society, reunification was immediately beneficial: their 'foreign' income now reached them direct. But for most DDR musicians such registration turned out to be impossible. The question was not who wrote their songs but who owned their copyrights. East German composers and lyricists had, in effect, (and without any option) assigned them to the state (which had thus handled any international licensing). The East German state no longer existed and, worse, under the terms of reunification was, anyway, adjudged to have been illegal. Its copyrights thus passed into the public domain. There was a marked discrepancy here between the treatment of the authors of music and records (and films and television programmes) and the authors of books. East German writers' copyrights were still protected: they were taken to have an individual right in their work deriving from the individual process of written production (and West German law acknowledged the moral rights of 'high' artists). East German musicians, by contrast, had only been able to produce records (and have their compositions performed) within the state system. They were not then – and are not now – assigned any *individual* rights in their music. Hence the bitterness: under the communist system they were obliged to assign their copyrights to the state if they wanted to make music publicly at all; under the capitalist system, they therefore have no property rights in their old songs at all. At the precise moment when their music could be treated as a commodity, it turned out not to be theirs.

NOTE

1. The information here is based on an interview with Dr Peter Wicke of the Institute for the Study of Popular Music, Humboldt University.

Notes on Contributors

MARCUS BREEN works as a freelance journalist and documentary film-maker in Melbourne, Australia. He is the editor of *Australian Popular Music Perspectives 1, Missing in Action* (1987) and *2, Our Place Our Music, Aboriginal Music* (1989).

JOHN COLLINS now runs Bokoor Recording Studio, Accra, Ghana, after years of playing and recording with many West African musicians. He is currently a member of the Ghana National Folklore Board of Trustees and the Technical Director of the co-documentation programme of the University of Ghana's Institute of African Studies music archives. A revised edition of his classic book, *West African Pop Roots,* was published by Temple University Press, Philadelphia in 1992.

SIMON FRITH is co-director of the John Logie Baird Centre at the universities of Strathclyde and Glasgow and an editor of *Popular Music* and *Screen.* He has recently co-edited *Rock and Popular Music: Institutions, Policies and Politics,* Routledge 1993.

JANE M. GAINES is Associate Professor of English and Director of the Programme in Film and Video at Duke University, North Carolina. Her book *Likeness and the Law: Image Properties in the Industrial Age* (English title: *Contested Culture*) was published by the University of North Carolina Press in 1991.

STEVE JONES is Assistant Professor of Communication at the University of Tulsa, Oklahoma. His book *Rock Formations: Music, Technology and Mass Communication* was published by Sage in 1992. He has written articles on mass communication, popular music studies, virtual reality and communications technology. He is currently treasurer of the International Association for the Study of Popular Music.

DAVE LAING co-edits the *Financial Times* newsletter, *Music and Copyright.* With Phil Hardy he is presently preparing a new edition of *The Faber*

Companion to Twentieth Century Popular Music, which was published in 1990.

TÔRU MITSUI is Professor of Musicology and English at the University of Kanazawa. As teacher, researcher and translator he pioneered the study of popular music in Japan and currently chairs the International Association for the Study of Popular Music. In Japanese he has written a cultural history of jeans (1990) and a study of the governor/singer, Jimmie Davis (1989). His article 'Reception of the Music of American Southern Whites in Japan' appears in *Transforming Tradition*, edited by Neil Rosenberg, University of Illinois Press, 1993.

PAUL THÉBERGE is Assistant Professor in the Department of Communication Studies, Concordia University, Montreal. He is currently researching the musical instrument industry with reference to both musicians' practice and consumer markets.

Index of Subjects

Abba, 5, 13
Abdullah, Mohammed Ben, 148, 151, 153
Adowa, 148, 152
AFRA, 112
Aghadza, 148, 152
Akutagawa Yasushi, 143
AMCOS, 110–11
American Federation of Musicians, 113
Anyidoho, Kofi, 150, 153
arrangements, 12
ARIA, 111
Art of Noise, 61
ASCAP, 24
Athens Agreement, 37–8
Australian Copyright Council, 119

Beatles, 63
Bell, Bryan, 73–5
Bentley, Lionel, 9, 11, 16
Berne Convention, 9, 23, 24–5, 26–7, 39, 115–16, 127, 128–32, 133, 136, 138
Betamax, 3
Bettig, Ronald, 83
BIEM, 135
blank tape levy, 2, 4
BMI-Canada, 50
Bolkus, Nick, 99, 100, 101
Bonham, John, 71
Bor Bor Bor, 147, 155
Brecht, Bertolt, 164
Brooks, John, 5
Brown, James, 5, 7, 55, 75–6, 81
Buchanan and Goodman, 13–14
burlesque, 13–14

Canadian content, 45
Cartridge Television Inc., 3
Casely-Hayford, Beatie, 156
choreography, xiv
Christgau, Robert, 15, 16, 61

collaboration, x–xi
Collins, Phil, 56, 71
colourisation, 4, 83
compulsory license, 12, 25, 48–9
copycode, 36–7, 69
Copyright Administration, 155–7
Copyright Agency Ltd, 110
Copyright Board, 45, 50
Copyright Office, 78
Copyright Tribunal, 9–11, 17
Copyright Tribunal (Australia), 114–15
Coryton, Demitri, 141
CPRS, 49, 50
Curley, Tom, 76–7
Cutler, Chris, 78

dagarte, 152
Davis, Jimmie, 125
Deleuze, Gilles, 95
derivative work, 89
Die Dreigrosschenoper, 136

EC, xi–xiii, 32–4
Eisenberg, Evan, 78–9
Elektra, 61
EMI, 27–8

fair use, 8, 48, 57–9
Fels, Allan, 102–3, 118–19
first fixation, 29
folk music, 8, 80–1, 146–57
Foster, Stephen, 23
Frith, Simon, 80
Fujito Masato, 140

Gahu, 149
Ga Kpanlogo, 147
Garrett, Peter, 102–3, 109
GATT, 24, 33
Gillett, Charlie, 6

giri, 142
gome, 149
Grandmaster Flash, 81
Guatari, Felix, 95

Hague, Stephen, 7
Harrison, George, 40
Hatoyama Kazuo, 131–2
Hebdige, Dick, 80
Hedl, Robert D., 35
Homburg, Robert, 89
home taping, 2, 3, 30, 67–9

IFPI, 28, 113
IIPA, 32–3, 82
Industry Commission, 106, 114

JASRAC, 125, 136–40
Junglieb, Stanley, 76
Justified Ancients of Mu Mu, 4–6

karaoke, 125–6
Kelty, Bill, 103
kenri, 142
Keyt, Aaron, 62
'Koinobori', 141
Kostelanetz, André, 78
Kpando Konkoma Group, 147
kpanlogo, 147, 155

Lardner, James, 4–6
Lange, David, 14–15, 16
Levi's, 12
Lexicon, 4
Lincoln, Otoo, 147
Little, Rich, 75, 91
Live Aid, 33

McClary, Susan, 91
McGiverin, Bruce J., 15–16
Macquarie Broadcast Services, 112
Madama Butterfly, 137
Major Network, 112
Marks, Leonard, 95
M/A/R/R/S, 6–7, 9
Marx Brothers, 15
Masuzawa Takemi, 138–9
'Matsunoki Kouta', 141
MC Hammer, 82
MCPS, 10–11
Mixmaster Morris, 8
Mizuno Rentaro, 129–33, 136
moral rights, 9, 10–11, 12, 25
MTV Europe, xi
Musicians Union, 72

National Folklore Board of Trustees, 154–7
neighbouring rights, 23, 27–31, 44, 52–3

Obey, Ebenezer, 149–50
oral culture, 147
Oswald, John, 4, 19, 42, 58–61
'Ozashiki Kouta' 141

Patterson, Lyman Ray, 18–19
Parks, Gordon, 79
Philips, 37
Phonogram Convention, 31
piracy, 30–1, 69
Plage, Wilhelm, 135, 137–8
Polygram, 119
PPCA, 112–3
PPL, 28, 113
Porter, Vincent, 26–7, 28
Presley, Elvis, 18
PROCAN, 51–2
PRS, 24, 49, 50
PSA, 99–100, 101–2, 104–5, 117–20
public domain, 14–15

rap, 81
record rental, 126, 135
Reich, Steve, 79
Robinson, Spider, 40
Rome Convention, 28–30

SACEM, 24
sampling, xv, 4–19, 53–62, 70–8, 81–2
Sanjek, David, 19
Scitex, 4
serial copy management system, 36–7
sheet music, 22–3
Simon, Paul, 154
SOCAN, 41
Sony Corporation, 37. 126
Soviet copyright law, 90
Stewart, Stephen, 28, 31
Suisei-sha, 141
'Sukiyaki', 141
Swedish Folk Music Board, 157
Synthbank, 73–5, 78

Thom, J. C., 17–18
Tigari, 152
Tochuken Kumoemon, 134
Toop, David, 81
Tournier, Jean Loup, 27
Trade Practices Commission, 119
Train, Kenneth E., 99–100
translation, xiii, 135–6
TRIPS, 33–4
Tsikata, Fui, 150, 153
'Tulip', 141

Universal Copyright Convention, 115–16

Ware, Martyn, 7
Waterman, Pete, 6–7, 9
WEA, 5
Willis, Nathaniel Parker, 82–3
WIPO, 117, 148, 151–2

'Yesterday', 162

Zappa, Frank, 54–5, 76

Index of Cases

Allen v. *National Video Inc.* (1985), 94
Boosey v. *Jeffries* (1853), 22–3
Booth v. *Colgate-Palmolive Co.* (1983), 96
Chaplin v. *Amador* (1928), 96
Davis v. *Trans World Airlines* (1969), 87
DC Comics Inc v. *Board of Trustees* (1981), 14–15
Ellis v. *Donkor* (1990), 150
Gardella v. *Log Cabin Products Inc.* (1937), 90
The Gramophone Company v. *Cawardine* (1933), 27–8
Lahr v. *Adell Chemical Co.* (1962), 87, 88, 95
Lombardo v. *Doyle, Dane and Bernbach Inc.* (1977), 90
Lugosi v. *Universal Pictures Inc.* (1979), 93
Midler v. *Ford Motor Co.* (1989), 12, 86–97
Miller v. *Universal Pictures Inc.* (1969), 90
Onassis v. *Christian Dior–New York Inc.* (1984), 94
O'Sullivan v. *Biz Markie* (1991), 8, 75
Shaw v. *Time-Life* (1975), 90
Sinatra v. *Goodyear Tire and Rubber* (1970), 87, 88
Waits v. *Tracy-Locke Advertising Agency and Frito-Lay* (1990), 92

Index of Statutes

AUSTRALIA
Copyright Act (1968), 99–104, 107–9, 114

CANADA
Copyright Act (1924), 43–4, 48
  1971 Amendment, 44
  1988 Amendment, 43, 46–7, 49

GHANA
Law 110, 150–1

JAPAN
Copyright Act (1899), 127, 129–30
  1920 Amendment, 134–5
  1931 Amendment, 135
  1939 Amendment, 138
  1970 Amendment, 141

UK
Copyright Act (1833), 50
Copyright Act (1842), 22–3
Copyright Act (1911), 27
Copyright, Design and Patent Act (1988), 9
International Copyright Act (1838), 22

USA
Celebrity Rights Act (California Code 990), 93
Copyright Act (1909), 67, 89
  1971 Amendment, 16–17, 67, 91
Copyright Act (1976), 67, 87
Copyright Law Amendments (1856 and 1859), 89
Digital Audio Home Recording Act (1992), 35–6, 70
Omnibus Trade and Competitiveness Act (1988), 32–3